MW00603676

They call that man a statesman whose ear is tuned to catch
the slightest pulsations of a pocketbook, and to denounce as a
demagogue anyone who dares listen to the heart-beat of humanity.

—William Jennings Bryan, 1896

WILLIAM JENNINGS BRYAN

A DIFFERENCE MAKER

CORINNE LIVESAY

ISBN 978-0-9980305-0-0
Library of Congress Control Number: 2019938988

WEB COMPANION: bryan.edu/wjb or scan

For usage permissions, contact: library@bryan.edu

Book design and photo restoration: Curtis Jolley
Editorial assistants: Christiana Manthei, Kathryn Manthei, and Chloe Townsend
Printing: Starkey Printing Company, Chattanooga, Tennessee

Published by Bryan College
Dayton, Tennessee
www.bryan.edu

Contents

FOREWORD

Every generation has difference makers who greatly influence their culture—significant men and women whose courage, conviction, and fortitude have forged lasting change in the world. These influencers have empowered us to become what we are today, and many are still celebrated; others, however, fade into history unsung if the generations cease telling their stories. The life and tremendous influence of people like William Jennings Bryan, in whose memory Bryan College is named, deserve their memory and incredible legacy to be treasured for years to come.

Corinne Livesay, my wife of 40 years and first lady of Bryan College for the past 17, is a gifted career educator and author who saw the need for students and alumni of the College to understand the significance and uniqueness of Mr. Bryan. Three years ago, she set out to edit and publish a series of brief articles that had been part of the *Bryan Life* alumni magazine for several years. Written by members of Bryan's faculty, staff, and alumni, each installment portrayed a different aspect of Bryan's life and accomplishments. Although the idea was sound, the reality of editing disparate articles without a common thesis and structure was untenable.

Starting over, Corinne resolved to write a work that would highlight those forces which made Bryan such a powerful difference maker, as well as provide a picture of his personal life. This work is truly unique with the following qualities:

1. The book is organized into five distinct parts that illuminate his life and legacy, not as a longitudinal biography.

2. The book can be read selectively—one part at a time in any order.

3. The organization of the writing conveys concisely (often through tables and figures) the intended ideas.

4. The book provides a unique collection of 125 photos that bring life and understanding to the text.

5. The work includes a *Web Companion*, a free online resource that follows the outline of the book and provides access to videos, audio, eBooks, photos, and other resources for readers who want to dig deeper.

Corinne brings the qualities of an experienced business education writer to this book, succinctly telling a perhaps forgotten story of the significant impact William Jennings Bryan made during his well-lived life. Her perspective is not that of an historian; rather, she observes her subject and portrays him in such a way that within a few hours, one gains a lasting impression of who this man was and why he mattered.

Bryan was a godly man with a huge heart for God and the common men and women of our great country. Bryan clearly saw the abuses of power in America during the late 19th and early 20th centuries, and he championed the working man's cause for freedom from the oppression of the ruling class. The greatest oppression he warned against, especially as his thoughts matured during the last 20 years of his life, concerned the impact of teaching evolution as fact—not theory—in America's schools.

In an age without the Internet, it is remarkable that Bryan became a household name and one so widely admired by men and women of every level of society. During his lifetime, perhaps no other individual surpassed him in oratorical skills nor the intellectual content of the message that he delivered. Whether speaking on the Chautauqua circuit or writing in his widely read *Commoner*, Bryan effectively communicated his message and made a difference in the intellect of the American people.

It is unfortunate that many today do not recognize Bryan's name; or if they do, they remember him as the irrational buffoon portrayed in the play and movie *Inherit the Wind*. In Bryan's day thousands of children were named after him because he was perceived as a visionary leader, an inspiring man of the people, and a man of unimpeachable character—as one to be remembered and emulated.

In this book Corinne provides an accurate rendition of the Scopes trial, one of the most significant events in our nation's history that to this day highlights the creation/evolution issue. Whether man was made in the image of God by a supernatural creative act or whether man evolved from some matter by chance over millions of years is far more than just a scientific discussion. It goes to the heart of morality and truth. Human beings are either image-bearers responsible to an almighty God for their lives and actions, or they are directly responsible for their own lives without any other authority than that which society may impose.

Bryan increasingly understood the significance of mankind's supernatural creation as the foundation of the moral fabric of our culture, and that is why he faced opposition such as was manifest at the Scopes trial.

Corinne helps the reader see Bryan as the Great Commoner—the man who championed the rights and dignity of all Americans as the sacred calling of the church and duty of the state. She also highlights his work in promoting the passage of the so-called Progressive Amendments of income tax, direct election of senators, prohibition, and women's suffrage. His work extended to curbing the abuses of child labor and 12-hour workdays for those working in America's factories.

Bryan detested any unjust war and promoted Thomas Jefferson's admonition, "Peace, commerce, and honest friendship with all nations—entangling alliances with none." Bryan was the principal influence of the Democratic Party for nearly two decades and stands with Woodrow Wilson and Theodore Roosevelt as the three men who most shaped America's political culture during Bryan's time on the political stage.

His love of higher education was evident by his many university addresses, the scholarships that remain to this day for students attending those schools, and his desire to establish a Christian university. Perhaps the greatest memorial to William Jennings Bryan is Bryan College, established in 1930 as a school that would recognize the Word of God as the ultimate authority including its historical account of creation in Genesis. The 10,000 alumni of Bryan College are a testament to the life and ideals of Bryan—an appropriate living memorial to the impact and significance of a man of untiring energy, clear vision, and godly character. The College today stands on the shoulders of this great man, faithful to its charter and mission.

Utilizing her own unique format, Corinne Livesay has painted a picture of why this man was so cherished in this country and throughout the world and why his influence remains a vital component of the fabric of our society. For Bryan College, this book ensures that the vision in 1925 of the Bryan Memorial University Association to establish a university "as a memorial to William Jennings Bryan and to stand for the faith for which he fought" will long endure.

—Stephen D. Livesay, President
Bryan College

PREFACE

 We build temporarily or permanently; if we live for pleasure, we build for a day; but if we have the trust and highest conception of what we put into this world and measure up to our responsibilities, we build for the ages.

—William Jennings Bryan
Grove Park Inn, Asheville, NC (1913)

As I put the final touches on this book before it goes to press, I have been considering this question: "What was it that drew me to spend three years researching and writing a book about someone who already has had countless words written about him?" While the list is long, the most prominent answer came to me while I was reflecting on my parents' legacy in the context of the life lessons they instilled in me. I concluded that the lesson my parents lived out most consistently and faithfully also characterizes Mr. Bryan's life—"Wherever you are, make it better."

I admire people who make the world a better place—whether it is by how they love others well; live life with energy, enthusiasm, and excellence; build something amazing; are generous with what they have; and a million other ways.

People who make the world a better place inspire me to be a better version of myself—to be one who pushes past my selfish desire to seek ways to make my world better only for me and instead direct more of my energy toward making the world better for others.

As my words now join countless others written about Mr. Bryan, my hope is that they will help readers see *how* Mr. Bryan left the world a better place than he found it—and more importantly *why* he did so. And by extension, I hope each reader will be inspired to do the same in whatever realms of influence they walk and live and touch people each day. That is what writing this book has done for me.

ACKNOWLEDGMENTS

Many people came alongside me to help make this book a reality, and my heartfelt thanks go out to each of them for the important part they each fulfilled so capably. Bryan College colleagues who reviewed every chapter of my early rough draft were English professor Beth Impson, Bryan alumnus Larry Puckett, history professor Travis Ricketts, and special collections librarian Kevin Woodruff. Kevin also did whatever it took to get me past brick walls that I frequently ran into in my quest for finding necessary information, especially photos. Greek professor Jud Davis, biology professor Neal Doran and communications professors Reggie Ecarma and Michael Palmer reviewed subsequent drafts of select chapters and sections. Math professor Bob Simpson provided valuable research resources.

Several individuals came along to fund the expenses related to research (subscription to newspapers. com, for example) and photo acquisitions. While many of the photos used in the book are in the public domain, such as those acquired through the Library of Congress, others were quite expensive. Thanks to the generosity of Tom and Mary Frances Rudd Carlson, Dan and Kathryn Manthei, and my ever-supportive-of-this-project husband, Stephen, I was able to include every photo that I thought was needed to help me tell the Bryan story. A special thanks also goes to Marty Miller at the Nebraska State Historical Society and Edgar Bumanis at Bryan Health for both going the extra mile to help me with photo acquisitions.

My hat is off to mother-daughter copy editors Kathryn and Christiana Manthei, who improved chapters before they were typeset. Kathryn provided additional writing support in several areas. For example, after copy editing Chapter 2, she encouraged me to dig deeper to find out more about Bryan's descendants. As a result, I had the privilege of connecting with several of Bryan's great-grandchildren—Al Forsyth, Mimi Forsyth, William Jennings Bryan Forsyth, Larry Gray, Steven Hargreaves, Victoria Hargreaves, and Frances Pavley—and distant relative and family genealogy researcher Jeanne Rollberg, all of whom graciously provided additional family information.

Curtis Jolley took my pages filled with text, photos and captions, tables, and figure sketches and created a beautiful book design that presents tons of information in a visually appealing and easy-to-follow format. He regularly exhibited the patience of Job, cheerfully processing the steady flow of changes sent his way. I've come to greatly admire Curtis' big heart, great design talent, positive can-do attitude, work ethic, and kindness. As the book moved closer to final print, Chloe Townsend came on board to do the critical work of rewriting my awkward sentences; fixing punctuation errors; and polishing every word, phrase, and sentence in the book.

Lastly, I am most thankful for the love and support of my family: my husband wrote the book's foreword and planned our research trips to places such as Asheville, NC; Lincoln, NE; and Miami, FL. He bought us a home in a beautiful location in North Carolina, where I could go to for weeks at a time to research and write uninterrupted and to be near our daughter, Kara Woodworth, and her wonderful family. They provided welcome fun on my days off from the computer. They and our other two children, Brent and Katie Livesay, regularly encouraged me on my book-writing journey. Likewise, my brother, George Ryder, at critical points along the way, offered great advice and the nudges I needed to finish the book. Everyone who has been on the WJB book team has been a joy to work with, and each has contributed just what was needed to bring the book to life.

A WORD FOR MY READERS

I conclude with some key thoughts from each of the five parts of the book.

- **OVERVIEW AND BEGINNINGS:** The timeline of Bryan's life is bookended by two world-changing books (see Chapter 1 foldout), providing context for Bryan's life story that culminated with Bryan's last campaign that he described as follows: "In this fight I have the most intolerant and vindictive enemies I have ever met and I have the largest majority on my side I have ever had and I am discussing the greatest issue I have ever discussed" (see Chapters 14–15). I also found Mary Bryan to be a fascinating woman and the perfect life partner to help her husband accomplish all that God put him on this earth to do. You'll see her featured throughout the book in some unexpected places.

- **VICTORIES AND DEFEATS:** One of the first facts I remember learning about Mr. Bryan (everyone has to start somewhere) was that he was the Democratic Party's presidential nominee three times and lost all three times. My reaction then was "How unimpressive!" My reaction now, after learning so much more about this great Christian statesman, is "How impressive!" Even if you don't reach that same conclusion, see if you can find reasons why I did.

- **GIFTED COMMUNICATOR:** Those who aspire to improve their communication skills will learn much and will be inspired by the "Silver-Tongued Orator."

- **BRYAN'S LAST DECADE:** One might expect after learning about everything Bryan accomplished through the end of his tenure as U.S. secretary of state, that he would have been worn out and deserved to take life easy after that. However, in many regards, the final decade of Bryan's life was his most productive.

- **BRYAN REMEMBERED:** To see the myriad of ways that this "Difference Maker" is remembered is evidence of the certainty of the opening quotation. Mr. Bryan surely lived his life for the ages.

Corinne Livesay
Dayton, Tennessee

William and Mary Bryan in front of their home at 1625 D Street, Lincoln, NE, with their three children (L-R) Ruth; William Jr.; and Grace, c. 1896

PART 1

OVERVIEW & BEGINNINGS

> **"** You cannot judge a man's life by the success of a moment, by the victory of an hour, or even by the results of a year. You must view his life as a whole. You must stand where you can see the man as he treads the entire path that leads from the cradle to the grave—now crossing the plain, now climbing the steeps, now passing through pleasant fields, now wending his way with difficulty between rugged rocks—tempted, tried, tested, triumphant.
>
> —William Jennings Bryan
> "The Law and the Gospel" (1890)

As William Jennings Bryan described so eloquently in an 1890 speech given prior to serving his first term as U.S. congressman, evaluating a person's life requires a measure of patience and perspective. To aid in viewing Bryan's "life as a whole," the following timeline provides a bird's-eye view of significant events in Bryan's life set amid major events that happened during his lifetime.

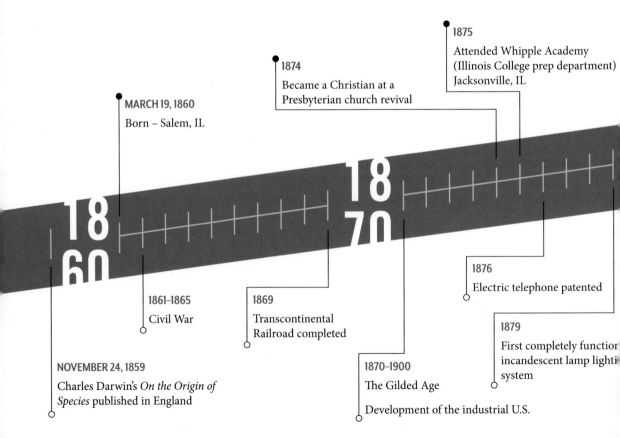

1875
Attended Whipple Academy
(Illinois College prep department)
Jacksonville, IL

1874
Became a Christian at a
Presbyterian church revival

MARCH 19, 1860
Born – Salem, IL

1876
Electric telephone patented

1861–1865
Civil War

1869
Transcontinental
Railroad completed

1879
First completely function[...]
incandescent lamp lighti[...]
system

NOVEMBER 24, 1859
Charles Darwin's *On the Origin of
Species* published in England

1870–1900
The Gilded Age

Development of the industrial U.S.

2 | BRYAN'S FAMILY

> A good name is more desirable than great riches;
> to be esteemed is better than silver or gold.
>
> —Proverbs 22:1 (NIV)

William and Mary are the focal point of the four-generation Bryan family tree. Because not all these family members are mentioned elsewhere in the book, information is provided about them following the family tree and in the *Web Companion* (bryan.edu/wjb).

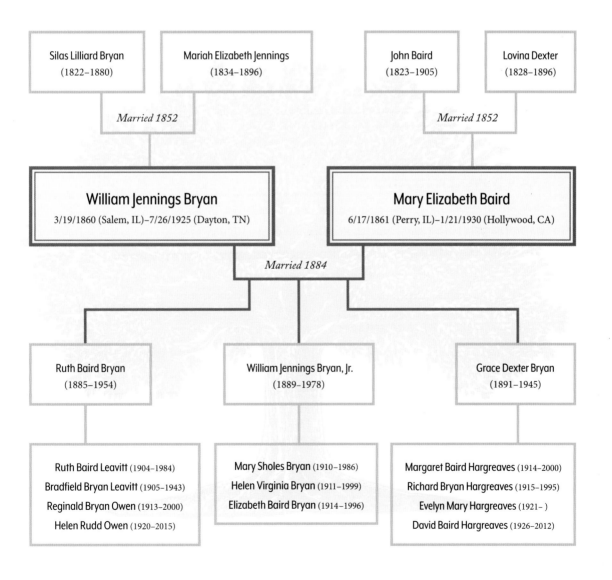

Silas Lilliard Bryan (1822–1880)	**Mariah Elizabeth Jennings** (1834–1896)

Married 1852

John Baird (1823–1905)	**Lovina Dexter** (1828–1896)

Married 1852

William Jennings Bryan
3/19/1860 (Salem, IL)–7/26/1925 (Dayton, TN)

Mary Elizabeth Baird
6/17/1861 (Perry, IL)–1/21/1930 (Hollywood, CA)

Married 1884

Ruth Baird Bryan (1885–1954)

William Jennings Bryan, Jr. (1889–1978)

Grace Dexter Bryan (1891–1945)

Ruth Baird Leavitt (1904–1984)
Bradfield Bryan Leavitt (1905–1943)
Reginald Bryan Owen (1913–2000)
Helen Rudd Owen (1920–2015)

Mary Sholes Bryan (1910–1986)
Helen Virginia Bryan (1911–1999)
Elizabeth Baird Bryan (1914–1996)

Margaret Baird Hargreaves (1914–2000)
Richard Bryan Hargreaves (1915–1995)
Evelyn Mary Hargreaves (1921–)
David Baird Hargreaves (1926–2012)

In this 1896 presidential campaign photo, Bryan (standing in the middle) is surrounded by his relatives in Salem, IL, on the front porch of his cousin Molly Webster's home. Bryan's parents were not alive to see him nominated for president. His father had died when Bryan was a 20-year-old college student, and his mother had died ten days before his nomination. In his *Memoirs* Bryan recounted his family's last visit with his mother in Salem for Christmas 1895 and stated that after her funeral the next summer he traveled directly to the 1896 Democratic National Convention in Chicago.[1]

BRYAN'S PARENTS AND SIBLINGS [2]

- **SILAS BRYAN** (1822–1880) was a state senator, lawyer, and circuit judge in Salem, IL.

- **MARIAH BRYAN** (1834–1896) homeschooled her children until they were 10 years old.

- Of Silas and Mariah's nine children, two sons and three daughters survived infancy.

- Bryan's younger brother, **CHARLES WAYLAND BRYAN** (1867–1945), supported Bryan's work by organizing his lecture tours, managing his campaigns, handling many of his financial affairs, and overseeing *The Commoner* operations. Charles' political career included two-time Lincoln mayor, three-time Nebraska governor, and 1924 VP Democratic candidate.

- Bryan's sisters came to Lincoln, NE, in the 1890s and made substantial contributions to Bryan's political career:

    FRANCES BRYAN MILLSON BAIRD (1858–1934), "Aunt Fannie," lived in a house Bryan built for her and her husband, James Baird (no relation to Mary Baird). Her son, William Bryan Millson, assisted in farming operations at Fairview (see "Fairview" on page 130) from about 1900 to 1912.

    NANCY LILLARD BRYAN (1869–1904) served her brother as a private secretary until her death.

    MARY ELIZABETH BRYAN ALLEN (1873–1962) served as the family historian. Her husband, Thomas Stinson Allen, was Bryan's law partner and campaign manager throughout his political career.

Siblings, c. 1921: (L-R) Charles W. Bryan, Mrs. J. B. Baird, Mrs. T. S. Allen, and Bryan. Bryan College's third president, Judson A. Rudd, visited Mrs. Allen many times in Lincoln, NE. His final visit was in 1958, after which her declining health kept her from receiving visitors. Upon Mrs. Allen's death in 1962, Bryan College received a $325,000 bequest from her estate (equivalent to more than $2.7 million in 2019). Her gift launched a major development program, including two dormitories, a gymnasium, and additional projects. (Everett Collection Inc/Alamy Stock Photo)

MARY ELIZABETH BAIRD'S PARENTS

- JOHN BAIRD (1823–1905) was a prosperous merchant in Perry, IL; he and LOVINA BAIRD (1828–1896) had only one child.
- Lovina and John lived with their daughter and Bryan from 1884 until their deaths.

WILLIAM AND MARY BRYAN AND FAMILY

WILLIAM JENNINGS BRYAN (1860–1925) and MARY ELIZABETH BAIRD (1861–1930) were married in 1884, five years after they first met while college students. They were engaged for four years, during which time William finished his schooling and established his law practice. For their wedding day, William had Mary's wedding ring inscribed with "Won, 1880 – One, 1884"[3]

In addition to their 3 children, 11 grandchildren, and 23 great-grandchildren—information about whom is provided in the remainder of the chapter—they welcomed another family member in 1898 under unusual circumstances. A 19-year-old Japanese youth presented himself at the Bryans' home and announced his desire to pursue his studies as a member of the Bryan household. He was taken into the Bryan family, treated as a son, educated at the public school and at the University of Nebraska, and went back to Japan in 1903 with the name of Yaschichira Bryan Yamashita. He returned to the U.S. in 1911 to attend Grace Bryan and Richard Hargreaves' wedding.[4]

The U.S. Minister to Denmark set sail with her family May 11, 1933, from Jersey City, NJ, to assume her new post in Denmark. Traveling with Ruth Bryan Owen, who is holding her granddaughter Kaywin (2), are (L-R) her daughters, Helen (12), and Mrs. W. P. Meeker, and her son, Bryan Owen. On the front row are her granddaughters Helen Meeker (5), and Ruth Meeker (9). (Acme News Pictures, Inc.)

Ruth attended the University of Nebraska and served as her father's traveling secretary during his third presidential campaign in 1908. She was a nurse to the British Army in the Middle East during the Egypt-Palestine campaign of 1915–1918. Like her father, she was a popular speaker on the lecture circuit, a politician, and an author. From 1926 to 1928 she taught public speaking at the University of Miami; the school's public speaking fraternity took its name, Rho Beta Omicron, from her initials. She was the first congresswoman elected from the South (Florida, 1929–1933) and the first American woman to represent the U.S. as a diplomatic minister to a foreign nation (U.S. minister to Denmark 1933–1936).[5]

Ruth had four children. Two were with artist **William Homer Leavitt** (m. 1903–1909; divorced), and two were with British Royal Engineers officer **Reginald Owen** (m. 1910–1927; widowed). In 1936 Ruth married **Captain Boerge Rohde** of the Danish Royal Guards at St. James' Chapel in Hyde Park, NY. President and Mrs. Franklin Roosevelt attended the ceremony, after which they hosted a wedding supper on the lawn of their Hyde Park estate.

RUTH BAIRD LEAVITT (1904–1984), known as "Kitty Owen," was a model for Maxfield Parrish's 1922–1923 *Life* magazine covers. She was one of two models in Parrish's famous *Daybreak*. Her grandfather (WJB) purchased the original painting in 1921 for $10,000 (nearly $143,000 in 2019). Upon his death, Kitty acquired the painting, never permitting it to be displayed until 1974 when she sold it for an undisclosed six-figure amount that was $20,000 above its appraised value. Its record purchase price was in May 2006 for $7.6 million by actor Mel Gibson and his wife Robin.[6]

Kitty had four children; three were with **William P. Meeker** (m. 1923–1933; divorced): **Ruth "Wendy" Meeker, Helen (Meeker) Bilby**, and **Katherine "Kaywin" Windsor Meeker**. The fourth was with **Robert Lehman** (m. 1934–1951; divorced): **Robert Owen Lehman**. She was also married to **Jonas Reiner** until his death in 1956 and to **Derek Spence** until his death in 1971.

BRADFIELD BRYAN LEAVITT (1905–1943) was known as "John Baird Bryan" after his maternal grandparents adopted him following his parents' divorce. See photo on page 126 of John with his grandfather and Woodrow Wilson. At his 1922 high school graduation from the boys' college prep school, McCallie, Chattanooga, TN, his grandfather (WJB) gave the commencement address. John attended the University of Wisconsin, published three slim volumes of poetry, became a Shakespearean stage actor, and played minor roles in four Hollywood films.[7]

REGINALD "BRYAN" OWEN (1913–2000) stated that one of his fondest childhood memories was when his mother gave him two walk-on roles in the feature film *Once Upon a Time/Scheherazade* (1922) that she independently financed, produced, and directed.[8] Bryan's political debut resulted in his losing a bid for the Democratic nomination for the Colorado House of Representatives from Denver in 1954.[9] Bryan married **Marie Louise Weber** in 1938 and had five children: **Kent Weber Owen**, **Donald Baird Owen**, **Donna Marie (Owen) Waring**, **Regis Mary (Owen) Miller**, and **Jenna (Owen) Rose**.

HELEN "RUDD" OWEN (1920–2015) married **Harrison Brown**, geochemist and professor of science at California Institute of Technology, in 1951; and they made Pasadena, CA, their home. She inherited her mother's talent for creative writing, art, politics, and lecturing. Rudd visited Dayton, TN, twice in 1960. On March 20, 1960, she delivered a speech entitled "Politics and the Responsibility of Citizenship," at Bryan College's Founders' Day Convocation "commemorating the Centenary of William Jennings Bryan 1860–1960 and the Thirtieth Year of Bryan College." On July 21, 1960, she attended the premier of Stanley Kramer's movie, *Inherit the Wind*, that coincided with the 35th anniversary of the Scopes trial (see photo).[10]

Helen "Rudd" Brown chats with Bryan College's fourth president, Theodore C. "Ted" Mercer (left) and John Scopes (right) during Dayton's Scopes Trial Day celebration on July 21, 1960. (BCA)

Bryan's family photo taken during his first congressional campaign in 1890

Portraits of Bryan and his family; (L-R) Grace, Ruth, Mary, and William, Jr.; lithograph, c. October 1896, with quotations from Bryan's "Cross of Gold" speech (LOC LC-DIG-pga-03796)

William, Jr., with (L-R) Helen, Mary, and Elizabeth

William, Jr., graduated from the University of Arizona (UA) and Georgetown Law School. He was assistant U.S. attorney in Arizona where he was involved with YMCA, local Democratic Party, and UA Board of Regents. He later practiced law in Los Angeles and was appointed by President Franklin Roosevelt to the post of Los Angeles Collector of Customs. He and his wife **Helen Berger** (m. 1909–1927; divorced) had three daughters. In 1930 William, Jr., married **Ellen Bent Balinger** in Los Angeles.

MARY SHOLES BRYAN (1910–1986) married **Alfred Smith Forsyth** in 1933 and had three children: **Mary "Mimi" Bryan Forsyth**; **Alfred Smith Forsyth, Jr.**; and **William Jennings Bryan Forsyth**. She was an artist and illustrator who used the professional name "Bryan Forsyth." Examples of her work include illustrating Mari Sandoz's *Love Song to the Plains* and sculpting the Sandoz bust located in the Nebraska Hall of Fame, Nebraska State Capitol.

HELEN VIRGINIA BRYAN (1911–1999) graduated from the American Academy of Dramatic Arts in New York City c. 1933 and married **Robert Peter Touyarot** in 1934. They had one son, **Robert Alexander Touyarot**.

ELIZABETH "BETTY" BAIRD BRYAN (1914–1996) married **John Ralph Gasser** and had four children: **Peter Degauntran Gasser**, **Josephine "Jody" Jennings Gasser**, **Robin Rhodes Gasser**, and **Gay "Michelle" Gasser**. After Betty and John's divorce, she married **Arthur J. Adams** in 1956. Betty was a school teacher and after retirement pursued her passion for photography. She exhibited print and color slides in international salons, won 42 medals, and served as a judge in international competitions.

Bryan with his daughter Grace (Mrs. Richard Hargreaves) and Grace's three children (L-R) Bryan, Margaret, and baby Evelyn, May 27, 1922 (Bettmann/Getty Images)

Grace attended Hollins Institute in Virginia and edited "William Jennings Bryan: Biographical Notes, His Speeches, Letters and Other Writings" (unpublished manuscript, Bryan Manuscript Collection, Library of Congress). Grace and her husband **Richard Hargreaves** (m. 1911–1929; divorced) had four children:

GRACE "MARGARET" HARGREAVES (1914–2000) met **Herman Gray** at the Federal Housing Administration in Los Angeles where they both were employed, and they married in January 1942. Herman served in the U.S. Navy as an electrician's mate on a supply ship in the Pacific during World War II. They had two sons, **Philip Laurence "Larry" Gray** and **Michael Lewis Gray**.

RICHARD "BRYAN" HARGREAVES (1915–1995) served in the U.S. Navy as a chief photographer's mate during World War II and the Korean War. He photographed every major WWII battle in the Pacific, such as Pearl Harbor, and received 17 Navy awards for his service, including the prestigious Air Medal. He married **Antonina Barnett** September 7, 1951, in Santa Barbara, CA; and they had one daughter, **Victoria Bryan Hargreaves**. Bryan is buried at Arlington National Cemetery next to his grandparents and his mother.

EVELYN MARY HARGREAVES (1921–), the last surviving Bryan grandchild—98 years old in 2019—is a graduate of the University of Southern California. She married Captain **Noble W. Jones** on September 7, 1943, choosing the birthday shared by her father, who had died in 1941, and her brother Bryan. Their two children are **Frances Meldrim (Jones) Pavley** and **Richard Noble Jones**.

DAVID BAIRD HARGREAVES (c. 1925–unknown), the Bryan's youngest grandson, unveiled his grandfather's statue that was dedicated by President Franklin Roosevelt in Washington, DC, May 3, 1934; see photo on page 138. David married **Kathleen Anne Makey** in 1951; they had one son, **Steven Hargreaves**.

BRYAN THE FAMILY MAN: A PRESS PERSPECTIVE

Published between 1908 and 1923, the following newspaper stories (quoted verbatim) provide a glimpse into Bryan's family life.

1. **NEW YORK, NY, 21 April 1908**—William J. Bryan's grandson, little Bryan Leavitt, gave the Democratic leader a bad scare today.

   Mr. Bryan had gone to the pier to meet the steamer Minnehaha, upon which Mrs. Bryan, her daughter, Mrs. Ruth Leavitt, and Mrs. Leavitt's two children were returning from a several months' visit to Europe.

   When the steamer swung in at the pier, Mr. Bryan was one of the first on board. He found Mrs. Bryan and Mrs. Leavitt awaiting him on the upper deck. His granddaughter, Ruth, also was there, but little Bryan was nowhere to be seen. A search which extended over the ship from one end to the other was not successful. Finally, his mother found him where he had hidden, under a berth in his mother's stateroom.

   When he was drawn out of his hiding place, little Bryan threw himself into his grandfather's arms; and the big crowd which had gathered on the deck watched the meeting with enthusiastic appreciation.

   From the pier the family went at once to the Hoffman House. Mr. Bryan was obliged to leave them at once to fill an engagement in Trenton, N. J. He returned to New York this evening, however, to remain with his family until they leave for Nebraska tomorrow.

   Mrs. Bryan and Mrs. Leavitt said they had a delightful trip abroad. They traveled extensively throughout Southern Europe, visiting Italy, Greece, Turkey, and other countries.[13]

   HERMOSA BEACH, CA, 12 July 1915—"The former secretary spent four hours in a launch on a fishing trip five miles out in the Pacific today with his son and a party of friends. He returned tonight in fine spirits with a string of eleven beauties, weighing 25 pounds and said it 'was the best luck I ever had in fishing.'"[16]

2. **SALEM, IL, 27 August 1908**—During the day Mr. Bryan divided most of his time with the Bryan and Jennings branches of his family. After luncheon he rode out to the country and placed flowers on the graves of his parents, and on his way back to the city inspected the new Bryan-Bennett library.[14]

3. **WASHINGTON, DC, 6 October 1913**—Mrs. William Jennings Bryan, wife of the Secretary of State, is setting an example in economy. She has learned to run the big limousine car of the Bryans like an expert. Mrs. Bryan dispenses with the chauffeur during their motor jaunts. With her on a run to Maryland fields to pick golden rod were the Secretary, Mrs. William Jennings Bryan, Jr., and her small grandchildren.[15]

4. **WASHINGTON, DC, 23 November 1913**—Soon after 11 o'clock the Secretary was at his desk, going over correspondence with department chiefs, when his little grandson, John Bryant [sic] Leavitt, walked in, dressed in frontier costume, with a little shotgun on his shoulder. "Grandpa," said the boy, "you promised to go duck hunting at 11 o'clock. You're late already. Let's go." Mr. Bryan quickly dismissed his assistants, saw there were no dispatches of importance requiring his attention, and with his grandson set out for an afternoon's sport.[17]

Bryan with his granddaughters, Mary and Helen Bryan, referred to in the 6 October 1913 story on the preceding page (LOC LC-DIG-ggbain-13516)

5. **HUTCHINSON, KS, 17 August 1920**—[From a story about Bryan dropping other engagements to visit the home of 95-year-old admirer, who had expressed her wish to meet him before she died.] Mr. Bryan and Grandma Naylor chatted about their families, their children and grandchildren. "I've got nine grandchildren now" said "Grandpa Bryan." "Well, that's more than I've got, for I've only got five grandchildren," replied Grandma Naylor. "But I've got you beat anyway, for I've got ten great-grandchildren." "Yes, you've got me beat," admitted Mr. Bryan. "But I've been used to being beat," he added with a chuckle.[18]

6. **HOLLYWOOD, CA, 29 September 1923**—Mr. and Mrs. Richard L. Hargreaves entertained at a garden party on Saturday afternoon, marking the thirty-ninth wedding anniversary of Mrs. Hargreaves' parents, Mr. and Mrs. William Jennings Bryan. Their beautiful home on Ogden Drive was elaborately decorated, and a feature of the color scheme in the gardens was an arrangement of flags. From a balcony, musicians played during the hours of receiving. More than 200 guests were entertained, and the affair was one of great distinction. Assisting the host and hostess were William Jennings Bryan, Jr., ... A feature of the afternoon was a poem by Walt Mason . . . written especially for this occasion by the people's poet, who is a longtime friend of William Jennings Bryan.[19]

Four generations of Bryans pictured at the Bryans' Marymont home on January 5, 1925. This is the first time Mrs. Bryan was photographed following an illness that left her an invalid. In the photo are the following: Mr. and Mrs. Bryan (on left); daughter Ruth (sitting by Mrs. Bryan); granddaughters (Ruth's two daughters), standing (L-R), Kitty (Mrs. William Meeker) and Helen; and the Bryans' first great-grandchild, Ruth (Kitty's daughter), who was born during the 1924 Democratic National Convention. (Bettmann/Getty Images)

3 | PREPARATION

Jesus provides us with a template for preparing for a life of service as set forth in Luke 2:52 (ESV): "And Jesus increased in wisdom [mentally] and in stature [physically] and in favor with God [spiritually] and man [socially]." This chapter uses that framework for examining Bryan's preparation and concludes with a section about Bryan's wife.

MENTAL GROWTH

Using Webster's speller books, *McGuffey Readers*, and a geography book, Bryan's mother home-schooled Bryan and his siblings until each became 10 years old, when they entered the public schools. At 15, Bryan went to school in Jacksonville, IL, graduating from Whipple Academy and then from Illinois College (B.A.) where he was selected as valedictorian.

Bryan's education was based on instruction in the liberal arts of logic, grammar, and rhetoric, and included six years of Greek and four years of Latin. Bryan was not known as the brightest student but rather as a hard worker with a retentive memory who used his time wisely. He was thorough in preparations and actively sought out extracurricular experiences and public speaking opportunities that would allow him to hone his craft.[2]

Bryan, pictured third from right in the 1880 photo on the next page, participated in an oratorical contest with students from nine Illinois colleges. Bryan

Bryan, c. 1865 (NSHS RG3198-15-02)

won second place and $50 in prize money with which he bought Mary's engagement ring.[3] The lady in the photo is Jane Addams, who in 1931 was the first woman from the U.S. to win the Nobel Peace Prize. The Bryans' daughter, Ruth, while a college student in the summer of 1903, worked in Chicago at Addams' Hull House, an experience that impacted her interest in the problems of America's youth, a cause she championed throughout her life.[4]

The Illinois College Rambler student newspaper (1881) said of Bryan, "He intends to study law, making it the steppingstone to the arena of politics." While attending Union College of Law (later known as Northwestern University School of Law), Chicago, IL, where he earned his LL.B., he worked in the office of Lyman Trumbull, Abraham Lincoln's friend and a U.S. senator (IL).

PHYSICAL GROWTH

Being the eldest son on a 520-acre farm, Bryan was accomplished at farm work by the time he was 14. He fed and watered the stock, milked the cows, cut the wood that heated their home, handled a plow, and rounded up cattle on horseback. After he became famous, Bryan credited those years of hard work for giving him strength, stamina, and good health for his often-grueling travel schedule.

SPIRITUAL GROWTH

Bryan grew up in a home where Bible reading, praying, and singing hymns and Sunday school songs were common practices. Throughout his childhood, he attended Sunday school at his mother's Methodist church in the morning and at his father's Baptist church in the afternoon. At the age of 14 he became a Christian at a revival led by a traveling minister from the Cumberland Presbyterian Church.[5] He then helped to establish a small congregation with about seventy other teenagers. Throughout high school and college, Bryan regularly attended the local Presbyterian church, where he brought many young men with him. Bryan also joined the YMCA and was several times elected chaplain of Sigma Pi, a campus literary society that doubled as a fraternity.

SOCIAL GROWTH

The home Bryan grew up in was known as one that regularly opened its doors to guests. As Bryan recalled in his *Memoirs,* "The spare bedroom was set apart for the special entertainment of politicians and divines." He also remembered with fondness the annual tradition of inviting the ministers of every denomination in Salem to their family dinners and that he "knew all the ministers as 'Brother.'"[6] While in Jacksonville for prep school and college, Bryan lived with a family relation, Dr. Hiram Jones, who was an Illinois College trustee, a prominent physician, philosopher, and faculty member. Dr. Jones mentored Bryan and introduced him to his prestigious friends and colleagues such as Ralph Waldo Emerson, Bronson Alcott, Henry Ward Beecher, and Robert Ingersoll.

BRYAN'S WIFE'S PREPARATION AND CONTRIBUTIONS TO HIS SUCCESS [7]

Mary Elizabeth Baird attended the Jacksonville Female Academy (absorbed by Illinois College in 1903) during the same years Bryan attended Illinois College. Bryan graduated (Class of 1881) as valedictorian. The next day Mary graduated as valedictorian of her class.

After they were married in 1884, she took classes at Illinois College, a practice unheard of for a married woman at the time. She later studied law under Bryan's instruction, and was admitted to the bar in Nebraska in 1888. She said she pursued that goal to be able to put herself in closer touch with her husband and to assist him in his work, which she did in countless ways.

These photos of Mary Elizabeth Baird and William Jennings Bryan were taken in 1880, about the time they first met as college students. NSHS RG3198-15-05 (WJB photo)

Historian Michael Kazin says that Bryan's career wouldn't have been possible without Mary's contributions. "She managed his correspondence, helped prepare his speeches, edited his articles, and on occasion even negotiated with his fellow politicians. . . . For many years, Mary and Will shared a large double desk that allowed them to work across from each other (see photo). It was a fitting symbol of the enterprise they built together."[8]

In preparation for Bryan's 1908 presidential campaign, Mary took German classes at the University of Nebraska so she could read and translate European economic and political positions for her husband.

Their daughter Ruth, Florida's first congresswoman, said of her mother, "I would like to emulate her. She is a thoroughly feminine woman with the mind of a thoroughly masculine man."[9] Ruth reflected that her father's career "was strengthened by my mother. She was the critical audience who helped to bring to fullest flower his gift of eloquence."[10]

Mr. and Mrs. Bryan ran the 1908 presidential campaign, handled much of Bryan's extensive correspondence, and collaborated on his books and speeches from the lower-level study of their Fairview home; see "Fairview," page 130. (Author's photo)

Bryan with newspapermen, Washington, DC, c. 1913 (LOC LC-DIG-hec-04021)

PART 2

VICTORIES & DEFEATS

> **"** My place in history will depend on what I can do for the people and not on what the people can do for me.
>
> —William Jennings Bryan[1]

INTRODUCTION

In a letter penned in 1895, Bryan expressed the political beliefs that guided many of his actions. He wrote that "'All men are created equal' is the most important" truth in the Declaration of Independence because "it is the most fundamental and comprehends all the others. Its application now would solve aright the questions which vex the civilized world and would both remove the abuses of legislative power . . . and add to the laws . . . additional statutes as are necessary to protect each citizen in the enjoyment of life, liberty and the pursuit of happiness."[2]

Although Bryan never won the country's top office, he wielded significant influence during his 34-year career in public service. This chapter presents three facets of Bryan's statesmanship: the many domestic reforms he advocated that were eventually adopted, the major role he played in reshaping the Democratic Party, and the significant influence he had while secretary of state.

STATESMAN:

1: one versed in the principles or art of government; especially: one actively engaged in conducting the business of a government or in shaping its policies;

2: a wise, skillful, and respected political leader.

Merriam Webster

Bryan was U.S. representative from Nebraska from 1891–1895. He sent this telegram to congratulate his fellow Democrat, President Grover Cleveland, on his inauguration as president, March 4, 1983. (LOC.gov/item/pin3101)

PROGRESSIVE LEGISLATION CHAMPIONED BY BRYAN

When asked how he could be a progressive in politics and a fundamentalist in religion, Bryan replied, "Government is man-made and therefore imperfect. It can always be improved. But religion is not a man-made affair. If Christ is the final word, how may anyone be progressive in religion. I am satisfied with the God we have, with the Bible and with Christ."[3] Progressive reforms Bryan championed are presented under four categories:

Beginning in 1890, Bryan advocated for the popular election of senators to replace the system of senators being elected by state legislatures. Under Bryan's influence, this goal was included in four Democratic Party platforms; and Bryan spoke in support of it from hundreds of platforms for 20 years. On March 31, 1913, with Mrs. Bryan at his side, he signed the proclamation announcing the ratification of the 17th Amendment. (NSHS RG3198-49-01)

1. **Political Reform:** 16th Amendment (graduated income tax); 17th Amendment (direct election of senators); 18th Amendment (prohibition of liquor); 19th Amendment (women's suffrage); regulation of campaign contributions; voting reform.[4]

2. **Economic Reform:** Federal Reserve Act; regulations regarding trusts and monopolies; Federal Trade Commission; Federal Farm Loan Act; government control of currency and banking; tariff reform.

3. **Public Policy:** Pure Food and Drug Act (1906); Federal Meat Inspection Act (1906); government regulation of the railroad and telegraph/teleophone; establishment of Departments of Health, Education, and Labor; promotion of public parks; defense of rights of minorities.[5]

4. **Labor Reform:** workers' compensation; minimum wage; eight-hour work day; improved conditions for seamen and railroad employees.

During the coal strike of 1902 that threatened the nation's industrial engine and its people dependent on coal for heat, President Theodore Roosevelt hinted he would use troops to seize and work the mines. Bryan advocated arbitration.

(L-R) Andrew Carnegie, steel magnate; Bryan; James J. Hill, railroad executive; and John Mitchell, United Mine Workers president, were among those President Roosevelt called to the White House during the coal strike of 1902. (LOC.gov/item/2016870950)

On October 2, 1902, Roosevelt called to Washington ten representatives of government, labor, and management to arbitrate a resolution (see photo). On October 23 the 163-day coal strike ended.[6]

INFLUENCE ON THE DEMOCRATIC PARTY

Bryan remained in the forefront of the Democratic Party in large part because of his ability to create coalitions and hold them together through his commanding presence and persuasive communications.

- Bryan dominated the Democratic Party for 16 years, from 1896–1912, "a length of time almost without parallel among American party leaders. Even after 1912, he remained among a handful of the most influential Democrats until his death 13 years later."[7]

Bryan (standing at front of platform in middle of photo) at 1912 DNC in Baltimore.

- Bryan wrote or greatly influenced large portions of the Democratic Party platforms for 1896, 1900, 1904, 1908, and 1912. Those of 1900 and 1908 were almost solely Bryan's work.

- Descriptions of the Democratic Party before and after Bryan:

  "Before Bryan, the Democratic Party was a conservative party of Civil War losers. After Bryan, the party was a progressive alliance of small businesses, farmers, blacks, and blue-collar workers."[8]

  Bryan worked with others to maintain the Democratic Party's "new commitment to a positive concept of government, its commitment to restraining great concentrations of economic power, and its commitment to increasing the role of the citizen in the political process."[9]

One significant example of Bryan's prominent role in the party is how his political influence is credited in leading to Woodrow Wilson's victory after 56 ballots during the deadlocked 1912 Democratic National Convention in Baltimore. After Wilson won the election, he invited Bryan to Trenton, NJ, and offered him the position of secretary of state, December 21, 1912 (photo). Bryan served Wilson well by working with Congress on his behalf to carry out his wishes on many significant issues. (LOC LC-DIG-ggbain-11195)

July 5, 1915, Bryan gave a pro-peace speech at the Panama-Pacific International Exposition in San Francisco, which was attended by more than 120,000 people. One source described Bryan's delivery that day as follows: "He had resigned from President Wilson's cabinet a little while before, and occupied the position of a sort of itinerant political clergyman, preaching peace in the midst of war and war's alarms, bravely holding aloft the ensign of human brotherhood when close to fifteen million men in Europe were trying to starve, blast, bayonet, and gas one another to death…"[10]

POLITICAL LEADERSHIP IN THE WORLD [11]

Bryan's major accomplishment as secretary of state (March 5, 1913 – June 9, 1915) was his negotiation of conciliation, or cooling-off, treaties, known officially as "Treaties for the Advancement of Peace." These treaties pledged the 30 signatories to refrain from hostilities during arbitration of disputes. The parties agreed that if they could not resolve a dispute, they would wait a year before going to war and would seek outside fact-finding.

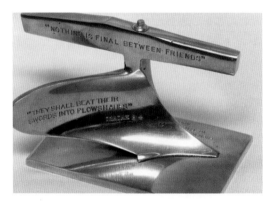

Bryan presented to each of the 30 diplomats a nickel-plated steel paperweight (the steel was composed of melted swords) cast into the shape of a plowshare (see photo at left). The inscriptions include a phrase from Isaiah 2:4—"They shall beat their swords into plowshares"—and two of Bryan's own epigrams—"Nothing is final between friends" and "Diplomacy is the art of keeping cool." These paperweights served as a symbol of his conviction that people everywhere desire peace and that governments must be restrained.

Bryan in many ways can be viewed as an American pioneer for international organization through his efforts in promoting peace arbitration and through his endorsement of the idea of the League of Nations, established in 1919 "to promote international cooperation and to achieve peace and security."

Bryan's resignation as secretary of state overshadowed many of his achievements, such as tariff reductions, Mexican and hemispheric relations, and his role in arbitrating an explosive immigration issue that threatened U.S.-Japanese relations.

Chief among the reasons that Bryan resigned was his disagreement with how Wilson responded to Germany after the sinking of the RMS *Lusitania*. Wilson ignored Bryan's counsel to follow mediation, or investigation of facts, as provided in the 30 peace treaties Bryan had negotiated. Despite Germany not being a signatory to those treaties, Bryan believed that Wilson should honor the principles established by the treaties.

While some Bryan critics characterize Bryan as a "pacifist," many of his actions indicate otherwise; for example,

- He served as a colonel in the Spanish–American War (1898).

- He supported every war declared by Congress while still advocating the principle of nonviolence. See "Political Crusades" on page 82 for more about Bryan's crusade for peace.

- He backed armed interventions in the Caribbean while secretary of state.

A three-mile petition for peace signed by 350,000 school children was presented to Secretary Bryan in 1915 to send to the leaders of the warring European nations. (LOC.gov/pictures/resource/hec.05443)

The simultaneous signing of four peace treaties with representatives from Great Britain, France, Spain, and China, September 15, 1914. More than half of the world's population was represented by the five officials who were seated at the State Department table. Mrs. Bryan (left) witnessed this event at the special invitation of her husband. (NSHS B915-375x)

Bryan's official portrait, painted for the Diplomatic Room of the Department of State, represents Bryan holding a copy of the peace treaties he negotiated.

5 | PRESIDENTIAL CAMPAIGNS

> The chief duty of governments, in so far as they are coercive, is to restrain those who would interfere with the inalienable rights of the individual, among which are the right to life, the right to liberty, the right to the pursuit of happiness and the right to worship God according to the dictates of one's conscience.

—William Jennings Bryan
The Royal Art (1914)

INTRODUCTION

Bryan was the Democratic Party's presidential nominee in 1896, 1900, and 1908. While he and Henry Clay share the record for each losing three presidential elections, Bryan alone holds the record for winning the most cumulative Electoral College votes without ever winning an election.

When President Harry Truman was asked why he thought Bryan never got elected, he responded, "I've given it a great deal of thought, but I've never figured it out. . . . The best I've come up with is that he was just too far ahead of his time, and the people in the East, the big-money people, were against him, and did everything they could to defeat him."[1]

Bryan compensated for his lack of financial backing by transforming the face of presidential politics. Prior to 1896 candidates stayed mostly in the background and the contest was between the parties. Bryan created the model seen in today's presidential campaigns where the candidates are constantly in the spotlight. Here are highlights from each of Bryan's campaigns, followed by the election results.

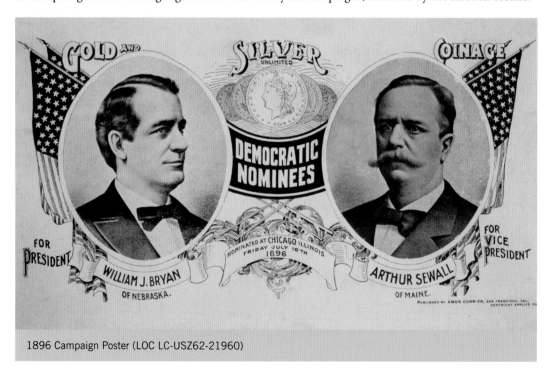

1896 Campaign Poster (LOC LC-USZ62-21960)

1896 PRESIDENTIAL CAMPAIGN[2]

On July 10, the day after delivering his "Cross of Gold" speech at the Democratic National Convention (DNC) in Chicago, IL, Bryan won his party's nomination on the fifth ballot. Bryan then won the nomination of the Populist, People's, and Silver Parties. William McKinley had won the Republican National Convention (RNC) nomination in St. Louis in June.

At age 36 Bryan became the youngest U.S. presidential nominee of a major party, a record he still holds. Other youngest presidential record holders are Theodore Roosevelt, the youngest to assume the presidency at 42, and John Kennedy, the youngest to run and win at 43.

Bryan acquired the "Great Commoner" nickname shortly after his nomination, when a railway executive offered to send Bryan back home in a private sleeper car. Journalist Willis Abbott objected, "Mr. Bryan, you should not accept this offer. You are the great Commoner, the people's candidate, and it would not do to accept favors from the great railroad corporations." Bryan declined the offer and wore the title with pride throughout his career.[3]

Mr. Bryan (left), Mrs. Bryan (right), and party on his campaign train car *The Idler* at Crestline, OH, 1896[4]

CAMPAIGN FIRSTS

- Bryan **pioneered the whistle-stop railroad tours** that remained part of American presidential politics into the 1950s. He crisscrossed the country and met voters in person. Usually accompanied by his family, he traveled over 18,000 miles by train in 3 months, visited 26 states and more than 250 cities, drew crowds as large as 70,000, and delivered over 600 speeches to about 5 million people.

- Bryan was the **first candidate to campaign in a car**. Hieronymous Mueller offered his 1895 Mueller-Benz for Bryan and his wife's use at two campaign stops in Decatur, IL, October 22, 1896 (see photo).

Bryan and Mueller are on the front seat. The rear seat is occupied by Mrs. Bryan, Mr. Bryan's secretary, and Mr. M. C. Irish of Decatur. (Hieronymus Mueller Museum)

- This was the first presidential election in which the **candidates used silent movies**. *Bryan Train Scene at Orange* (NJ) was filmed on September 23 and first shown at Proctor's Theatre in New York City on October 19, one week after *McKinley at Home* was first shown at the Olympia Music Hall in New York City.[5]

- This was the first presidential election for which the **candidates used mass-produced metal celluloid "pin back" campaign buttons.**

- **Bryan's campaign created the first voter database.** During the campaign Bryan received on average over 2,000 letters and telegrams a day from supporters, totaling 250,000 by election day. Bryan's brother and wife, Charles and Mary, created a card file in which they recorded information found in these letters (for example, party affiliation, job, and religion) and kept the files updated for 30 years. The files had about 200,000 names in 1897 and half a million by 1912. The information was used to create a mailing list for communicating with the Bryan network of supporters throughout Bryan's political career.[6]

- *The New York Times* published the results the day after the election, employing what is most likely **the first use of "news visualization"** (see map). Each state's winner was indicated with white for McKinley or black for Bryan, providing an easy way to see voting patterns.[7] Comparing this map's results with the map at the end of the chapter demonstrates the media bias against Bryan. Seven states were wrongly shown as white McKinley states instead of black Bryan states—KS, NE, NC, SD, VA, WA, and WY; no states were wrongly attributed to Bryan; and then-territories with no electoral votes—AZ, NM, and OK—were also white.

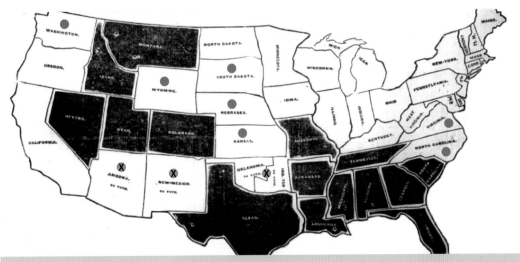

The front page of *The New York Times*, November 4, 1896, provides an example of media bias. These symbols, added to the original map, indicate the following: ● = Bryan states wrongly attributed to McKinley; Ⓧ = territories that say "NO VOTE" appear to be McKinley states because they are white.

BRYAN AT A DISADVANTAGE

Bryan's 1896 campaign is estimated to have raised less than 3 percent what McKinley's did ($425,000 vs. $16,500,000). In addition to Bryan's financial disadvantage, his campaign faced other challenges as outlined below:

- The Republicans distributed 120 million copies of 275 pamphlets, some as long as 40 pages, and translated in 9 languages.

- In Iowa alone 6,000 speakers were on the campaign trail for McKinley.

- Workers and businesses were pressured not to vote for Bryan. For example, workers who supported Bryan were fired or refused employment or told that a Bryan victory would force their company to close. Companies were sent large orders contingent on Bryan's defeat. Insurance companies promised to extend mortgages five years if Bryan lost.

1900 Campaign Poster (LOC LC-DIG-pga-02808)

- The press tended to be stridently anti-Bryan, as evidenced in how Bryan's platform was described in the July 10, 1896, edition of the *Philadelphia Press*: "It rests upon the corner stones of Communism and enthroned Anarchy. Such a noxious and nefarious profession of faith has never before been made in this country even by an escaped band of lunatics. The platform in every vital part appeals to everything that is low and debased and vicious in human nature."

- The Republicans paid voters for the time taken from their jobs to go vote. In Indiana, 30,000 voters were each paid $5 plus food and alcohol to vote for McKinley.

- Names from tombstones showed up on ballots; and in one district of 30,000 registered voters, 48,000 votes were cast.

- Some historians agree with Bryan's analysis that voting fraud stole about six states from Bryan; and a change of fewer than 20,000 votes in California, Oregon, Kentucky, Indiana, North Dakota, and West Virginia (some of which Bryan lost by only a few hundred votes) would have given him the presidency.[8]

1900 PRESIDENTIAL CAMPAIGN [9]

At the DNC in Kansas City, MO, on July 5, 1900, delegates nominated Bryan unanimously on the first ballot. Two weeks earlier, McKinley had won the nomination at the Philadelphia RNC.

The two presidential candidates campaigned as they did in 1896: McKinley from the front porch of his home in Canton, OH, and Bryan traveling 19,000 miles, delivering 546 speeches, and often putting in 17-hour days. Republican vice-presidential candidate Teddy Roosevelt, however, was determined to outdo Bryan in the oratorical arena; he traveled 3,000 more miles than Bryan and gave 127 more speeches than Bryan gave.

1908 Campaign Postcard

1908 PRESIDENTIAL CAMPAIGN [10]

At the DNC in Denver, CO, on July 11, 1908, delegates nominated Bryan on the first ballot with nearly 90 percent of the votes. His Republican Party opponent, William Howard Taft, had won the nomination about two weeks earlier at the Chicago RNC. Campaign firsts include the following:

- On the second day of the convention, July 8, Sen. Thomas Gore (former Vice President Al Gore's distant cousin) casually mentioned Bryan's name during a routine address. The 15,000 delegates and spectators burst into a **loud demonstration that lasted 87 minutes** in what "may have been the longest such event in American political history."[11]

- Bryan was the **first candidate to use audio media to spread his message to audiences on a vast scale.** In the process, he was the **first candidate to use "sound bites."** In May 1908 Bryan recorded ten speeches for Edison's National Phonograph Company. Due to wax cylinder space limitations, Bryan had to reduce each speech to about two minutes. Bryan's records went on sale in July. Taft made his recordings in August, and they went on sale in September. By October both candidates' records were strong sellers; however, the demand for Bryan's surpassed Taft's, with Bryan's sales exceeding 600,000. The records were played on home phonographs, at political club meetings, on city streets, and over telephone lines.[12]

- The **first mass media "debates"** occurred during this presidential campaign. A New York penny arcade played the recordings during mock debates using mannequins of Bryan and Taft. Phonograph dealers also hosted mock debates in their stores and in other venues.

Bryan riding in carriage in New York, 1908 (LOC LC-DIG-ggbain-02283)

ELECTION RESULTS [13]

	November 3, 1896		November 6, 1900		November 3, 1908	
Election Day	November 3, 1896		November 6, 1900		November 3, 1908	
Turnout	79.3%[14]		73.2%		65.4%	
Issues of the Day	Monetary System (Gold, Silver Standards) Financial Panic of 1893 | Tariffs		Liberty • Justice • Humanity | Anti-Imperialism | Spanish–American War		Shall the People Rule? | Bank Panic of 1907 Control and Regulation of Business Trusts	
Nominee	William McKinley	William Jennings Bryan	William McKinley	William Jennings Bryan	William Howard Taft	William Jennings Bryan
Home State	Ohio	Nebraska	Ohio	Nebraska	Ohio	Nebraska
Party	Republican	Democratic	Republican	Democratic	Republican	Democratic
Running Mate	Garret Augustus Hobart	Arthur Sewall	Theodore Roosevelt	Adlai Stevenson	James S. Sherman	John W. Kern
Estimated Spending[15]	$16,500,000	$425,000	$9,500,000	$425,000	$1,700,000	$750,000
Electoral Votes	271	176	292	155	321	162
States Carried	23[16]	22	28	17	29	17[17]
Popular Vote	7,112,138	6,508,172	7,228,864	6,370,932	7,678,395	6,408,984
Percentage	51.0%	46.7%	51.6%	45.5%	51.6%	43.0%

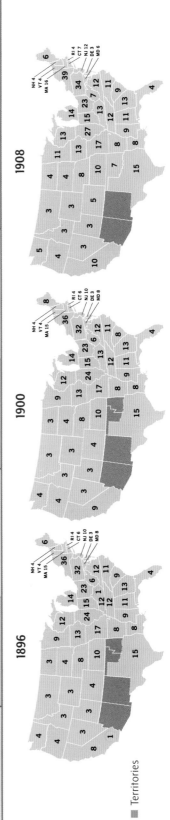

1908

1900

1896

■ Territories

> " Seest thou a man diligent in his business? He shall stand before kings.
>
> —Proverbs 22:29a (KJV)

B ryan resolved to use the significant influence he gained during his 1896, 1900, and 1908 presidential campaigns to promote democratic values and the causes he believed would improve life for ordinary Americans from the working and middle classes. This chapter outlines many of Bryan's activities between his presidential campaigns.

BETWEEN THE 1896 AND 1900 CAMPAIGNS [1]

- Authored the following books:
    - *The First Battle: A Story of the Campaign of 1896*
    - *Republic or Empire?: The Philippine Question*
    - *The Life and Speeches of Hon. Wm. Jennings Bryan*
- Launched a countrywide tour in early 1897 to speak on such themes as bimetallism, the encroachment of the trusts and money power on the rights of the people, and the evils of protective tariffs.

- Toured Mexico by train with Mrs. Bryan for three weeks in December 9, 1897. During their stay in Mexico City, President Diaz gave the Bryans a state carriage for their use and invited them to dine at Chapultepec Castle.[2]

- Appeared before the United States Supreme Court as an unpaid associate counsel in *Smyth v. Ames* 171 U.S. 163 (1898).[3]

- Increased his involvement in international affairs after the February 15, 1898, sinking of the naval ship USS *Maine* in Havana Harbor during the Cuban revolt against Spain, an event that became a major political issue in the United States and precipitated the Spanish–American War.

Bryan spoke at 16th International Christian Endeavor Convention, Central Park, San Francisco, July 7–12, 1897. (OpenSFHistory/ wnp37.01005.jpg)

After Col. Bryan contracted a weak case of typhoid fever, his wife (left) and daughter Grace came to care for him and stayed for several weeks. (State Archives of Florida)

- Joined the Nebraska militia on May 19, 1898, shortly after the outbreak of the Spanish–American War. Bryan was elected by the men to be colonel of the 2,000-man Third Nebraska Volunteer Infantry, nicknamed the "Silver Regiment." In July of 1898, Bryan's regiment joined the Seventh Corps at Camp Cuba Libre near Jacksonville, FL. They saw no active service but were plagued by typhoid fever and malaria. The war ended with the signing of the Treaty of Paris on December 10, 1898.

Col. Bryan is shown on horseback, leading the men of the Third regiment through the Exposition entrance of the Administration Arch into the Grand Court. (From the collections of Omaha Public Library)

- Used his influence to promote bringing a world's fair to Omaha, NE, in 1898. The Trans-Mississippi and International Exposition attracted over 2.6 million people from 26 countries and featured 4,062 exhibits. Bryan led his regiment in a military display at the Expo (see photo at left).[4]

- During the eighteen months leading up to the July 1900 Democratic National Convention, traveled the country giving speeches and being otherwise involved in various state campaigns and primary battles.

BETWEEN THE 1900 AND 1908 CAMPAIGNS [5]

- Authored the following books in 1900:

    - *The Second Battle, or, the New Declaration of Independence 1776–1900: An Account of the Struggle of 1900*

    - *Great Political Issues and Leaders of the Campaign of 1900*

- Launched his weekly newspaper, *The Commoner*, with the first issue published in January 1901 (see Chapter 9). Bryan used *The Commoner* to promote his reforms and stay connected to his loyal base of supporters. He was also a frequent contributor to other newspapers and various magazines.

- Broke ground in 1901 and moved into his second Lincoln, NE, home, Fairview, in 1903 (see "Fairview" on page 130).

- Used his influence to advocate for a wide variety of reforms, including popular election of senators, prohibition of corporations from contributing to campaign funds, demands for railroad regulation and for good roads, and demands to cease exploitation of child labor (1900–1904).

- Earned most of his annual income during summers by maintaining a full speaking schedule on the Chautauqua circuit (see "Chautauqua" on page 58). He would not accept pay when he spoke on Sundays or at patriotic, charitable, or religious gatherings.

- Embarked from New York with his son, William, Jr., on a two-month European tour on the RMS *Majestic* on November 14, 1903.[6] Bryan met with many heads of state and while in Russia spent several days with author Leo Tolstoy, whose influence can be seen in many of Bryan's actions, especially while he was secretary of state.

- Upon their return, plunged into the 1904 campaign and played a significant role at the Democratic convention in determining the party's platform.

(L-R) Unidentified man, Bryan's son, Leo Tolstoy, and Bryan outside Tolstoy's home, Yasnaya Polyana, in Russia, 1903

(L-R) Bryan, Mrs. Bryan, Grace, and guide in Egypt during world tour

- Departed from San Francisco for an 11-month world tour with his wife and two youngest children, William (16) and Grace (14), in September 1905 on the SS *Manchuria*.

   º Paid for the tour by giving speeches and writing weekly articles containing travelogue and political and religious commentary that were published in William Randolph Hearst's newspapers and several others and reprinted in *The Commoner*.

Inter-Parliamentary Union Conference, Westminster, London, England, 1906: (L-R) Bryan, Count Albert Apponyi (Hungary), and Baron D'Estournelles de Constant (France)

   º Visited Hawaii, Japan, Korea, China, the Philippines, Java, India, Burma, Egypt, Syria, Turkey, Lebanon, the Holy Land, Galilee, Greece, Hungary, Austria, Norway, England, Ireland, Spain, France, Switzerland, Belgium, the Netherlands, Germany, Russia, and other places.

   º Enthralled international listeners, including the Inter-Parliamentary Union in July 1906, with speeches on international peacekeeping. He spoke before other high-level audiences in Tokyo, India, the Middle East, Russia, and Europe.[7]

- Concluded world tour in August 1906 when he and his family arrived in New York Harbor. He was welcomed by nearly every prominent Democrat in the country and by thousands of enthusiastic people as he made his way from the harbor to the Victoria Hotel. See the three photos that conclude this chapter.

- Authored the following books between 1906–1908:
  - *The World's Famous Orations* (10 Vols.) – co-editor
  - *Letters to a Chinese Official: Being a Western View of Eastern Civilization*
  - *British Rule in India*
  - *The Old World and Its Ways*

- Secured the presidential nomination on the first ballot of the Democratic National Convention held in Denver in July 1908 and was on the road almost constantly from August until election eve.

Three photos show enthusiastic crowds greeting Bryan in New York City at conclusion of world tour.
1/3 Surrounded by reporters, friends, and political supporters, Bryan spoke from a tugboat in New York Harbor. (NSHS RG3198-36-05)

2/3 Throngs lined the street as Bryan and his entourage traveled down Broadway and passed the American Surety Building. (NSHS RG3198-36-12)

3/3 Bryan arrived (carriage in front of entrance) at Victoria Hotel, located at the intersection of 27th Street, Broadway, and Fifth Avenue, where he stayed until later that evening, when he gave a speech to an estimated 20,000 people in Madison Square Garden.[8] (NSHS RG3198-36-14)

> Belief in God gives courage. The Christian believes that every word spoken in behalf of truth will have its influence and that every deed done for the right weighs in the final account. What matters it to the believer whether his eyes behold the victory and his voice mingles in the shouts of triumph, or whether he dies in the midst of conflict!

—William Jennings Bryan
In His Image (1922)

While millions of people loved and admired Bryan, countless others opposed him. This chapter focuses on the following categories of critics and detractors: editorial cartoonists, journalists, and historians. Three examples of Bryan's responses to his critics conclude the chapter.

EDITORIAL CARTOONISTS [1]

Pictured here are a few of the many political cartoons that appeared on magazine covers and in newspapers from 1896–1925. *The Chicago Tribune* reported that "Bryan liked cartoons and took with extreme good nature the many caricatures of himself which appeared during his political career. 'I like as much as anybody,' he said, 'to see these cartoons of myself. I enjoy them immensely. And then cartoonists must live.'" [2]

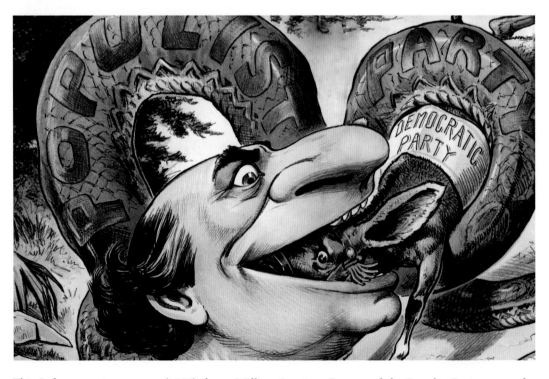

This *Judge* magazine cartoon (1896) shows William Jennings Bryan and the Populist Party as a snake swallowing up the mule representing the Democratic Party.

This November 7, 1900, illustration is one of many Bryan cartoons that appeared on *Puck* magazine covers. The full "Nevermore" caption reads, "On this home by horror haunted—tell me truly, I implore!—Is there—is there balm in Gilead? tell me, tell me, I implore! Quoth the Raven, 'Nevermore!'"

The illustration shows Bryan sitting at a desk on which are papers labeled "Free Silver Speeches." With a sorrowful look, he stares up at a raven perched on a bust of Pallas Athena. The raven wears a medallion labeled "Free Silver." Free Silver was the monetary platform on which Bryan ran his 1896 campaign, a policy that would expand the currency and help debtors, such as farmers.

This illustration appeared on the cover of the September 19, 1896, issue of *Judge*. It depicts Bryan standing atop a Bible, marketing the sales of a "crown of thorns" and a "cross of gold," both referencing his famous "Cross of Gold" speech (see page 52). The cartoonist characterized Bryan as "The Sacrilegious Candidate," adding that "No man who drags into the dust the most sacred symbols of the Christian world is fit to be President of the United States."

Vol XLIV No 2277

10 Cents a Copy
$4 00 a Year

HARPER'S WEEKLY

A Journal of Civilization

N E W   Y O R K   A U G U S T   11 : 1900

HE MADE IT ALL BY HIMSELF

This *Harper's Weekly* cover cartoon ridicules Bryan's role in shaping the Democratic Party's 1900 platform. It depicts a poorly constructed platform on which an impish Bryan has cobbled together "The Fierce Demopoptam from Kansas City,"—the Democratic Donkey, the Tammany Tiger, and the Populist Ostrich. Uncle Sam surveys the scene with a smirk on his face, and the caption reads, "He Made It All by Himself."

JOURNALISTS

Political historian Michael Kazin provided this context when he summarized 1896 press coverage of Bryan: "The campaign made compelling news. Most papers outside the Deep South and the Rockies supported McKinley, but his front-porch campaign lacked drama and spontaneity. In contrast, nearly every day with Bryan supplied an occasion either to ridicule the statements and habits of the 'boy Orator,' to marvel at his skill and endurance, or both."[3]

Quoted below are two of Bryan's harshest critics—Walter Lippmann (1889–1974) and H. L. Mencken (1880–1956).

Walter Lippmann was a writer, reporter, and one of three founding editors of *The New Republic*.

- In *Drift and Mastery* (1914), Lippmann wrote, "Bryan has never been able to adjust himself to the new world in which he lives. That is why he is so irresistibly funny to sophisticated newspapermen. His virtues, his habits, his ideas, are the simple, direct, shrewd qualities of early America. . . . he moves in a world that has ceased to exist."[4]

- In *A Preface to Politics* (1933), he said he did "not see the statesman in Bryan" and described Bryan as "a voice crying in the wilderness, but a voice that did not understand its own message." He added that "the scientific habit of mind is entirely lacking in his intellectual equipment" and concluded that "Bryan does not happen to have the naturalistic outlook, the complete humanity, or the deliberative habit which modern statecraft requires. He is the voice of a confused emotion."[5]

H. L. Mencken was one of America's leading journalists and covered the Scopes trial for the *Baltimore Sun*.[6]

In Mencken's autobiography, *My Life as Author and Editor*, he wrote, "I was against Bryan the moment I heard of him."[7] And Mencken's reporting on Bryan for some 20 years thereafter, especially his coverage of the Scopes trial, reflected his long-held hostility toward Bryan and his principles.

Through Mencken's trial reporting and his writing of Bryan's obituary, an obituary described as one of "the great masterpieces of invective in the English language,"[8] he created caricatures of Bryan, the proceedings, and the townspeople. Here are examples in each category:

- Mocked Bryan as an "old buzzard"; "tinpot pope"; "charlatan, a mountebank, a zany"; a "fundamentalist pope." Wrote, "It is a tragedy indeed to begin life as a hero and to end it as a buffoon."

- Called the proceedings a "universal joke" and dubbed them the "Monkey Trial."

- Ridiculed the townspeople, calling them "gaping primates," "yokels," and "rustic ignoramuses" who "never knew anything and never would."

- Wrote that Bryan's "one yearning was to keep his yokels heated up—to lead his forlorn mob against the foe. . . . He seemed only a poor clod like those around him, deluded by a childish theology, full of an almost pathological hatred of all learning, all human dignity, all beauty, all fine and noble things. He was a peasant come home to the dung-pile."[9]

When news of Bryan's death reached Mencken in Baltimore, he joked, "God aimed at Darrow, missed, and hit Bryan instead." To Joseph Krutch, fellow Scopes trial reporter, he said, "We killed the son-of-a-[expletive]!"[10]

HISTORIANS

Robert W. Cherny wrote in 1996 that historians have been fascinated with Bryan, at least in part, because of his longevity. After capturing his party's presidential nomination in 1896, at the age of 36, he remained the party's most important leader for the next 16 years. Thereafter, for the remaining 13 years of his life, Bryan continued to play an influential role among Democrats. Cherny categorized the works on Bryan into these four categories:[11]

DURING BRYAN'S POLITICAL PRIME	1920s & 1930s	LATE 1940s TO EARLY 1960s	BEGINNING ABOUT 1960
Mainly campaign biographies and "most are best forgotten."	Most were favorable toward Bryan.	Highly critical scholarly analyses that largely portrayed Bryan in a negative light.	Tended to be more balanced.
Two highly negative Bryan portrayals: • *The Boomerang or Bryan's Speech with the Wind Knocked Out* by James S. Barcus (1896).[12] • *Bryan (The Boy Orator of the Platte) Unveiled* by H. E. Bartholomew (1908). The last page wrongly predicted, "After the campaign Mr. Bryan, politically dead, will remain at Fairview in merited seclusion, for no one will care to hear him spout any more."[13] • The book titles during this period (see Chapter 18) generally indicate whether a book is pro- or anti-Bryan.	See Chapter 18 for books written about Bryan during this period.	• Historian Richard Hofstadter in 1948 presented Bryan as conventional, provincial, impractical, and expedient; he drummed repeatedly on Bryan's lack of intelligence.[14] • Historian Richard Challener in 1961 wrote this: "With his rejection of power politics, his penchant for moralizing, his addiction to platitudinous speeches, and his reliance upon the tenets of Christian pacifism, Bryan seems to be the symbol of virtually every error that is condemned by contemporary critics of the American diplomatic tradition."[15] • Textbooks followed suit as shown in a widely used history textbook (1963) that said Bryan "had not lent the [Democratic] party much in intellectual distinction."	Ten years after Cherny's analysis, Michael Kazin wrote *A Godly Hero: The Life of William Jennings Bryan*. Kazin stated that Bryan's mass appeal lifted him "to the top rank of American leaders" and that only "Theodore Roosevelt and Woodrow Wilson had a greater impact on politics and political culture during the era of reform" from the mid-1890s to the early 1920s.[16] Kazin's biography was recognized as one of the best books of the year by *The Washington Post, Chicago Tribune, Los Angeles Times,* and the *St. Louis Post-Dispatch.*

Secratary of State Bryan, on his way to deliver a Chautauqua address, meets Gov. William Mann of VA and discusses a new currency bill at the American Institute of Banking, Richmond, VA, 1913. (NSHS RG3198-PH-18-32)

BRYAN'S RESPONSE TO HIS CRITICS [17]

Bryan often had a good-natured response to his critics (see "University of Michigan" on page 158). Other times his response was of a more serious nature.

During the 1896 presidential campaign, "Rev. Cortland Myers of Brooklyn's Baptist Temple stated that 'the blood-stained banner of the cross' was endangered by the 'anarchist' Chicago platform—a document 'made in hell.' Scores of clergymen in other eastern cities agreed, although usually in cooler terms."[18]

Bryan "knew that many of his supporters viewed Christ . . . as 'the great emancipator and the great equalizer' and that they shared his contempt for haughty backsliders in clerical collars. The goldbugs might 'buy the ministers,' a young woman from upstate New York wrote to Bryan, but 'they cannot buy the congregations.'"[19]

During Bryan's tenure as secretary of state, the press widely criticized him when he used his summer vacation to conduct Chautauqua lectures for pay (see page 58). Here is Bryan's response:

I expect to lecture whenever I deem it desirable or necessary to do so and, I have not in the least altered the plans which were made at the time I assumed the duties of the office. The criticism that has been directed against my lecturing is no more bitter than the criticism I have undergone at other times and for other things during my connection with politics.

A part of this criticism is malicious, a part of it is partisan, and a part of it is based upon misinformation. That which is malicious will answer itself, that which is partisan will be accepted as such, that which is based upon misinformation will cease when the critics are better informed.

No man should enter public life if he objects to criticism, and he cannot stay in public life if he permits criticisms to turn him from doing what he thinks is right. He must decide his duty for himself and is answerable to the public for any mistakes he makes. I regard lecturing as an entirely legitimate field. I lectured before I was nominated for the presidency; I lectured between campaigns; I shall continue to lecture, and I shall not believe that any person whose opinion is worth having will think the less of me because I do so. This closes the lecture subject for the present.[20]

More than a decade later, Bryan reopened the subject when he wrote in his *Memoirs*: "The President approved of my Chautauqua work—which, by the way, occupied fifteen days in two years. I had less vacation than any clerk in my department; other secretaries were able to travel without criticism. . . . President Taft lectured at Chautauqua after he was elected; Vice President Marshall and Speaker Clark while they were in office. Nobody ever criticized them. . . . There was no reason why I should be criticized for putting in a part of my vacation time lecturing."[21]

A large crowd gathered in anticipation of hearing Bryan deliver a speech during his campaign train's five-minute stop at the Monroe Railroad Station (NY) at 11:15 a.m., October 24, 1908.

PART 3

GIFTED COMMUNICATOR

8 | ORATOR

> Eloquent speech is not from lip to ear, but rather from heart to heart.
>
> —William Jennings Bryan
> Preface to *The World's Famous Orations* [1]

INTRODUCTION

Mary recalled in the Bryans' *Memoirs* a significant event that launched her husband on a trajectory that led to his renown as one of the most popular public speakers in American history. She described as follows the incident that occurred when Bryan was 27, shortly after he got into Nebraska politics:

> He had spoken in a town in the western part of the state, came home on a night train, and arrived at daybreak. I was sleeping when he came in, and he awakened me. Sitting on the edge of the bed, he began: 'Mary, I have had a strange experience. Last night I found that I had power over the audience. I could move them as I chose. I have more than usual power as a speaker. . . . God grant I may use it wisely.' And as it was his custom all through life to carry to his Heavenly Father any new development, he prayed. [2]

Nine years later, Bryan's "more than usual power as a speaker" propelled him into the political limelight when he delivered his "Cross of Gold" speech in Chicago, IL. The "Cross of Gold" speech and the one that became known as "The Last Message," which he prepared 29 years later in Dayton, TN, bookended the thousands of speeches Bryan made during his time on the world stage.

"Cross of Gold" (July 1896). The day after he delivered his "Cross of Gold" speech at the Democratic National Convention, Bryan won his party's nomination and became the Democratic presidential candidate. [3]

- With Bryan's theme of "free silver," he represented the voice of farmers and western miners who believed the fixed Eastern money markets of the "gold standard" left them with limited currency, inadequate credit sources, and looming foreclosures.

- This speech is known as a masterpiece of political-religious oratory, exemplified in the closing: "You shall not press down upon the brow of labor this crown of thorns; you shall not crucify mankind upon a cross of gold."

- Following his speech, delegates shouted, cried, threw handkerchiefs, and stomped their feet for a full forty minutes, twice as long as Bryan had spoken. *The New York World* reported that "everyone seemed to go mad at once." [4]

- "In every presidential year since 1896, feature writers have retold the story of [Bryan's] triumph and deemed his speech the most famous one ever made in any American party convention and one of the world's great orations." [5] See speech text on pages 168–172.

"The Last Message" (July 1925). Bryan intended for "The Last Message" to be his closing argument at the Scopes trial. However, it became Bryan's unspoken speech because the trial ended abruptly when Darrow asked the jury to return a guilty verdict so the case could be appealed to the Tennessee Supreme Court. Bryan spent several days following the trial preparing the text for release to the press.

- Five days after the trial ended and about an hour before his passing, Bryan had a telephone conversation with George F. Milton, editor of *The Chattanooga News*. Milton reported that Bryan told him, "I feel that this is the mountain peak of my life's efforts. I only regret that I did not have the opportunity to make it at the close of the trial."

- Milton said the last penciled proof correction Bryan made near the end of the 15,000-word speech was to finalize the wording on the phrase "with hearts full of gratitude to God."[6]

- Bryan's hope for its widespread publication was fulfilled: The Associated Press and the United Press sent the entire speech to all their clients. The International News Service sent almost half of the text.

- See page 124 for more about this speech.

Although many factors contributed to Bryan's success as a public speaker, these three stand above the rest and serve as an outline for this chapter:

Bryan delivering speech in New York City, c. 1906

- **Possessed innate abilities.** Bryan's exceptional oratorical powers were reinforced by his extraordinary strength and stamina.

- **Connected uniquely with audiences.** Bryan connected with, understood, and persuaded his listeners, and gave voice to their concerns in a way few political leaders have been able to achieve.

- **Drew crowds wherever he spoke.** Bryan drew crowds and touched his listeners wherever he spoke—before political audiences; during international travel; on the Chautauqua circuit; and at religious, civic, and educational events.

POSSESSED INNATE ABILITIES

Bryan's desire to use wisely his ability to move his audiences guided his career during which he delivered over 6,000 scheduled speeches and countless unscheduled ones. Among the nicknames by which he was known were "The Silver-Tongued Orator," "The Boy Orator of the Platte,"[7] "The Voice of Hope of the People," "The Orator of Small-Town America," and "The Mouthpiece for Jeffersonian Democracy."

Nebraska Democrats nicknamed him "Bryan the Invincible," declaring that he "thoroughly believes what he says, and his entire lack of artfulness makes him invincible." A fellow Lincoln, NE, attorney stated, "By your personal magnetism you won all the hearts; and by the force of your eloquence and the irresistible character of your logic and argument, you vanquished the enemy."[8]

Bryan's career occurred during an era when mass media was mainly limited to newspapers and there were no voice amplification options. Nevertheless, the *Washington Post* reported the day after Bryan's death that "his voice has been heard, probably, by more people than any man on earth."[9] While many factors contributed to such an achievement, these four stand out:

1. HE POSSESSED A MESMERIZING VOICE.[10]

Foes as well as allies said Bryan was "the most compelling speaker they'd ever heard." Their reasons for saying so often began with a description of the quality of his voice: "sonorous and melodious," "deep and powerfully musical," "soothing but penetrating," "free, bold, picturesque," "clear as a cathedral bell," and "sometimes familiar as if in personal conversation, at other times ringing out like a trumpet."[11]

Although Bryan had no microphone or loud speaker, his voice could reach everyone in arenas with 20,000 seats and could cover great distances outdoors. One local paper reported that when Bryan spoke at the Boulder, CO, Chautauqua in 1900 that "his booming voice could be heard a mile away on the University of Colorado campus (the roar was heard, though exact words were indiscernible)." Experts indicate that breath control techniques enabled Bryan to project his voice loudly and for long periods of time.[12] In addition, Bryan's diction was "clear, precise, and rendered with a slight prairie twang that passed for no accent at all," which "ensured that listeners could understand every word."[13]

Bryan addressing thousands assembled at Madison, IN, Chautauqua, July 6, 1901 (LOC LC-USZ62-10014)

2. HE MANIFESTED EXTRAORDINARY STAMINA AND ENERGY.

Examples of Bryan's stamina and energy abound from his 18,000-mile 1896 presidential whistle-stop campaign (see "1896 Presidential Campaign" on page 29) to his grueling Chautauqua circuit speaking schedule. This story about Bryan after the 1920 Democratic National Convention in San Francisco is revealing. He was 60 years old, weary after his involvement at the convention, and scheduled to embark immediately on a three-week Chautauqua tour ending in Salt Lake City. The circuit manager assigned a husky 22-year-old man to assist Bryan. As they rushed to make train connections in the summer heat and slept wherever they could, the young man "managed to keep within sight of Bryan's coattails." After they finished their three-week tour, Bryan's assistant "took to his bed and slept a week." Meanwhile, Bryan wired home to his wife, "I am in splendid physical shape and rested up from the convention."[14]

3. HE WROTE HIS OWN SPEECHES.

Bryan never used speechwriters. Early in his career he memorized his speeches; later he spoke extemporaneously from an outline and only wrote speeches that had official importance. When speech copy was required for publication, Bryan dictated the speech to a secretary without using notes. His wife, who did much of the research for his quotations and historical references, said that when a subject was familiar to him, he spoke entirely without notes. She marveled at his expansive, well-ordered memory that enabled him to recall ideas, stories, facts, and figures and use them with great effect.[15]

4. HE EXPLOITED AVAILABLE MASS MEDIA OPTIONS.

Examples of mass media options that Bryan used to connect with his audiences include the following:

- For 22 years he published his own paper, *The Commoner* (see Chapter 9), in which many of his speeches appeared.

- He was an early adopter of emerging mass media technology, such as silent movies and phonograph records (see 1896 and 1908 presidential campaign firsts in Chapter 5) and commercial radio (see "Radio Evangelist" on page 61).

- The press found Bryan to be a source of compelling news throughout his public career. After Bryan's death a reporter pronounced that the press should build a memorial to him "because he was to the world of news what Babe Ruth is to baseball—the real drawing card."[16]

CONNECTED UNIQUELY WITH AUDIENCES

Bryan's popularity as a speaker perhaps can be best explained by his belief expressed in the chapter's opening quotation, "Eloquent speech is not from lip to ear, but rather from heart to heart."

His communication style was undeniably genuine and unfeigned:

> Nearly every observer agreed that Bryan was a 'magnetic' speaker. The allusion to a power of nature is instructive. He appeared to be free from all doubt, ambivalence, and insincerity. Whether talking to Mary in their sitting room or to thousands of people in a park or metropolitan arena, he uttered the same sentiments in a mode of unapologetic sentimentality.[17]

Gaining insights about Bryan's heart and his perspective regarding his listeners' hearts helps to explain Bryan's unique connection with his audiences.

Bryan's Heart

While no one can ever know another person's heart, these insights provide a glimpse into Bryan's:

- While a Nebraska congressman (1893), he told his wife shortly before delivering an important speech that he had prayed to be used as "an instrument in the hands of Providence of doing some good for my country."[18]

- Bryan naturally merged his faith with his political career. He used his renown as a politician and orator as a platform to share his faith with those who otherwise might never darken the door of a church. His political speeches often included biblical allusions, and his religious speeches often included political allusions. Bryan recounted during an 1896 campaign stop in Fredericksburg, VA, that "a gentleman in the audience, in an outburst of enthusiasm, shouted: 'Bryan, I am not a Christian, but I am praying for you.' This gave me an opportunity to suggest that the people of that community had an additional reason for desiring my election, because, if they could convince the gentleman of the efficacy of prayer, they might make a Christian out of him."[19]

- While serving as a colonel in the Spanish–American War (1898), he wrote to his wife: "If I consulted my own happiness I would forsake public life forever, but I am not free to please myself. I have consecrated whatever talents I may have to the service of my fellow men. To aid in making the government better and existence more tolerable to the producer of wealth, is my ambition."[20]

- While commenting on his most popular Chautauqua lecture, "Prince of Peace" (1913), Bryan explained, "I offer no apology for speaking upon a religious theme, for it is the most universal of all themes. I am interested in the science of government, but I am more interested in religion than in government. I enjoy making a political speech—I have made a good many and shall make more—but I would rather speak on religion than on politics."[21]

Bryan standing, holding hat, speaking to crowd at the Santa Fe, NM, Fair, c. 1913 (LOC LC-USZ62-50422)

Bryan's beliefs about the people he served and to whom he spoke influenced and shaped his message:

- Bryan expressed what he believed to be the qualities of "the goodness of the American people" in the introduction of his *Memoirs* by enumerating "their patriotism, their moral courage, their high ideals, their willingness to sacrifice for their convictions—the virtues that not only make popular government possible but insure its success."[22]

- Bryan explained how his audience influenced the shift in his message from politics to religion: "After the election of 1900 there was no certainty of my being a candidate again . . . . I felt free to devote more time to religious addresses, . . . I thought that possibly I might reach and influence some young men who avoided the churches. . . . that I might make a defense of the Christian religion and reach some who might not be so easily reached from the pulpit."[23]

- Mary said of her husband, "It is not too much to say that Mr. Bryan has remained the most popular Chautauqua lecturer in this country for thirty years. Each year when he returned from his tours he had not only spoken to, but had listened to, the mind of America. He had had an opportunity to know what America was thinking and he had helped America to make up her mind."[24]

DREW CROWDS WHEREVER HE SPOKE

As discussed in earlier chapters, Bryan drew large crowds for political speeches he delivered at venues such as the Democratic National Convention arenas and coliseums; Westminster in London, England; and Madison Square Garden in New York City.

To provide another perspective, this section includes information on the Chautauqua lecture circuit that Bryan traveled nearly every summer for three decades and will conclude with examples of civic, religious, and educational venues at which he spoke (see Figure 8-1).

FIGURE 8-1	SPEECH VENUES

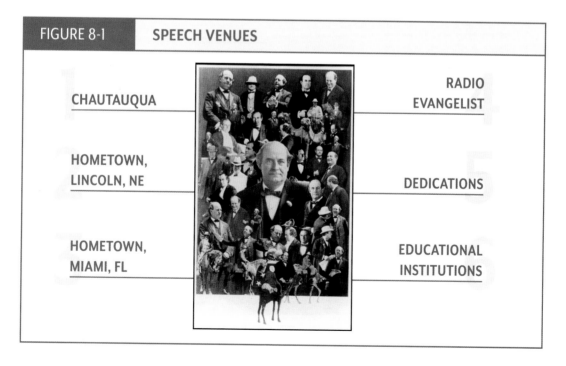

CHAUTAUQUA

HOMETOWN, LINCOLN, NE

HOMETOWN, MIAMI, FL

RADIO EVANGELIST

DEDICATIONS

EDUCATIONAL INSTITUTIONS

Bryan's Chautauqua summer lecture tours provided a major source of income from 1895–1925, when he was widely considered to be the most popular lecturer on the circuit.[25] The effect of the Chautauqua movement by providing cultural stimulation and intellectual inspiration was somewhat similar to the effect of 21st century TED talks.[26] The following provides more insights about Chautauqua history, Bryan's earnings, his reputation, and his lecture topics.

CHAUTAUQUA HISTORY [27]

- Chautauqua was founded in 1874 as a summer school for Sunday school teachers on the shores of Lake Chautauqua in western New York. Shortly thereafter independent Chautauquas, or assemblies, sprang up across the country. Soon lyceum bureaus were used by the assemblies to book their talent.

- The goal of the circuit Chautauquas was "to offer challenging, informational, and inspirational stimulation to rural and small-town America."

- The movement peaked in the mid-1920s, when circuit Chautauqua performers and lecturers appeared in more than 10,000 communities in 45 states to audiences totaling 45 million people.

- Bryan called Chautauqua a "potent human factor in molding the mind of the nation." Woodrow Wilson during World War I described it as an "integral part of the national defense." Theodore Roosevelt said that Chautauqua is "the most American thing in America."

Keokuk County
Chautauqua ⹀ Institute
August 14⹀23, 1905,
S I G O U R N E Y ,   I O W A

COL. WILLIAM JENNINGS BRYAN

MONDAY, AUGUST 21, 2 P. M.
The greatest orator of our time. Thousands of people assemble to hear him wherever he goes.

The opportunity of a life time to hear America's most noted Speakers and Musicians

- The Great Depression brought an end to most circuits; however, many sites continue to this day to provide a modern-day Chautauqua experience in New York, where the movement began, as well as in several other states.[28]

EARNINGS

- Estimates regarding Bryan's annual summer earnings on the circuit range between $50,000 and $100,000. His standard rate was $250 per speech, plus half the proceeds over $500. He generally delivered two speeches a day, sometimes more.

- "He was the best drawing card Chautauqua ever knew. He was the highest-paid lecturer and brought the most money into the box office. The circuit lucky enough to lure the old war horse away from competition knew to a certainty that would be its most successful season. He was good for 'forty acres of packed Fords, anywhere, at any time of the day or night.'"[29]

REPUTATION ON THE CIRCUIT

Bryan had no flaws from Chautauqua's perspective:

- He consistently drew record crowds; everyone could hear and see him.

- He could hold the attention of young and old and send all of them away satisfied.

- No conditions kept his audiences away, and no travel delays kept Bryan from showing up, even if it meant getting to his destination after midnight. In Sioux Falls, SD, for example, his audience was still there and shouting when he arrived after midnight. He talked from 12:40–2:08 a.m., and the "listeners left him as reluctantly as he left them."

- Throughout the grueling 60–120 consecutive days of daily speeches in the midwest summer heat, Bryan was the "same even-tempered, uncomplaining, kindly man . . . and his final oration of the season was as full-bodied and convincing as the first."

- He didn't need to be entertained, spoke as easily to the trainmen as to the governor, and was also fine with just sitting and thinking.

- Bryan had no vices even of the smallest that had to be hidden from his audience.

- He didn't require any special accommodations and didn't mind if he had to wash in a common basin on a bench behind the tent, or sleep on a pile of blankets in the crew tent. He could sleep anywhere for any length of time and wake up refreshed.

- "Bryan had a sweetness of spirit that endeared him to the thousands upon thousands—many millions, actually—who heard him speak. There was no bitterness, no malice, no verbal jabs at his political opponents. America, he said time and again, had been good to him. He held no resentment against anybody. He was incapable of holding a grudge."[30]

Chautauqua manager Charles F. Horner described the audience response to Bryan as follows: "I think that there is but one word that can correctly define the feeling of the Chautauqua audience for Mr. Bryan. There was respect, of course, admiration and even affection. But overall there was one quality which seemed never to be absent, and that was reverence."[31]

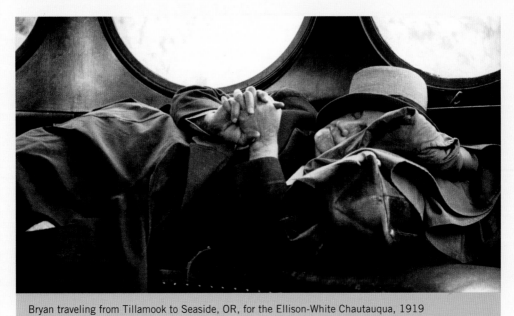

Bryan traveling from Tillamook to Seaside, OR, for the Ellison-White Chautauqua, 1919
(NSHS RG3198-65)

2. Hometown, Lincoln, Nebraska [32]

- The Bryans were very involved in Lincoln's civic and religious life. They were active in the YWCA and YMCA. Mrs. Bryan helped organize the Lincoln chapter of the Sorosis Club, the first professional club for women in the U.S. Bryan made himself available, free of charge, as a speaker at local high school, church, and civic events. He declined invitations to accept political speaking engagements on Sundays. "Normally, Bryan was at home on Sundays—whether in Lincoln, Washington, or Miami" and he and his family regularly attended church.[33]

- Bryan was a church elder at Westminster Presbyterian Church, serving communion to Woodrow Wilson during Wilson's 1912 visit to Fairview. The Bryans also worshiped at the small Normal Methodist Church to become better acquainted with their neighbors, and both Bryans taught Sunday school there when their travel schedules permitted.

- Bryan and Adolphus Talbot established a law practice in Lincoln in 1887. In 1891 they founded The Round Table Club, a non-partisan debating club that provided a venue for Lincoln's leaders to debate political, legal, and business issues.

Bryan (front row, 3rd from left) with his Normal Methodist Church men's Sunday school class (NSHS RG3198-67-03)

Caption on bottom right: "Neath Palms & Sunshine | William Jennings Bryan's Presbyterian Tourist Bible Class | Miami, FLA, Feb 6th 1921" (LOC LC-USZ62-126497)

3. Hometown, Miami, Florida

- Considered to be "even more eloquent when preaching than when talking politics. . . . For virtually all his adult life Mr. Bryan was a Sunday school teacher. . . . A decade ago, when he moved to Florida, he began teaching a Bible class in a grove at Miami. . . . His class was one of the prides of his life."[34] (See photo above.) By 1923 "Bryan's Bible Talks" were carried by 110 newspapers across the country and had an estimated readership of 20–25 million.[35]

- Mary described the class setting as "beneath the open sky, under the shade of graceful palms, and on the shore of our beautiful Biscayne Bay." She told the story of a man who was among the many who greeted her husband after the class, and Bryan responded to his compliment saying that he was hoping to reach people who never go to church. The man replied: "I am sure you had some of them here this morning. I was standing in the aisle near the front and a man was interfering with my view. I asked him to stand over a little, and he rejoined, 'You go to hell. I will stand where I damn please.'" Another of Mary's stories was about a four-year-old boy who attended the class with his grandmother. Afterward he said, "I am not going back to my own Sunday school anymore; I am coming to Mr. Bryan's class." His grandmother said, "Why should you want to leave your own Sunday school?" The boy replied, "But, Grandma, God can see us here."[36]

4. Radio Evangelist

- Bryan delivered sermons via radio stations in Pittsburgh, Los Angeles, Miami, and elsewhere, "making him one of the first evangelists to exploit the new medium."[37]

- One such sermon was broadcast October 25, 1922, to an audience of an estimated 60 million. His 10-minute address was aired on Salt Lake City, UT, radio station KZN (known as KSL today) that began broadcasting in May 1922 and was among the first radio stations in the western U.S.[38]

5. Dedications

- Bryan delivered the keynote speech at the dedication of the Sam Houston Memorial, Huntsville, TX, 1911.[39]

- Bryan spoke to a crowd of thousands at the dedication of the Lincoln Monument, a bronze statue of Abraham Lincoln at the Nebraska State Capitol, Lincoln, NE, 1912.[40]

- Bryan addressed 400 distinguished men of the South during his speech at the grand opening banquet of Grove Park Inn, Asheville, NC, 1913.[41]

6. Educational Institutions

- Bryan spoke at many colleges and universities, including the University of Michigan, the University of Florida, Brown University, Dartmouth, Harvard, Moody Bible Institute, Bible Institute of Los Angeles (Biola University), Wheaton College, Lane Theological Seminary, Union Theological Seminary, and Princeton.[42]

- Bryan delivered an address to the students of Washington and Lee University, Lexington, VA, in the spring of 1908, which inspired the launch of the Washington and Lee Mock Convention. The Mock Convention has occurred every four years since 1908, except for the 1920 and 1944 elections, and has the reputation for being the most accurate student-run mock political convention in the country.[43]

- He emphasized the importance of oratory for the development of a new Japan in a speech on the ideal of education and the American educational system to about 8,000 Japanese students at Waseda University, Tokyo, October 18, 1905.[44]

- Bryan was the commencement speaker at Salem High School, May 16, 1919, in his hometown of Salem, IL. Among those graduating that day was John T. Scopes, who by a curious twist of fate, was named the defendant in the 1925 Scopes trial (see Chapter 15).

9 | THE COMMONER

> If you are going to accomplish anything in this country, you must have faith in your form of government, and there is every reason why you should have faith in it. . . . It is best, not because it is perfect, but because it can be made as perfect as the people deserve to have. It is a people's government, and it reflects the virtue and intelligence of the people.

—William Jennings Bryan
In His Image (1922)

INTRODUCTION

Bryan made the above statement during a series of nine lectures he delivered to students at a Richmond, VA, seminary. What Bryan said leading up to the statement provides context for it: "We are told that without faith it is impossible to please God, and I may add that without faith it is impossible to meet the expectations of those who are most interested in you." He followed with a discussion of the four areas of faith that students must possess if they are to do a great work: faith in themselves, faith in humanity, faith in the form of government under which they live, and faith in God.[1]

The Commoner audience was educated and motivated in all four faith areas as the content over the course of its 768 issues "reveals the gradual extension of Bryan's interest from political to moral reforms."[2] This chapter tells the story of how *The Commoner* came to be; its audience, naming, and purpose; its content, financing, circulation, and format; and its employees and end of publication.

FOUNDING & DURATION

Bryan had the idea of founding and managing his own paper during his tenure as editor of the *Omaha World-Herald* (1894–1896).

- Wanted to publish a national journal that would serve as a forum for reform, discussing issues of national and international concern.
- Sought the advice of his friend, Orlando Jay Smith (1842–1908), co-founder, president, and general manager of the American Press Association (APA), who provided technical advice and helped shape the character of *The Commoner*.[3]
- Opened *The Commoner* office in Lincoln, NE, shortly after his 1900 election defeat and published the first edition on January 23, 1901. Wrote in the January 31, 1902, edition, "Both writing and speaking furnish such agreeable occupation that one does not notice the loss of a little thing like the presidency."[4]
- Published 768 issues in its 22-year run through April 1923. Issues are available as part of the Library of Congress's *Chronicling America: American Historic Newspapers* online collection.[5]

The Commoner.

VOL. I. NO. 1.   LINCOLN, NEBRASKA, JANUARY 23, 1901.   **$1.00 a Year.**

William J. Bryan.

Editor and Proprietor.

The Commoner.

Webster defines a commoner as "one of the common people." The name has been selected for this paper because THE COMMONER will endeavor to aid the common people in the protection of their rights, the advancement of their interests and the realization of their aspirations.

It is not necessary to apologize for the use of a term which distinguishes the great body of the population from the comparatively few, who, for one reason or another, withdraw themselves from sympathetic connection with their fellows. Among the Greeks "Hoi polloi" was used to describe the many, while among the Romans the word "plebe" was employed for the same purpose. These appellations, like "the common people," have been assumed with pride by those to whom they were applied, while they have been used as terms of reproach by those who counted themselves among the aristocratic classes. Within recent years there has been a growing tendency in some quarters to denounce as demagogic any reference to, or praise of, the common people.

One editor in a late issue of his paper takes exception to the phrase and says:

This expression is an ill-chosen one and should have no lodgment in the vocabulary of an American patriot and statesman. If we sought its origin, we would look for it in that specious demagogy which has evolved the professional politician, arrayed country against town—the farmer and his sons and daughters against the business and professional men and their sons and daughters—capital against labor, and built up against neighbors the impregnable barriers of prejudice and hate.

This quotation is reproduced because it fairly represents the views of those who criticize the expression. It has, however, an eminently respectable origin. In the same chapter in which Christ condensed man's duty to his fellows into the commandment: Thou shalt love thy neighbor as thyself; in the same chapter in which he denounced those who devour widows' houses and for a pretense make long prayers—in this same chapter it is said of Him: The common people heard Him gladly.

No higher compliment was ever paid to any class.

The term, the common people, is properly used to describe the large majority of the people—those who earn their living and give to society a fair return for the benefits bestowed by society—those who in their daily lives recognize the ties which bind together the mass of the people who have a common lot and a common hope. Sometimes they are called "the middle classes" because paupers and criminals are excluded on the one hand, while on the other hand some exclude themselves because of wealth or position or pride of birth. The common people form the industrious, intelligent and patriotic element of our population; they produce the nation's wealth in time of peace and fight the nation's battles in time of war. They are self-reliant and independent; they ask of government nothing but justice and will not be satisfied with less. They are not seeking to get their hands into other people's pockets, but are content if they can keep other people's hands out of their pockets.

The common people do not constitute an exclusive society—they are not of the four hundred; any one can become a member if he is willing to contribute by brain or muscle to the nation's strength and greatness. Only those are barred—and they are barred by their own choice—who imagine themselves made of a superior kind of clay and who deny the equality of all before the law.

A rich man, who has honestly acquired his wealth and is not afraid to intrust its care to laws made by his fellows, can count himself among the common people, while a poor man is not really one of them if he fawns before a plutocrat and has no higher ambition than to be a courtier or a sycophant.

THE COMMONER will be satisfied if, by fidelity to the common people, it proves its right to the name which has been chosen.

A Living Fountain.

Jeremiah gave to literature a beautiful and striking figure when, in charging the children of Israel with apostasy, he said:

They have forsaken me, the fountain of living waters, and hewed them out cisterns, broken cisterns, that can hold no water.

One is reminded of this forcible simile today when a large number of our people seem inclined to turn back to the once discarded doctrine of empires. To compare self-government with an arbitrary form of government is like comparing a living fountain with a broken cistern.

When the people are recognized as the source of power the government is perpetual because the people endure forever. The government then responds to their desires and conforms to their character; it can be made as good as they deserve to have and they are satisfied with it because it is their own handiwork. If it has evils those evils are endured because the people recognize that they themselves are to blame and that it is within their power to apply any needed remedy.

A government resting on force is, on the other hand, ever unstable because it excites hatred rather than affection and is continually at war with human nature; it is in constant antagonism to that universal sentiment which is defined as the love of liberty.

All history sustains the self-evident truths which form the foundation of a government deriving its just powers from the consent of the governed. All history condemns a political structure which appeals only to fear and relies upon bayonets for its support.

How the Tariff Aids the Trusts.

A recent number of the Hardware Dealer's Magazine contains an interesting comment on the methods of the wire nail trust. It says:

A statement which recently emanated from Pittsburg has attracted some attention and comment among hardware men. The points that were sought to be made were as follows: In 1898 there were produced in the United States 7,418,475 kegs of wire nails. These cost the consumer $1.31 per keg. There were exported during the same year 307,194 kegs, at about $1.55 per keg, the foreigner paying a higher price than the home customer. These same nails sold at $1.11 per keg on an average during 1894.

During the last year there were manufactured 7,599,522 kegs, at an average price of $2.57 to the domestic buyers. In the meantime, 752,781 kegs were exported, at about $1.40 per keg. The American customers of the steel wire nail makers paid about $17,506,124.37 for the balance of the manufactured nails (about 6,846,741 kegs). Had the American consumers been privileged to buy at the quotations granted the foreign buyers, the Americans would have saved about $8,010,686.97 on their purchase.

More than eight millions of dollars! This measures the extortion practiced upon the hardware merchant, but this must be increased by the merchant's profit, if his profit is estimated upon a percentage basis, before it measures the extortion practiced upon the consumer.

And yet some are so devoted to a protective tariff as not to protest against import duties which enable trusts to sell at home at a high price while they sell abroad at a low price.

The Vice-Presidency.

It has been intimated that Vice-President-Elect Roosevelt is desirous of receiving more consideration at the hands of the President than has, as a rule, been given to those occupying his position. Whether or not the report is true is not material, but the ambition, if he does entertain it, is an entirely worthy one.

Why has the Vice-President been so generally ignored by the Chief Executive? It is said that Mr. Breckenridge was only consulted once by President Buchanan, and then only in regard to the phraseology of a Thanksgiving Proclamation. This incident was related to a later Vice-President who was noted for his skill at repartee and he replied, with a twinkle in his eye: "Well, there is one more Thanksgiving Day before my term expires."

According to the constitution the Vice-President succeeds to the office in case the President dies, resigns, is removed, or becomes unable to discharge the duties of the office. The public good requires that he should be thoroughly informed as to the details of the administration and ready to take up the work of the Executive at a moment's notice. The Vice-President ought to be ex-officio

---

NAMING & PURPOSE

Bryan stated the following in the opening paragraph of *The Commoner's* first article:

 Webster defines a commoner as 'one of the common people.' The name has been selected for this paper because *The Commoner* will endeavor to aid the common people in the protection of their rights, the advancement of their interests, and the realization of their aspirations.

Highlights of Bryan's description of "the common people" are as follows:

- To critics Bryan explained the expression's "eminently respectable origin" as follows: "In the same chapter in which Christ condensed man's duty to his fellows into the commandment: Thou shalt love thy neighbor as thyself; in the same chapter in which he denounced those who devour widows' houses and for a pretense make long prayers—in this same chapter it is said of Him: 'The common people heard him gladly.' No higher compliment was ever paid to any class."

- "The common people form the industrious, intelligent and patriotic element" that "produce the nation's wealth in time of peace and fight the nation's battles in time of war."

- "They are not seeking to get their hands into other people's pockets but are content if they can keep other people's hands out of their pockets."

- "The common people do not constitute an exclusive society . . . any one can become a member if he is willing to contribute by brain or muscle to the nation's strength and greatness."[6]

Bryan in front of *The Commoner* office in Lincoln, c. 1906 (NSHS RG3198-54-3)

CONTENT

The paper reprinted Bryan's major speeches as well as many of the interviews and articles he did for other publications. It was an important channel for disseminating Bryan's political, social, and religious views. Other content included political cartoons; household, topical humor, and mail columns; and writings on patriotic themes.

FINANCIAL PLAN

The paper was supported by sales (annual mail subscriptions, $1 per year; newsstand price, 5 cents per issue) and advertising revenue. Advertisers included publishers of Bibles and religious materials, food companies, clothing manufacturers, and the like. Despite the loss of significant potential revenue, *The Commoner* accepted no advertising from liquor or tobacco companies or monopolistic trusts.

CIRCULATION & FORMAT

- Sales of the first 8-page issue surpassed 50,000 copies.

- By 1906 the paper had increased to 16 pages, half of which was advertising. Circulation was 145,528. Other publications, including major east coast newspapers, accepted Bryan's invitation to reprint for free any part of *The Commoner*, thus gaining an even larger audience than circulation numbers reflected.[7]

- At its peak the weekly paper had circulation of nearly 275,000; the mailing list included addresses in every U.S. state and several hundred addresses in Europe.

- In July 1913, shortly after Bryan became secretary of state, publication changed from weekly to monthly and doubled its size to 32 pages.

EMPLOYEES & END OF PUBLICATION

- Bryan was editor and proprietor, and his wife, Mary, often contributed editorials.

- Brother Charles was business manager and later associate editor and publisher.

- Brother-in-law Thomas Allen, a Lincoln lawyer, assisted Charles with management tasks and wrote columns.

- Richard Metcalfe, who had produced presidential campaign biographies of Bryan for the *Omaha World-Herald* in 1896 and 1900, left the *World-Herald* in 1901 to become *The Commoner's* associate editor.

- The publication office had a staff of 50–75, many of whom were female; employees were paid 50 percent over prevailing wage rates and observed an eight-hour day. They received paid holidays and enjoyed a lavish annual summer picnic.

- Publication ended with the April 1923 edition because Bryan lived in Florida and Charles was inaugurated as Nebraska's new governor in March 1923. After the books were closed, Bryan designated that the surplus of $7,500 (equivalent to nearly $112,000 in 2019) be distributed to the employees with each receiving a cash bonus based on years of service.[8]

Company picnic at River View Park, Crete, NE; Bryan, second from left (NSHS RG3198-44-03)

10 | BOOKS AND SPEECHES BY BRYAN

> **"** | The words of the godly are a life-giving fountain.
>
> —Proverbs 10:11 (NLT)

Bryan's published books and speeches are organized chronologically by topic. The *Web Companion* (bryan.edu/wjb) provides full citations and links to eBooks that are available for most titles.

AUTOBIOGRAPHY & COMPILATIONS

1900   *The Life and Speeches of Hon. Wm. Jennings Bryan*

1902–08 *The Commoner Condensed* (7 vols.; see Chapter 9)

1906   *The World's Famous Orations* (10 vols.)

1909   *Speeches of William Jennings Bryan* (2 vols.)

1917   *Heart to Heart Appeals*

1925   *The Memoirs of William Jennings Bryan*

CAMPAIGNS

1896   *The First Battle: A Story of the Campaign of 1896*

- Sold 200,000 copies within the first nine months, making it one of the best-selling books of the time.

- Bryan contributed to free silver organizations his share of the $750,000 revenue from *The First Battle*, which sold for $3.75 per copy.

- "In farm homes across the South and West, it soon occupied a place alongside the Bible. Its title alone made it clear that Bryan would continue the fight."[1]

1900   *Great Political Issues and Leaders of the Campaign of 1900*

1900   *The Second Battle: An Account of the Struggle of 1900*

INTERNATIONAL TRAVEL & GOVERNMENTS

1904   *Under Other Flags: Travels, Lectures, Speeches*

1906   *British Rule in India*

          Letters to a Chinese Official: Being a Western View of Eastern Civilization

1907   *The Old World and Its Ways*

Bryan in his home library, c. 1900

POLITICS (SOME TITLES INCLUDE RELIGIOUS THEMES)

1894 *Speeches of Congressman Bryan of Nebraska in the House of Representatives During the 52nd and 53rd Congress: Extracts from the Congressional Record*

1895 *Silver and Gold or Both Sides of the Shield: A Symposium of the Views of All Parties on the Currency Question as Expressed by Their Leading Advocates*

1896 *Cross of Gold*

1899 *Republic or Empire?: The Philippine Question*

1900 *Imperialism (Flag of an Empire)*

1907 *Masterful Tributes to the Memory of President Lincoln*

1908 *Guaranteed Banks: Topeka, KS, August 27, 1908*

An Ideal Republic

The Railroad Question

1912 *The Forces that Make for Peace: Address at the Mohonk Conferences on International Arbitration*

The Signs of the Times: To Which Is Added Faith, An Address Delivered Before Several Colleges

A Tale of Two Conventions

1913 *Mr. Bryan's Peace Plan*

1914 *The People's Law*

The Royal Art

1915 *Address of the Secretary of State Delivered at the Opening Session of the Pan American Financial Conference*

The Causeless War and Its Lessons for Us

Neutrality. Correspondence Between the Secretary of State and Chairman, Committee on Foreign Relations

Why Abstain? Address Delivered by Secretary Bryan at Philadelphia, March 15, 1915

1916 *Prohibition*

1917 *Address of Hon. William Jennings Bryan to the Forty-Ninth General Assembly of the State of Missouri*

World Peace: A Written Debate Between William Howard Taft and William Jennings Bryan

RELIGION & ORIGINS

1910 *The Fruits of the Tree*

1914 *The Making of a Man*

Man

The Message from Bethlehem

The Price of a Soul

1914   *The Prince of Peace*

       The Value of an Ideal

- Bryan's target audience in *The Prince of Peace* and *The Value of an Ideal* were young people so that he might "make a defense of the Christian religion and reach some who might not be so easily reached from the pulpit."[2]

- He first delivered *The Value of an Ideal* in 1901 and *The Prince of Peace* in 1904 on the Chautauqua circuit. Together he delivered these two speeches over 3,000 times in the U.S. and in nearly every foreign country he visited, including Canada, Mexico, Japan, the Philippines, India, Egypt, and Israel.

- *The Prince of Peace* was his most widely published and most often delivered lecture. (See Appendix B on page 173).

1917   *The First Commandment*

1921   *The Bible and Its Enemies*

1922   *In His Image*

- Based on nine lectures given at a Richmond, VA, Presbyterian seminary, the book sold over 100,000 copies within a few months of publication.

- Mary wrote in their *Memoirs*, "This week spent in the Theological Seminary was a very happy one. He spoke several times of the joy it gave him to speak connectedly upon such themes to a body of students and expressed a hope that if he lived to be old, he might arrange lectures at a series of colleges, and 'you can go with me and meet these pleasant friends,' he said."[3]

- Bryan explained his intentions in delivering the lectures as follows:

> In these lectures I have had in mind two thoughts, first, the confirming of the faith of men and women, especially the young, in a Creator, all-powerful, all-wise, and all-loving, in a Bible, as the very Word of a Living God and in Christ as Son of God and Saviour of the world; second, the applying of the principles of our religion to every problem in life. My purpose is to prove, not only the fact of God, but the need of God, the fact of the Bible and the need of the Bible, and the fact of Christ and the need of a Saviour.[4]
>
> I present my appeal to the young to accept Christ and to enter upon the life He prescribes, not because they may *die* soon but because they may *live*. They need Christ as their Saviour *now* and they need Him as their guide throughout life.[5]

1922   *The Menace of Darwinism*

1923   *Famous Figures of the Old Testament*

       Orthodox Christianity Versus Modernism

1924   *Is the Bible True?*

       Shall Christianity Remain Christian?: Seven Questions in Dispute

1925   *Christ and His Companions: Famous Figures of the New Testament*

       The Last Message of William Jennings Bryan (See pages 53 and 124.)

11 | MEMORABLE QUOTATIONS

This chapter presents 30 quotations attributed to Bryan, organized under 10 topics.

CHARACTER

The desire to seem, rather than to be, is one of the faults which our age, as well as other ages, must deplore. Appearance too often takes the place of reality. . . . Sham is carried into every department of life, and we are being corrupted by show and surface. We are too apt to judge people by what they have, rather than by what they are.[1]

To form character is to form grooves in which are to flow the purposes of our lives. . . . There is character formed by our association with each friend, by every aspiration of the heart, by every object toward which our affections go out—yea, by every thought that flies on its lightning wing through the dark recesses of the brain.[2]

Congressman Bryan, c. 1893

EDUCATION

The purpose of education is not merely to develop the mind; it is to prepare men and women for society's work and for citizenship.[3]

An education is incomplete which does not place a noble purpose behind mental training and make the hands willing to work. The work should ultimately be the largest work of which the hands are capable, but at all times it should be the work that most needs to be done. That education is also defective which so inflames one's vanity or so shrivels one's heart as to separate him in sympathy from his fellows.[4]

FAITH

A belief in God is fundamental; upon it rest the influences that control life.[5]

Belief in God is almost universal, and the effect of this belief is so vast that one is appalled at the thought of what social conditions would be if reverence for God were erased from every heart.[6]

GOD'S WORD

The wisdom of the Bible writers is more than human; the prophecies proclaim a Supreme Ruler who, though inhabiting all space, deigns to speak through the hearts and minds and tongues of His children.[7]

[The Bible] holds up before us ideals that are within sight of the weakest and the lowliest, and yet so high that the best and the noblest are kept with their faces turned ever upward. It carries the call of the Savior to the remotest corners of the earth; on its pages are written the assurances of the present and our hopes for the future.[8]

If we desire rules to govern our spiritual development, we turn back to the Sermon on the Mount. . . . The Old Testament gave us the law; the New Testament reveals the love upon which the law rests.[9]

LAW, POLITICS, AND GOVERNMENT

Having behind us the producing masses of this nation and the world, supported by the commercial interests, the laboring interests, and the toilers everywhere, we will answer their demand for a gold standard by saying to them: "You shall not press down upon the brow of labor this crown of thorns; you shall not crucify mankind upon a cross of gold."[10]

The great political questions are in the last analysis moral questions.[11]

Law is but the crystallization of conscience; moral sentiment must be created before it can express itself in the form of a statute.[12]

If we are going to make any progress in morals, we must abandon the idea that morals are defined by the statutes; we must recognize that there is a wide margin between that which the law prohibits and that which an enlightened conscience can approve.[13]

Artist's depiction of Bryan after his "Cross of Gold" speech at the 1896 Democratic National Convention (William Robinson Leigh, *McClure's Magazine*, April 1900, 536)

ORATION

[The orator] borrows from the philosopher his principles, from the poet his language, from the warrior his courage, and mingling with these his own enthusiasms, leads his hearers according to his will.[14]

An orator is a man who says what he thinks and feels what he says.[15]

Eloquence may be defined as the speech of one who *knows what he is talking about* and *means what he says*—it is *thought on fire*.[16]

As long as there are human rights to be defended; as long as there are great interests to be guarded; as long as the welfare of nations is a matter for discussion, so long will public speaking have its place.[17]

ORIGINS (SEE CHAPTER 14)

It is desirable that the student should study the sciences taught in schools, but it is more than desirable—it is *necessary*—that he shall understand the science of *how to live*. If it were necessary to choose between the two, it is more important that he should know the *Rock of Ages* than the *age* of rocks.[18]

The parents have a right to say that no teacher paid by their money shall rob their children of faith in God and send them back to their homes skeptical, or infidels, or agnostics, or atheists.[19]

The Theistic evolutionist tries to occupy a middle ground between Christians who accept the Bible account of man's creation and the atheistic evolutionists who reject God entirely; but consistency finally carries most of them on to the progressive rejection of all that is vital in the Bible.[20]

The contest between evolution and Christianity is a duel to the death. . . . If evolution wins, Christianity goes—not suddenly, of course, but gradually, for the two cannot stand together.[21]

SERVICE

The essence of patriotism lies in a willingness to sacrifice for one's country, just as true greatness finds expression, not in blessings enjoyed, but in good bestowed.[22]

Christ deserves to be called the Prince of Peace because He has given us a measure of greatness which promotes peace. When His disciples quarreled among themselves as to which should be greatest in the Kingdom of Heaven, He rebuked them and said: "Let him who would be chiefest among you be the servant of all." Service is the measure of greatness; it always has been true; it is true today, and it always will be true, that he is greatest who does the most of good. And how this old world will be transformed when this standard of greatness becomes the standard of every life![23]

STANDING FOR TRUTH

There is . . . a great advantage in an investigation that brings out the facts, for disputed facts between nations, as between friends, are the cause of most disagreements.[24]

One can afford to be in a minority, but he cannot afford to be wrong; if he is in a minority and right, he will someday be in the majority.[25]

If Christians are as grateful to God, to Christ, and to the Bible as they should be, they will give attention to every problem that affects the individual, the community, and the larger units of society and government. They will consider it their duty to carry their religion into business and politics and to apply the teachings of Christ to every subject that affects human welfare.[26]

WISDOM & SUCCESS

Christ gives us a vision of our possibilities and the strength to realize them.[27]

But if each day we gather some new truths, plant ourselves more firmly upon principles which are eternal, guard every thought and action, that it may be pure, and conform our lives more nearly to that Perfect Model, we shall form a character that will be a fit background on which to paint the noblest deeds and the grandest intellectual and moral achievements; a character that cannot be concealed, but which will bring success in this life and form the best preparation for that which is beyond.[28]

Love makes money-grabbing seem contemptible; love makes class prejudice impossible; love makes selfish ambition a thing to be despised; love converts enemies into friends.[29]

If it be true, as I believe it is, that morality is dependent upon religion, then religion is not only the most practical thing in the world, but the first essential.[30]

Bryan addresses crowd from the speaker stand at the cornerstone laying ceremony for Sibley Memorial Hospital, which is today part of Johns Hopkins Health System, Washington, DC, 1911. (LOC LC-DIG-hec-01651)

12 | INFLUENCER

> **"** ... How joyful are those who fear the Lord and delight in obeying his commands. ... Their good deeds will be remembered forever. They will have influence and honor.
>
> —Psalm 112:1, 9 (NLT)

While every chapter provides examples of Bryan using his influence to make a difference[1] this chapter will look at the topic from two perspectives: (1) how history has evaluated the significance of Bryan's influence and (2) how individuals expressed Bryan's influence on them personally.

HISTORY'S EVALUATION

The two rankings highlighted in the below graphic provide impressive examples of how history views Bryan's influence.[1] The millennium ranking, released in 1998, was determined by allocating point values to world figures on five criteria: lasting influence, effect on the sum total of wisdom and beauty in the world, influence on contemporaries, singularity of contribution, and charisma.[2]

The second ranking, published in *The Atlantic* magazine in 2006, asked 10 historians to compose their own lists of the 100 most influential Americans of all time by using this broad definition of *influence*: "a person's impact, for good or ill, both on his or her own era and on the way we live now." The balloting was averaged and weighted, giving extra points to candidates that appeared on multiple ballots.[3]

> ### *1,000 YEARS, 1,000 PEOPLE: RANKING THE MEN AND WOMEN WHO SHAPED THE MILLENNIUM*
>
> #911 – WILLIAM JENNINGS BRYAN

> ### *THE 100 MOST INFLUENTIAL AMERICANS OF ALL TIME*
>
> #36 – WILLIAM JENNINGS BRYAN

In *Almost President: The Men Who Lost the Race but Changed the Nation*, Scott Farris states that even after losing his third bid for the White House, Bryan "was still idolized by millions. ... [I]t was the magic of the 1896 campaign that had bonded his followers to him in a way almost unprecedented in American history. His image hung like an icon in a million American homes next to portraits of Jesus."[4]

SORROW IN THE AMERICAN HOME

Published in the *Chicago Daily Tribune*, July 27, 1925, the day following Bryan's death[12]

INDIVIDUALS' EXPRESSIONS

Mary described her husband's ability to connect deeply with so many individuals when she wrote, "His was a genius for friendship composed of a warm interest in his fellowmen and an impulse for generous affection which always met the stranger more than halfway." She revealed the most repeated statement in the thousands of letters she received after her husband's death was "He was my friend."[5]

Throughout Bryan's career in the national spotlight, he received hundreds of thousands of letters from admirers who asked him for a favor, told him their troubles, asked for his prayers, and told him how his words and example had profoundly changed their lives.[6] Here are a few examples of the latter:

- A young Presbyterian cleric from Michigan in 1916 wrote, "I want you to know that I am one of the thousands of young men in this country that you have helped into lofty conceptions of life and its meaning. I am a better citizen, and by the grace of God, a better minister for having heard you."[7] In a 1923 letter to Bryan, Texas Governor Pat M. Neff told him that he had first heard Bryan speak in Austin, TX, when Neff was a college student, and several times thereafter. Neff stated, "I have gotten much inspiration from your life and from your addresses."[8]

- Several accounts of individuals converting to Christ appear in Bryan's *Memoirs*:

  - After he spoke to nearly 5,000 men at a YMCA meeting in Indianapolis and afterward to a smaller group of younger men, the superintendent told Bryan that 17 boys came up after Bryan left and said they wanted to begin a Christian life.

  - A missionary teacher in Tokyo, Japan, told Bryan she had a class of 13 Japanese boys and that 10 of them had converted to Christianity because of Bryan's "Prince of Peace" talk.

  - After another talk, four young men came to tell him of their coming to Christ. Bryan followed up afterward and gave each of them one of his books.[9]

- Bryan's wife shared a "curious coincidence" regarding Bryan's funeral services that were held in New York Avenue Presbyterian Church, Washington, DC, where she and Bryan had worshiped (see photo on page 123). She was asked if she wished Dr. Joseph Sizoo to conduct the service because he was filling the pulpit while the pastor was in Europe. "I assented, although this clergyman was personally unknown to me. It came then as a complete surprise and as a coincidence of dramatic impressiveness to learn that Dr. Sizoo had been brought into the ministry through the influence of one of Mr. Bryan's speeches, and that fact added weight to his impressive and beautiful address."[10]

- On December 4, 1925, the General Council of the Presbyterian Church in Atlantic City, NJ, adopted a memorial to Bryan declaring that Bryan would be "sorely missed wherever men meet to plan for a good work or Christian cause." It described Bryan as a "man who 'being dead, yet speaketh'" asserting that 'he speaks in the thousands of young men whose ambition he awakened and turned into noble channels of endeavor.'"[11]

Bryan; his sister-in-law, Elizabeth; and his brother, Charles, leaving the White House after visiting President Calvin Coolidge, March 18, 1925. W. J. Bryan was in Washington, DC, to attend the annual meeting of the Presbyterian General Assembly, of which he was a member. (LOC LC-H234- A-9520, Harris & Ewing Photographs)

PART 4

BRYAN'S LAST DECADE

13 | CALLINGS AND CRUSADES (1915–1925)

> *Each day marks out our duty for us, and it is for us to devote ourselves to it, whatever it may be, with high purpose and unfaltering courage. Whether we live to enjoy the fruits of our efforts or lay down the work before the victory is won, we know that every well-spoken word has its influence; that no good deed is ever lost.*
>
> —William Jennings Bryan
> *Man* (1914)

Two significant changes—one personal, the other political—set the stage for Bryan's last decade. First, the Bryans left Nebraska's harsh winters and by 1921 transitioned to living full time in Miami, a decision mainly driven by the need to be in a more suitable climate for Mary's worsening arthritis. Second, Bryan held no government position and had no plans to run for office.

After resigning as secretary of state on June 9, 1915, Bryan told many audiences, "I resigned only when I became convinced that the opportunities for service were larger outside the Cabinet."[1] Bryan gave a preview of how he would serve when he responded to a reporter who asked him if he were quitting politics. He smiled and told a story about a tenderfoot who asked an old mountaineer, "Have you lived here all your life?" The mountaineer replied, "Not yet."[2]

Bryan addressed 15,000 delegates at the Sixth World Christian Endeavor Convention, July 9, 1921, in Central Park, NY, following the delegates' parade along Fifth Avenue.

CHANNELS OF SERVICE

Perhaps the resoluteness to serve others that marked Bryan's youth and endured until his final days can be attributed to the Apostle Paul's words in 1 Corinthians 13:13 (NIV): "And now these three remain: faith, hope and love. But the greatest of these is love." Bryan's character was built on those qualities, and his character enabled him to persevere in using these channels of service—his heart, his voice, and his pen—as he pursued the callings and crusades of his final decade.

HIS HEART	HIS VOICE	HIS PEN
Bryan revealed his heart when he said the following: "The teachings of Christ apply to the structure and administration of government as well as to the life and conduct of the individual."[3] "Whether I speak on politics, on social questions, or on religion, I find the foundation of my speech in the philosophy of Him who spake as man never spake; who gave us a philosophy that fits into every human need and furnishes the solution for every problem that can vex a human heart or perplex the world."[4]	Bryan put his energy, zeal, and oratorical skills to work as he crisscrossed the country to speak • **to the people** on his summer Chautauqua lecture tours, at political rallies, before religious and business groups, and on high school and college campuses, • **on the people's behalf** as he addressed state legislators, met with political and religious leaders, used his continued influence within the Democratic Party, and gave testimony before congressional committees.	Bryan was a prolific writer in his final decade, authoring books, magazine articles, and a nationally syndicated newspaper column. Bryan continued to educate and motivate his constituents through the monthly publication of *The Commoner*.

Bryan loved young people, desired to influence them, and spoke on countless campuses (see "A Difference Maker in Higher Education" on page 157). On this occasion he was the guest of a Fullerton (CA) High School cooking class at Hotel Shay in 1917. The students, under the supervision of their instructor, Miss Catherine Caldwell, prepared a multi-course breakfast for Bryan prior to his speech to the student body.

POLITICAL CRUSADES

While Bryan advocated for many political issues and reforms during his last decade, this section will focus on three of his most significant crusades. Six months after he resigned as secretary of state, Bryan wrote in the December 1915 issue of *The Commoner*, "The voters of the country are turning with earnestness to three great issues which promise to be ready for decision within the next few years—Peace, Prohibition and Woman's Suffrage."[5]

This section will examine each of the three great issues in detail.

PEACE

- **Reasons Bryan supported peace.** After Bryan's resignation as secretary of state, he promoted peace in many speeches. In June 1915 Bryan said, "If others desire that our flag be feared, let us prefer that it shall be loved; if others would have the world tremble in awe at the sight of it, let us pray that the plain people everywhere may turn their faces toward it and thank God that it is the emblem of justice and the hope of peace. I desire that my country shall maintain the national honor which such a flag represents."[6]

  In February 1917 Bryan said, "If civilization is to advance, the day must come when a nation will feel no more obligated to accept a challenge to war than an American citizen now feels obligated to accept a challenge to fight a duel. . . . If there ever was a time . . . when a nation was justified, aye, compelled to be patient and exercise Christian forbearance, that time is now and our nation is the nation."[7]

- **Result.** Congress declared war on Germany on April 6, 1917.

- **Bryan's subsequent actions.** Upon hearing of Congress's declaration of war, Bryan immediately wired President Wilson: "Believing it to be the duty of the citizen to bear his part of the burdens of war and his share of its perils, I hereby tender my services to the Government. Please enroll me as a private whenever I am needed and assign me to any work I can do."

  In the April 1917 edition of *The Commoner*, Bryan wrote, "The nation has entered the war. Men differed as to the wisdom of going into the war, but the government has acted, and there is no longer division. The people are one—they all stand behind the President and congress who bear the grave responsibility of leading the country through war to peace. 'Our lives, our fortunes and our sacred honor'—all these are pledged to support of the government through every hour until the end."[8]

  In the October 1917 edition of *The Commoner*, Bryan wrote, "Patriotism requires some to give their lives; it requires some to give their money; it may require some to hold their peace rather than risk creating dissension or discord."[9]

- **Ultimate outcome.** Ranked among the deadliest conflicts in human history, World War I ended in victory for the Allies on November 11, 1918.

  Michael Kazin wrote that in retrospect, Bryan "was quite correct to oppose American entry into the Great War. It was not a conflict that history has justified. The main consequence . . . was a great bitterness from which grew . . . Fascism, Nazism, and Bolshevism. Bryan also foresaw that Wilson, by rejecting compromise, would lose the fight over the peace treaty and deprive the League [of Nations] of the one powerful nation that might have halted the drift toward a second world war."[10]

Both Bryan and evangelist Billy Sunday (on right) used their respective platforms to support prohibition. In July 1920 the Prohibition Party at its national convention in Lincoln, NE, tried unsuccessfully to draft Bryan and Sunday to head its party's national ticket.

PROHIBITION

- **Reasons Bryan supported prohibition.** "Throughout his lifetime Bryan saw intoxicants as the nation's worst enemy and the liquor traffic its greatest evil. He viewed the drinking of alcohol as a sin against the individual, against society, and against God. Drink, he reasoned, brought no advantage, decreased a man's efficiency, imparted a constitutional weakness to one's offspring, was a waste of money, formed a dangerous habit, caused poverty and crime, and from a Christian standpoint, provided a poor example."[11]

- **Result.** The 18th Amendment to the U.S. Constitution, which established the prohibition of "intoxicating liquors" in the United States, was ratified January 16, 1918, and went into effect January 17, 1920.

- **Bryan's subsequent actions.** Bryan publicized the benefits of prohibition and advocated for more effective methods of enforcement.[12]

  At the University of Florida, he promoted the idea of students and faculty signing a pledge not to use intoxicating liquor as a beverage. All the faculty and 75% of the students signed the pledge cards.

  The idea was apparently not accepted as readily elsewhere despite Bryan's pointing out in his letter to one university president in 1923 that two instructors from a North Carolina institution were fired after they were discovered making wine in a bathtub.[13]

- **Ultimate outcome.** Enforcement was inefficient and costly, sometimes resulted in violence, and was impacted by corruption.

  Prohibition was in effect for 13 years and was repealed in 1933 by ratification of the 21st Amendment.

WOMEN'S SUFFRAGE

- **Reasons Bryan supported women's suffrage.** Bryan valued the moral force that he believed women would bring to the ballot box. He argued that mothers have a right to a voice in determining the environment in which their children live.

  Mrs. Bryan was also a national figure on this and the prohibition issue. She was an official with the Woman's Christian Temperance Union and the National American Woman Suffrage Association. She lobbied congressmen's wives to urge their husbands to support both constitutional amendments.

- **Result.** The 19th Amendment to the U.S. Constitution was ratified August 18, 1920, and granted American women the right to vote.

- **Bryan's subsequent actions.** Once it was ratified, Bryan's work on its behalf ended.

- **Ultimate outcome.** The 100-year anniversary of the amendment's ratification will be celebrated in 2020.

The June 14–16, 1916, Democratic Convention was held at the St. Louis Coliseum. Bryan endorsed Woodrow Wilson to lead the Democratic Party's ticket for a second time, which Wilson did. Afterward, Bryan campaigned for Wilson, and Wilson won the presidential election. See the next page for details about Bryan's involvement at the convention and afterward. (LOC LC-DIG-ggbain-22022)

INFLUENCE ON THE DEMOCRATIC PARTY

One year and six days after resigning as secretary of state, Bryan's continued influence on the Democratic Party was evident, as described below, when he gave an unscheduled speech before the delegates at the 1916 Democratic National Convention. This table provides highlights of Bryan's participation at the 1916, 1920, and 1924 conventions, his subsequent campaigning for the candidates, and the outcomes of the elections.

1916	1920	1924
Bryan's Participation at the Democratic National Conventions		
St. Louis, MO—(see photo at left) This was the first convention in 20 years that Bryan did not serve in any official capacity as either a candidate, platform committee member, or delegate. He attended as a newspaper syndicate reporter. At the end of the second day cries from the delegates, "Bryan! Bryan!" resulted in a motion being passed to suspend the rules and allow a non-delegate to give a speech.[14] His 45-minute address "was interrupted forty times by applause. When Bryan left the platform, every delegate lined up to shake his hand."[15]	*San Francisco, CA*—Efforts by many were made to secure Bryan's fourth nomination for president, but Bryan chose not to run. He attended as a Nebraska delegate and was hired again as a syndicate reporter. This was the first DNC that used microphones. Bryan served on the Platforms and Resolutions Committee—but had little influence on the writing of the platform and the naming of the candidate. Bryan declined to vote on the final ballots leading up to the 44th ballot, when James Cox won the nomination.	*New York, NY*—Again many called upon Bryan to consider a fourth run for the White House, but he declined. He attended the convention as a Florida delegate. He was chairman of the subcommittee on resolutions where hot debates ensued over several of the planks. He proposed many candidates who were not accepted by the delegates. Despite Bryan's opposing the selection of John W. Davis (who won on the 103rd ballot), Davis surprisingly chose Bryan's brother Charles as his running mate. "He had failed worse than in 1920 in exerting a commanding power in a Democratic convention, and it was with tears in his eyes that he told Senator Thomas Heflin of Alabama, after the convention, that he had never been so humiliated in his life."[16]
Bryan's Campaigning for the Candidates		
He campaigned in 20 states from September until the election, averaging 4–5 speeches a day. Wherever he went he spoke to overflow crowds.[17]	Bryan did not campaign.	Bryan campaigned in 15 states from September until the election and gave more than 100 speeches.

1916	1920	1924

Election Results (Electoral Votes)

Democrats Win (Wilson/Marshall) 277	**Republicans Win** (Harding/Coolidge) 404	**Republicans Win** (Coolidge/Dawes) 382
Republicans (Hughes/Fairbanks) 254	**Democrats** (Cox/FDR) 127	**Democrats** (Davis/C. Bryan) 136
In the states where Bryan campaigned, 15 out of 20 went to Wilson, and Senator Thomas Walsh of Montana called Bryan's role in Wilson's victory "the factor most transcendent in importance."[18]		**Progressives** (LaFollette/Wheeler) 13

BRYAN'S LAST POLITICAL DECISION

Bryan received requests from all corners of the state to run as a candidate for Florida senator in 1922. While he seriously considered doing so, in the end he declined. However, in early 1925 Bryan reversed that decision and announced he would campaign for election to the United States Senate in the 1926 midterm congressional elections. Even though his death in July 1925 meant he never pursued this goal, it is still interesting to note the factors that apparently prompted the decision[19]:

- His strong showing in the Florida primaries of 1924, having received 42,000 more votes than any other delegate candidate and a higher vote total than any of the candidates in the presidential primary;

- "His desire to reduce his itinerant crusading so he could spend more time with his ailing wife";

- His feeling that it was his "last opportunity to render a service to the party which has made me what I am and given me all I have. I regard a union of the South and West as the only

Bryan, a Florida delegate, at the 1924 Democratic National Convention in New York (NSHS RG3198-19-11)

hope of the party. Being a resident of the South and acquainted with the West, and having an influence, . . . I believe I can render the party more service than any other man now in the Senate or likely to be there during the next few years."

BRYAN'S EARNINGS

Up until 1920, Bryan's income came from his writing, lectures, and real estate investments (see Chapter 16). From 1920–1925, income from these sources increased, and he added a new income source, through employment at a law firm.

WRITING

Bryan's writing during his last decade included the following:

- He published 14 books and speeches (see Chapter 10). In addition, he began writing his memoirs that Mrs. Bryan finished after his death; and he wrote in July 1925 what was titled after his death *The Last Message* (see page 52).

- He received $12,000 from the Central Press Association for covering the national political conventions in 1920.[20]

- He continued as editor and proprietor of *The Commoner* through its final edition in April 1923 (see Chapter 9).

He started teaching the Sunday School class in 1918 at Miami's First Presbyterian Church. With its popularity among locals and tourists, it quickly outgrew the church and moved to nearby Royal Palm Park (see photo). Attendance ranged from 2,000–6,000 each week (see "Hometown, Miami, FL" on page 61). Newspaper syndication of his Bible class talks began with 68 papers in 1921. He earned $21,000 in 1923 when syndication reached 110 newspapers with readership between 20–25 million.[21]

Royal Palm Park was part of Miami's first luxury hotel, the Royal Palm Hotel (photo background) built by railroad magnate Henry Flagler. Due to damage caused by the Great Miami Hurricane in 1926, the hotel and park bandstand where Bryan led his class were demolished in 1930. Today this area is occupied by Metropolitan Miami (condos, hotel, retail shops, cinema, dining, and museum).

LECTURES

George Merrick, founder and developer of Coral Gables, one of the first planned communities in America, paid Bryan as much as $100,000 in fees and property to speak about the benefits of living in Florida.[22] As Miami's "First Citizen," Bryan had been speaking for many years on this topic to as many as 500 weekly guests who attended the Bryans' open houses at Villa Serena (see page 135).

From January–March 1925, every day except Sunday, Bryan spoke to the crowds that filled the wooden grandstands surrounding the city's Venetian pool. People came from all over the country to tour the community in part due to the work done by the sales representatives at the Coral Gables sales offices in every major U.S. city. They also came to hear Bryan speak and to enjoy special events, such as alligator wrestling and water shows featuring the likes of Olympic star and future Tarzan Johnny Weissmuller. *The Miami News* added to the promotional value that Bryan brought to Merrick's city by frequently publishing Bryan's entire speech.

Bryan at Coral Gables' Venetian Pool near Miami, 1925 (State Archives of Florida/Fishbaugh)[25]

On March 13, 1925, hundreds of dignitaries attended the groundbreaking for Coral Gables' Biltmore Hotel (National Historic Landmark). Bryan gave the keynote address; at the conclusion of the ceremony, he boarded a steam-powered excavating machine and began clearing the grounds.

On April 30, 1925, Bryan was the featured speaker at the inauguration ceremony of the arrival of the first trolley car that linked Miami and Coral Gables.

When news of Bryan's death reached Coral Gables, Merrick "grieved not only for the death of a friend and supporter but for the greater loss to the University of Miami, which Bryan had championed for more than a decade and in whose future he had planned to have a key role."[24] (See "University of Miami" on page 159.)

Following the 1926 Great Miami Hurricane that resulted in an early start to the Great Depression for the region, Coral Gables filed for bankruptcy in 1929. Today Coral Gables is a thriving and prosperous city with 11 properties listed in the National Register of Historic Places—the Venetian Pool being one of them.[25]

PROPERTY

The Bryans' 1913 decision to build Villa Serena proved to be a wise investment. Miami property values increased 1,000% between 1909 and 1924. At the time of Bryan's death in 1925, his real estate holdings in Miami, Los Angeles, and Lincoln were worth more than $600,000 (equivalent to more than $8.5 million in 2019).[26]

LEGAL COUNSEL

Bryan was employed in 1921 by the law firm of Douglas, O'Bear, and Douglas with the title of Counsel in International Law. Located in Washington, DC, the law firm specialized in obtaining American loans for Latin America and representing American citizens in international controversies in that region.[27]

INFLUENCE ON RELIGION IN AMERICA

Bryan influenced religion in America in a variety of ways:

- **Bryan's church was among the most influential churches in America**. First Presbyterian Church of Miami was named one of the eight most influential churches in the United States during the time when Bryan's FPC Sunday Bible classes were syndicated.[28]

Bryan stands ready to deliver his first sermon broadcast by radio, March 12, 1922.
(Westinghouse Electric Corporation Photographs)

- **Bryan was one of the first radio evangelists**. Bryan's first sermon using radio was delivered from the pulpit of Point Breeze Presbyterian Church, Pittsburgh, PA, March 12, 1922 (see photo). It was broadcast on KDKA, after which he received more than 5,000 letters from listeners.[29] He continued to use the medium to deliver sermons from Miami, Los Angeles, Salt Lake City, and elsewhere.

- **Bryan spoke at churches across America**. In Los Angeles, for example, Bryan preached at R. A. Torrey's Church of the Open Door and Aimee Semple McPherson's Foursquare church, Angelus Temple. When he spoke on the topic "Is the Bible True?" at Angelus Temple in back-to-back services in 1924, he filled the nearly 4,000-seat auditorium both times before he left to give the evening sermon at First Methodist Church.[30] McPherson sent Bryan a telegram during the Scopes trial, which read, "Ten thousand members of Angelus Temple with her millions of radio church membership send grateful appreciation of your lion-hearted championship of the Bible against evolution and throw our hats in the ring with you."[31]

- **Bryan was one of the Chautauqua's most popular summer lecturers from 1895–1925.** Two of his most requested speeches were "The Value of an Ideal" and "The Prince of Peace." This quotation is from the former:

> If I can leave but one thought with the young men who honor me by their presence on this occasion, let it be this thought—that we must all have food and clothing and shelter, and must either earn these things or have them given to us, and any self-respecting young man ought to be ashamed to sponge upon the world for his living and not render unto the world valuable service in return. . . . What we need today is an ideal of life that will make people as anxious to render full service as they are to draw full pay—an ideal that will make them measure life by what they bestow upon their fellows and not by what they receive.[32]

- **Bryan became the chief spokesman for the fundamentalist movement.** Despite being out of sync with major fundamentalist leaders on several issues, such as his belief that the church should enter the political arena to help solve social and economic problems, Bryan was in perfect sync with them regarding "an unshakable belief in the infallible word of the Bible and a determination to eliminate the teaching of evolution from the nation's public schools."[33]

The following statement is from Bryan's defense of the essential doctrines reaffirmed by the Presbyterian General Assembly in May 1923 (see "The Presbyterian Church" on page 107). This quotation shows Bryan's view of the evolutionist theory on the origin of man and provides a segue to the next chapter.

> The evolutionary hypothesis is the only thing that has seriously menaced religion since the birth of Christ, and it menaces all other religions as well as the Christian religion, and civilization as well as religion—at least, this is the conviction of a multitude who regard belief in God as the most fundamental of all beliefs and see in Christ the hope of the future.[34]

14 | ON THE ORIGIN OF MAN

> So God created man in his own image, in the image of God created he him.
>
> —Genesis 1:27 (KJV)
>
> And without faith it is impossible to please him, for whoever would draw near to God must believe that he exists and that he rewards those who seek him.
>
> —Hebrews 11:6 (ESV)

INTRODUCTION

As is common for anyone in public life, Bryan had supporters and detractors for every cause that he advanced. However, his stand for biblical creationism spurred more debate, inspired more action and gained more admiration among his constituents, and garnered more ridicule from his detractors than any other reform he pursued—both while he was living and after his death. Here are two examples of Bryan's response to ridicule:

RIDICULE	RESPONSE
One cartoonist portrayed Bryan as abandoning his hunt for the Republican elephant to pursue the Darwinian monkey into the jungle.	Bryan wrote the cartoonist a friendly letter in which he defended the cartoonist's right to exaggerate and then went on to say, "However, if you would be entirely accurate you should represent me as using a double-barreled shotgun, firing one barrel at the elephant as he tried to enter the treasury and another at Darwinism—the monkey—as he tried to enter the school room."[1]
In a March 5, 1922, *New York Times* article, Professor E. G. Conklin stated, "Apparently Mr. Bryan demands to see a monkey or an ass transformed into a man, though he must be familiar enough with the reverse process."	Bryan responded with a letter to the editor on March 7, 1922, about the paper publishing the views of Professors Conklin and Osborn (see "Using the Press" on page 108): "You have rendered a distinct service to your readers in bringing two distinguished 'tree men' down from their arborial lodging to terra firma. . . . The answers of the professors whom you selected have exhibited all the characteristics of their class. They misrepresent their opponents, look with contempt upon those who do not exhaust the alphabet in setting forth their degrees, and evade the issue which they pretend to discuss . . . . [I]t is evident that they regard the discovery of the bones of a five-toed horse as a greater event than the birth of Christ."[2]

This chapter examines the complex topic of origins from three perspectives with the goal of helping the reader understand why Bryan crusaded against what he came to regard as the "menace of Darwinism." Presented first is a framework for answering the origins question and includes examples of how the language and arguments have changed in the nearly 100 years since Bryan launched his anti-evolution campaign; second are reasons why Bryan entered the evolution fray; and lastly are the anti-evolution strategies he employed.

ANSWERING THE HUMAN ORIGINS QUESTION

In November 1859 (four months before Bryan's birth) a book was published that many regard as "the most influential academic book in history" and refer to as the book that "has changed the way we think about everything."[3]

That book was Charles Darwin's *On the Origin of Species by Means of Natural Selection, or the Preservation of Favoured Races in the Struggle for Life.*

Darwin's *Origin of Species* went through six editions during Darwin's lifetime (1809–1882). Revisions dealt with counter-arguments and included corrections and responses to religious objections.

- The fifth edition (1869) for the first time included the phrase "survival of the fittest," attributed originally to philosopher Herbert Spencer in his 1864 *Principles of Biology.*
- The sixth edition (1872) for the first time included the word "evolution," though all the editions used "evolved," and "On" was dropped from the book's title.

The following table outlines three basic belief systems that answer the question of human origins. Bryan's answer was based in Belief System #1. Darwin used Belief System #2 in *The Origin of Species* and his later work, *The Descent of Man, and Selection in Relation to Sex* (1871).[4] More details about how Belief System #3 answers this question will be discussed later in the chapter.

	Belief System #1		Belief System #2	Belief System #3
Source	Bible		Science	Bible and Science
Beginning	God		Evolution	God-Guided Evolution
Known as	Creationism		Atheistic Evolutionism	Theistic Evolutionism
Bryan's Remarks	"Three sentences from Genesis comprehend more of vital truth than has been written in all the volumes of science issued from the presses of the world. "First: 'In the beginning God created the heaven and the earth'—the alpha of all history. "Second, reproduction according to kind: 'And God said, Let the earth bring forth the living creature after his kind, cattle, and creeping things, and beast of the earth after his kind, and it was so.' "Third: 'And God said, Let us make man in our image.' This is the most important sentence of the three. Ignorance of the beginning of all things does not affect the philosophy of life as much as it is affected by the theory of man's origin. Even the law of reproduction according to kind is not so vital to man as his kinship with the Heavenly Father."[5]		"Atheistic evolution denies the existence of God and this arouses indignation. "Theistic evolution, on the other hand, lulls the young Christian to sleep with the assurance that evolution recognizes God and offers a more sublime method of creation than the Bible accords. "Theistic evolution and atheistic evolution travel together until they reach the origin of life; at this point the theistic evolutionist embraces the atheist, tolerantly if not affectionately, and says, 'I beg your pardon, but here I must assume a Creator.'"[6]	

Since Bryan's day, arguments to support each belief system have advanced significantly. For example, the concept of evolution was poorly defined prior to the 1930s–1950s' "evolutionary synthesis." The modern synthesis involved the unification of the biological sciences, including botany, zoology, paleontology, genetics, and ecology.[7] Evolution in Bryan's day lacked precise definitions of species, populations, and even genes. This made the grounds for argumentation much more philosophical than scientific.

Likewise, a clearly articulated concept of creation science was still decades away. The rough outlines of "creation science" began to emerge in the 1960s with the publication of *The Genesis Flood* by John C. Whitcomb and Henry M. Morris and the founding of the Creation Research Society.[8]

While many of Bryan's arguments continue to be used by today's creation scientists, others have not stood the test of time or have been framed more clearly with new terms and explanations. Here are four such examples:

1. Reproduction according to kind, as Bryan referenced ("Second" in the belief systems table), is an attribute of microevolution. However, the concepts of microevolution and macroevolution weren't introduced until 12 years after Bryan's death.[9] Microevolution is observable "change below the species level" whereby created kinds can interbreed. For instance, all dog varieties can interbreed and are of one species. Macroevolution, on the other hand, is unobservable "change above the species level" that happens over thousands or millions of years and is a "hypothetical process of unlimited variation that evolutionists believe transforms one kind of living organism into a fundamentally different kind" (reptiles into birds, apes into people). As scientists continue to research, debate, and discuss macroevolution, it would be interesting to hear how Bryan's creation–evolution arguments might have been different if he were to have had access to the research and ideas now discussed by scientists from each of the three belief systems.[10]

2. Bryan's discussion of "survival of the fittest," Darwin's mechanism of natural selection, represented the best thinking available in Bryan's day but falls short today. For example,

   - Bryan did not distinguish between "Darwinism" and "Social Darwinism."[11] While today the theory of Social Darwinism is largely discredited, in Bryan's day there were many evidences of the concept of survival of the fittest being applied to social structures, a topic discussed on page 98.

   - Bryan's arguments regarding theistic evolution (see pages 105–106) would have been more compelling had he associated survival of the fittest with theistic evolution, as today's creation scientists do with arguments such as the following:[12]

     a. The logical result of theistic evolution makes God the author of disease, pain, suffering, violence, and death—all of which, according to theistic evolution, preceded the creation of man.

     b. Theistic evolution makes God an inefficient Creator because it took Him billions of years to reach His crowning achievement—the creation of man in His own image; and in order to do so, He had to use a death-driven process whereby only the strong survive.

     c. Theistic evolution denies truths that are the heart of the gospel, such as that death came into the world only after Adam sinned, that the wages of sin is death, and that Jesus came to the earth for the purpose of breaking the power of death by paying the penalty for man's sins.

3. When Bryan focused on what people could relate to, how the evolutionary theory strikes at the very core of man's purpose, some inferred that his apparent lack of concern about whether evolution applied to rocks, plant life, and the animal kingdom cast doubt on the inerrancy of scripture.

    Bryan stated, "The only part of evolution in which any considerable interest is felt is evolution APPLIED TO MAN. A hypothesis in regard to the rocks and plant life does not affect the philosophy upon which one's life is built. Evolution applied to fish, birds, and beasts would not materially affect man's view of his own responsibilities except as the acceptance of an unsupported hypothesis as to these would be used to support a similar hypothesis as to man."[13]

    That inference, however, overlooks the fact that Bryan worked tirelessly to protect the doctrine of inerrant verbal inspiration of the Bible. A good example is presented later in the chapter under strategy number five, "Influencing the Clergy" on page 105.

4. Bryan's concession during the Scopes trial that the earth was far older than 6,000 years and the days of creation were probably longer than 24-hour days seems to contradict his belief in the inerrancy of scripture. Two facts help put Bryan's comments in the context of his times. First, George McCready Price, a creationist whom Bryan had asked (but was declined) to be an expert witness at the Scopes trial, had advised Bryan not to discuss science at the trial.[14] Second, Bryan's "views on Genesis were consistent with the best of Evangelical scholarship of the time,"[15] as evidenced by Bryan's statement made nearly two years before the Scopes trial: "According to the interpretation placed upon it by orthodox Christians, the day mentioned in the account of creation was of indefinite duration."[16]

UNDERSTANDING WHY BRYAN ENTERED THE CREATION–EVOLUTION BATTLE

This section presents two perspectives for understanding why Bryan put so much of his time and energy into fighting Darwinism: first, a timeline to introduce Bryan's first publicly stated view of Darwinism; second, contributing factors to explain why Bryan decided to launch an anti-evolution campaign in 1920.

BRYAN'S EARLY VIEW OF DARWINISM

Figure 14-1 provides a timeline with highlights of Bryan's changing view of Darwinism.

Bryan stated his early views of evolution in "The Prince of Peace," first delivered in 1904 (published in 1914) and known as his most often delivered speech (see Appendix B).

- "There are difficulties to be encountered in religion, but there are difficulties to be encountered everywhere. If Christians sometimes have doubts and fears, unbelievers have more doubts and greater fears. I passed through a period of skepticism when I was in college. . . . It was at this period that I became confused by the different theories of creation. But I examined these theories and found that they all assumed something to begin with."

- "Those who reject the idea of creation are divided into two schools, some believing that the first germ of life came from another planet and others holding that it was the result of spontaneous generation. . . . [I]f we accept the doctrine of spontaneous generation, we cannot explain why spontaneous generation ceased to act after the first germ was created."

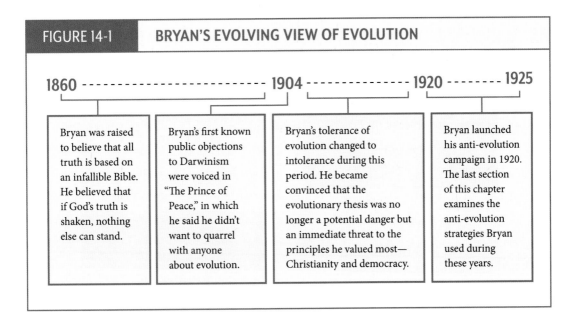

FIGURE 14-1   BRYAN'S EVOLVING VIEW OF EVOLUTION

1860 - 1904 - - - - - - - - - - - - 1920 - - - - - - - 1925

Bryan was raised to believe that all truth is based on an infallible Bible. He believed that if God's truth is shaken, nothing else can stand.	Bryan's first known public objections to Darwinism were voiced in "The Prince of Peace," in which he said he didn't want to quarrel with anyone about evolution.	Bryan's tolerance of evolution changed to intolerance during this period. He became convinced that the evolutionary thesis was no longer a potential danger but an immediate threat to the principles he valued most—Christianity and democracy.	Bryan launched his anti-evolution campaign in 1920. The last section of this chapter examines the anti-evolution strategies Bryan used during these years.

- "Go back as far as we may, we cannot escape from the creative act, and it is just as easy for me to believe that God created man as he is as to believe that millions of years ago He created a germ of life and endowed it with power to develop into all that we see today."

- "I object to the Darwinian theory . . . because I fear we shall lose the consciousness of God's presence in our daily life, if we must accept the theory that through all the ages no spiritual force has touched the life of man and shaped the destiny of nations."

- He noted other moral and logical objections and concluded with, "But, I repeat, while I do not accept the Darwinian theory I shall not quarrel with you about it; I only refer to it to remind you that it does not solve the mystery of life or explain human progress."[17]

BRYAN'S LATER VIEW OF DARWINISM

The second perspective identifies four factors that help explain why Bryan changed his 1904 view ("I shall not quarrel with you") to his 1920 view when he launched his anti-evolution campaign (Figure 14-2) that began with his October 1920 speech, in which Bryan described Darwinism as "the most paralyzing influence with which civilization has had to contend during the last century." (See "Equipping His Constituents" on page 102.)

Perhaps looking to Mary Bryan is the best way to understand what motivated her husband to take on the evolution battle. Bryan wrote to her on their 31st wedding anniversary, "The flame of love that the first sight of you kindled in my youthful heart glows on undiminished. You have been my only real companion for more than three decades—the sharer of every secret and the partner of every purpose."[18] Using Mary's insights,[19] Bryan's words, and other experts' analyses, this section will examine four factors (see Figure 14-2) that help to explain why Bryan entered the battle against Darwin's theory that was widely accepted as fact in Bryan's day.

FIGURE 14-2	WHY BRYAN FOUGHT THE EVOLUTION BATTLE

His Faith	**His Belief in the Supernatural**
His Position on the Separation between Church and State	**His View of Darwinism as a Menace**

1. **Bryan's Faith.** Mary explained, "A source of tremendous strength to Mr. Bryan was his freedom from doubt. . . . This may be explained by his conviction that man was much too puny and finite to understand the ways of God. He said more than once: 'What do these men know? Pitting their poor little knowledge against omniscience! The infinite power which rules and controls is far beyond our finite mind.'"[20]

   In 1921 Bryan published his first anti-evolution article in *The Commoner*. Because he believed that the evolutionary theory undermined God's existence, Bryan began the article by discussing six influences that control life and that are based on a belief in God: "a sense of responsibility to the Creator for every thought and word and deed," "prayer," "personal immortality," "the spirit of brotherhood," "belief in the Bible," and "a belief in Christ." He stated later in the article that to accept that Darwinism explains the almost infinite number of creatures we see about us "requires more faith in CHANCE than a Christian is required to have in God."[21]

2. **Bryan's Belief in the Supernatural.** One hindrance to many people's ability to believe the biblical account of creation is their desire to explain "the beginning" using only natural processes. Bryan, however, believed in the supernatural acts of God, as Mary pointed out when she wrote, "Miracles, a troublesome question to many, did not perplex him." She summarized his views on the supernatural with an excerpt from Bryan's *Seven Questions in Dispute*:

> Miracles are performed today—miracles as marvelous as anything recorded in Holy Writ. . . . The feeding of five thousand with a few loaves and fishes is not nearly so great a mystery nor, measured by man's rules, so seemingly impossible as the cleansing of a heart and the changing of a life. The spiritual gravitation that draws a soul toward heaven is just as real as the physical gravitation that draws matter toward the earth's center. We judge the law of gravitation by the influence it exerts; the proof of the spiritual law is as abundant and as conclusive. . . . There are realities in the spiritual world which science cannot explain because spiritual things are spiritually discerned, but these things are no less demonstrable than the things with which science deals.[22]

Bryan summarized the relationship between Darwinism and the supernatural as follows: "Darwinism discredits the things that are supernatural and encourages the worship of the intellect—an idolatry as deadly to spiritual progress as the worship of images made by human hands."[23]

3. **Bryan's Position on the Separation between Church and State.** Mary explained that Bryan "was a firm believer in the doctrine of complete separation of Church and State. He believed in absolute equality before the law of all religious denominations. . . . He believed in his religion with all his might, and with all his soul, and with all his strength, but he thought that it was unworthy of the true religion to ask or accept any favors from the State. He believed that all sects should advance their religion by their own efforts and at their own expenses, unaided by the State."

Mary further explained Bryan's reasoning: "He argued that if the power of the State could not be properly used to advance religion, it followed as a matter of course that the power of the State must not be used to attack religion."

She provided this example from the preamble of a resolution Bryan wrote, and the Florida legislature passed, in 1924:

> Whereas, the public schools and colleges of this State, supported in whole or in part by public funds, should be kept free from any teachings designed to set up and promulgate sectarian views, and should also be equally free from any teachings designed to attack the religious beliefs of the public. . . . Therefore, it is the sense of the Legislature of the State of Florida that it is improper and subversive to the best interest of the people of this State for any professor, teacher or instructor in the public schools and colleges of this State, supported in whole or in part by public taxation, to teach or permit to be taught atheism or agnosticism or to teach as *true* Darwinism or any other hypothesis that links man in blood relationship to any other form of life.[24]

Michael Kazin said of Bryan as follows: "Respecting the separation between church and state, he never asked his fellow Democrats to endorse his views on evolution."[25]

4. **Bryan's View of Darwinism as a Menace.** Between 1904 and 1920, Bryan saw growing evidence that the Darwinian theory was undermining religion and democracy in America in the following three areas:

Undermining of Children's Faith. Mary described a powerful motivator for Bryan's anti-evolution campaign as follows: "His soul arose in righteous indignation when he found from the many letters he received from parents all over the country that state schools were being used to undermine the religious faith of their children." She continued, "Repeated indications of unbelief, especially among college students, puzzled him. Upon **investigation** [emphasis added] he became convinced that the teaching of evolution as a fact instead of a theory caused the students to lose faith in the Bible, first, in the story of creation, and later in other doctrines which underlie the Christian religion."[26]

Examples of what Bryan was hearing include the following:

- A student at the University of Wisconsin complained to him of his professor of German, who asserted that all thinking men were agnostics.

- He heard that in one of the classrooms at Bryn Mawr College, a vote was taken to determine the existence of God—and God lost, 43 to 23.

- A congressman and three ministers informed him that their sons, after studying evolution at divinity school, had lost their faith.[27]

The **investigation** to which Mary referred came from two main sources:

- His personal conversations with students during his many visits to colleges and high schools throughout the country.
- His reading of Bryn Mawr College psychology professor James H. Leuba's 1916 book, *The Belief in God and Immortality, a Psychological, Anthropological and Statistical Study*. In this study, Leuba contends that most students entered college believing in a personal God, but "on leaving college, from 40 to 45 percent . . . deny or doubt the fundamental dogmas of the Christian religion."[28]

Modernism and Higher Criticism. Higher criticism—a key issue in the Fundamentalist–Modernist controversy—threatened the ordinary citizens' confidence in reading and understanding the Bible for themselves and caused many to believe that it is necessary to seek out the higher critics to explain to them what God meant in the Old and New Testaments.[29]

Fundamentalists' initial concern was how Modernism, or biblical liberalism, gave "a figurative interpretation to . . . some scriptural passages based on the application of textual higher criticism."[30] The Fundamentalists recognized, as stated by World Christian Fundamentals Association president William Bell Riley, that "basal to the many forms of modern infidelity [modernism] is the philosophy of evolution."[31]

Bryan described higher critics as those who "are trying to make the Bible suit the men who are criticizing it. . . . The Higher Critics who are trying to please such men are attempting the impossible task of suiting the Bible to a skeptical brain. The brain that is controlled by a heart that has love and faith in it does not need to be converted to the Bible—and no other kind can be converted to it. If I understand the average Higher Critic, he is an egotist who thinks himself above the Bible and looks down upon it. He puts the Bible upon an operating table and cuts out what he regards as the diseased parts. When he gets through, the Bible is no longer the Book of Books; it is just a 'scrap of paper.'"[32]

Social Implications of Darwinism. The Great Commoner called the public's attention to the attacks on human rights and human dignity that were being perpetrated as a result of individuals and nations embracing Darwin's survival-of-the-fittest ideas. While viewpoints vary on the influence Darwin's ideas had on cutthroat competition, war, racism, and eugenics,[33] this section examines those topics from how Bryan, who was ever concerned about defending the weak against the assaults of the strong and powerful, viewed what was happening 100 years ago. Bryan believed that applying Darwin's ideas to society "justified an economic jungle both at home, where a [John D.] Rockefeller could demonstrate his 'fitness' by driving out competition and controlling an industry, and abroad, where nations engaged in deadly struggle and ruthlessly tried to impose their wills on others. The doctrine of the fittest, in Bryan's estimation, encouraged industrial exploitation, war, and imperialism—evils against which he never tired of battling."[34] Bryan often spoke of two books that convinced him to take up the battle against evolution:

- *The Science of Power* (1918)[35] by Benjamin Kidd, a highly respected social theorist in both academic and lay circles, who also wrote *Social Evolution* in 1894, a widely read book on the implications of evolution.[36] Kidd said that Germany's nationalism, materialism, and militarism stemmed from the social Darwinian hypothesis. Bryan stated, "Kidd goes so far as to charge that '[Friedrich] Nietzsche's teaching represented the interpretation of the popular Darwinism delivered with the fury and intensity of genius.' And Nietzsche . . . denounced Christianity as the 'doctrine of the degenerate,' and democracy as 'the refuge of weaklings.'"[37]

- *Headquarters Nights: A Record of Conversations and Experiences at the Headquarters of the German Army in France and Belgium* (1917) by Vernon Kellogg, a Stanford University professor, who co-authored the 1908 textbook *Evolution and Animal Life*. Kellogg gives an account of the conversations he heard as an American war relief worker at the German Great General Staff headquarters. He "was appalled . . . at the justification for war and German supremacy advanced by these officers . . . . They not only proposed an evolutionary rationale but advocated a particularly crude form of natural selection."[38]

While eugenics is generally associated with Germany, it also had a significant presence in the U.S as indicated by the actions of these three American eugenicists[39]:

- Charles B. Davenport published his views on eugenics in *Heredity in Relation to Eugenics* (1911), in which he promoted mass compulsory sterilization of the unfit.

- Harry S. Laughlin outlined his strategy to inculcate eugenics discussion in the minds of all Americans at the National Conference on Race Betterment in 1914, which involved nationwide instruction "to lobby for legal restraints of marriage and habitation of the unfit, to agitate for the segregation of those identified as unfit, and finally to use sterilization . . . if the unfit are released into society."

- Harry C. Sharp was the first to impose sterilization on prison inmates (1902), which he saw as the only rational means of eliminating a "most dangerous and hurtful class" of people.

Although the laws varied regarding intent and extent and were "frequently edited, amended, and erased," sterilization laws were adopted by 12 states: Indiana, Washington, California, and Connecticut in 1909; Iowa, Nevada, and New Jersey in 1911; New York, Kansas, Michigan, and North Dakota in 1912; and Oregon in 1913.

"Throughout the early 1900s, multiple American eugenics societies convened to discuss compulsory sterilization legislation, segregation for the unfit, and screening for defectives in the population."[40]

The following statements from Bryan's *Last Message* provide further insight into how Darwin and Bryan viewed the social implications of survival of the fittest.

- Bryan quoted from Darwin's *The Descent of Man*:

  "With savages, the weak in body or mind are soon eliminated; and those that survive commonly exhibit a vigorous state of health. We civilized men . . . do our utmost to check the process of elimination; we build asylums for the imbecile, the maimed, and the sick; we institute poor laws; and our medical men exert their utmost skill to save the life of everyone to the last moment. . . . Thus the weak members of civilized society propagate their kind. No one who has attended to the breeding of domestic animals will doubt that this must be highly injurious to the race of man. It is surprising how soon a want of care, or care wrongly directed, leads to the degeneration of a domestic race; but excepting in the case of man himself, hardly anyone is so ignorant as to allow his worst animals to breed."[41]

- Bryan's rejoinder to Darwin's stated position:

"Darwin reveals the barbarous sentiment that runs through evolution and dwarfs the moral nature of those who become obsessed with it. . . . All of the sympathetic activities of civilized society are condemned because they enable 'the weak members to propagate their kind.' Then he drags mankind down to the level of the brute and compares the freedom given to man unfavorably with the restraint that we put on barnyard animals."[42]

An astonishing coincidence is worthy of note. During the Scopes trial, on July 18, 1925, Adolf Hitler's *Mein Kampf* [My Struggle], in which he called for the improvement of the race by the elimination of inferior people, was published in Germany.

EXAMINING BRYAN'S ANTI-EVOLUTION CAMPAIGN

After her husband's death Mary reflected, "Just why the interest grew, just how he was able to put fresh interest into a question which was popular twenty-five years ago, I do not know." Her explanation was based on her summary of what an editorialist had written about why Bryan regularly was the subject of front-page news: "Whenever Mr. Bryan took a stand upon any subject, the matter at once became an issue. People began to fall in line. Sides grew distinct. The public divided and stood ready to do battle." She concluded, "The vigor and force of the man seemed to compel attention."[43]

Bryan wrestled with many heavyweights over the course of his career, including banks, big business interests, and the Republican Party. He described what was to become his final heavyweight opponent— those who promoted the theory of evolution—when he wrote on July 3, 1925, "In this fight I have the most intolerant and vindictive enemies I have ever met and I have the largest majority on my side I have ever had and I am discussing the greatest issue I have ever discussed."[44]

He stated the purpose of his fight during a "fierce, cacophonous debate" at the 1923 General Assembly of the Presbyterian Church regarding his resolution that "provided that no part of the Educational Fund of the Presbyterian Church should support instruction that teaches as proved fact either Darwinism or any other evolutionary hypothesis that linked men in a blood relationship with any other form of life." During Bryan's summation he stated to a Modernist detractor, "Did you do more than I did to put across women's suffrage? Did you do more than I did to put across the election of Senators by direct vote of the people? Did you do more than I did to levy an income tax so that those who had the wealth would have to pay for it? There has not been a reform for twenty-five years that I did not support and I am now engaged in the biggest reform of my life. I am trying to save the Christian Church from those who are trying to destroy her faith."[45]

Bryan developed a well-crafted battle plan based on his unique combination of strengths—his extraordinary sense of audience and the press, ease with the public, and political acumen—to awaken widespread public interest in the creation–evolution debate.

The Bryans in Coconut Grove, Miami, FL, at their daughter Ruth's home, Chota Khoti, c. 1925 (BCA)

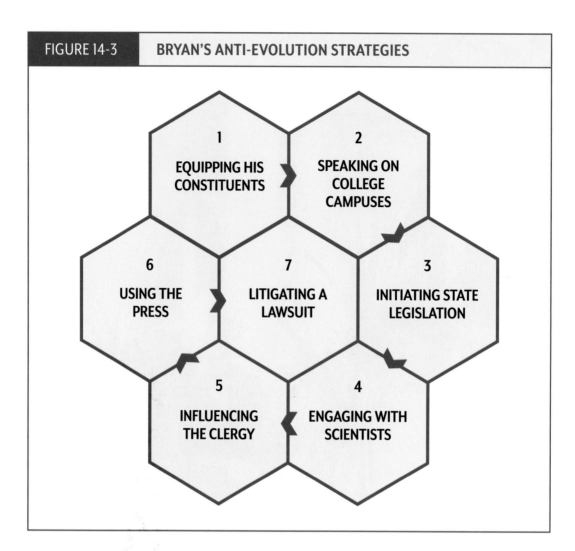

FIGURE 14-3   BRYAN'S ANTI-EVOLUTION STRATEGIES

The remainder of the chapter explores the strategies Bryan employed in his crusade against evolution that are outlined in Figure 14-3.

1. EQUIPPING HIS CONSTITUENTS

Bryan, as he had with other reforms throughout his career, appealed to his constituents to stand and fight with him for this cause; and he equipped them with reasoned arguments and writings for the battle.

- In October 1920 Bryan addressed the World Brotherhood Congress in Washington, DC, where he surprised his audience by announcing he had changed his speech title from "World Brotherhood and World Peace" to "Brother or Brute?" In that speech he expressed his "growing conviction" that "the doctrine, commonly known as the Darwinian theory, that traces man's ancestry back to the brute is the most paralyzing influence with which civilization has had to contend during the last century. When one begins his family tree with the beasts of the field, ancestor worship becomes a dangerous religion, not to speak of the possibility of his borrowing his ethics from the jungle."[46]

- Bryan published his first major attack on Darwinism in the April 1921 edition of *The Commoner*, "The Menace of Darwinism."[47]

- Bryan also began delivering his "Menace of Darwinism" speech in 1921 at Bible conferences and on the Chautauqua circuit and did so for the remainder of his life. Large crowds were attracted to hear the lecture that Bryan began, not with an attack on evolution, but rather in answering the question of mankind's role and purpose in the universe:

> When the mainspring is broken, a watch ceases to be useful as a timekeeper. A handsome case may make it still an ornament and the parts may have a market value, but it cannot serve the purpose of a watch. There is that in each human life that corresponds to the mainspring of a watch—that which is absolutely necessary if the life is to be what it should be, a real life and not a mere existence. That necessary thing is a belief in God. Religion is defined as the relation between God and man, and Tolstoy has described morality as the outward expression of this inward relationship.[48]

"The Menace of Darwinism" and a second anti-evolution lecture Bryan introduced later that year, "The Bible and Its Enemies," were published in various formats for distribution by the thousands to ministers, fundamentalist laymen, politicians, and college students."[49]

2. SPEAKING ON COLLEGE CAMPUSES

Bryan often faced opposition when he spoke about evolution on college campuses. He raised a furor, for example, when he charged that "students were forced to state views about God they really did not hold in order to pass their examinations, as at Wellesley College and the Universities of Kentucky and Wisconsin."[50] Here are examples of positive and negative responses he received on college campuses[51]:

- In November 1920 Bryan gave a Sunday address at the University of Michigan to an audience of 4,500, after which he received many critical letters, including one from Rev. Arthur W. Stalker of the First Methodist Church in Ann Arbor. Stalker "criticized him for the false alternatives he had posed and claimed that until his speech, the issue of evolution had been a dead one for most of the Michigan students. He intimated that Bryan would lose his influence with the people if he continued speaking along these lines." Likewise, following the speech, a philosopher and a scientist publicly denounced what Bryan had said. This criticism resulted in Bryan's expanding and elaborating his arguments and printing 5,000 copies of the new speech for distribution, sending many of them to Michigan.

- In the fall of 1921 he stirred controversy when he spoke at Middlebury College in Vermont, and again in early 1922 when he addressed a crowd of 2,000 at the University of Wisconsin at Madison. Similar results occurred when he visited Dartmouth College and Harvard,[52] Yale, and Brown Universities.

- Two of his campus lectures delivered in 1921 were published as follows:
    - *In His Image* is based on a series of nine lectures Bryan presented at Union Theological Seminary (known today as Union Presbyterian Seminary), Richmond, VA. The first lecture was entitled "In the Beginning—God" and the fourth, "The Origin of Man." *In His Image* was promoted as "Bryan's Answer to Darwin" and was one of the most influential religious books of the time, selling over 100,000 copies.
    - *The Bible and Its Enemies* was published following the address Bryan delivered at the Moody Bible Institute of Chicago.

3. INITIATING STATE LEGISLATION

Bryan reiterated two points in every address he gave on the legislative efforts at the state level. The anti-evolution law should, first, **contain no penalties:** "We are not dealing with a criminal class and a mere declaration of the state's policy is sufficient"; and second, **only prohibit the teaching of evolution as a fact:** "a book which merely contains it as an hypothesis can be considered as giving information as to views held, which is very different from teaching it as a fact."

In May 1923 Florida adopted a resolution that Bryan drafted that met his criteria (see "Separation Between Church and State" on page 97). In the months that followed, Bryan addressed state legislatures, advised their members in framing bills, and urged New York and Chicago mayors to ban the teaching of evolution as a fact in their city schools.[53]

Two state laws were passed that did not meet Bryan's criteria:

- March 1923—Oklahoma legislature passed a textbook bill barring the use of all texts teaching the Darwinian theory.

- March 1925—Tennessee's Butler Act prohibited teachers from denying creation and teaching evolution and included penalties for violating the law. The law was challenged later that year in the Scopes trial (see Chapter 15).

4. ENGAGING WITH SCIENTISTS

Bryan debated with scientists in a series of articles published in *The New York Times* (1922). See page 108.

The American Association for the Advancement of Science (AAAS) published an article in 1922 entitled "Quotations: William Jennings Bryan on Evolution" that included the following Bryan quotations[54]:

> Christians do not dispute the right of any teacher to be agnostic or atheistic, but Christians do deny the right of agnostics and atheists to use the public school as a forum for the teaching of their doctrines.
>
> The Bible has in many places been excluded from the schools on the ground that religion should not be taught by those paid by public taxation. If this doctrine is sound, what right have the enemies of religion to teach irreligion in the public schools? If the Bible cannot be taught, why should Christian taxpayers permit the teaching of guesses that make the Bible a lie?
>
> The Christians who want to teach religion in their schools furnish the money for denominational institutions. If atheists want to teach atheism, why do they not build their own schools and employ their own teachers?
>
> We stamp upon our coins "In God We Trust"; we administer to witnesses an oath in which God's name appears; our President takes his oath of office upon the Bible. Is it fanatical to suggest that public taxes should not be employed for the purpose of undermining the nation's God?
>
> As religion is the only basis of morals, it is time for Christians to protect religion from its most insidious enemy [Darwinism].

In *The Scientific Monthly*, a University of Chicago professor wrote about the "lamentably great hiatus that has long existed and has been also long widening between men of science and the unlearned multitude." He suggested that Bryan and his followers demonstrate that "every advance by men of learning over the religious and political philosophy of the Revolutionary Fathers has widened the breach between the many who support and the few who promote science—so slow is the task of raising the general level of intelligence."

The author added, "Mr. Bryan speaks not for himself alone; he remains what he has for so long been, both the interpreter and prophet of a great mass of men whose political and religious aspirations find no more commanding articulation. Addressing himself to 'the heart and mind of the average man,' Bryan speaks for, as well as to, a substantial group of sturdy Americans."[55]

Bryan appeared to be aware of those that characterized him as being against scientific advancements by actions such as these:

- He sang the praises of science when he wrote in *The Last Message*, "Give science a fact; and it is not only invincible, but it is of incalculable service to man." That statement was followed by a long list of scientific advances that have done so much good for society, such as the use of steam and electricity; the phonograph, telephone, and radio; the sewing machine, tractor, and automobile; and the advances in curing typhoid, yellow fever, diphtheria, and pneumonia. He further stated as follows:

> Science is a magnificent force, but it is not a teacher of morals. It can perfect machinery, but it adds no moral restraints to protect society from the misuse of the machine. It can also build gigantic intellectual ships, but it constructs no moral rudders for the control of storm-tossed human vessels. It not only fails to supply the spiritual element needed, but some of its unproven hypotheses rob the ship of its compass and thus endanger its cargo.
>
> In war, science has proven itself an evil genius; it has made war more terrible than it ever was before. Man used to be content to slaughter his fellowmen on a single plane—the earth's surface. Science has taught him to go down into the water and shoot up from below and to go up into the clouds and shoot down from above, thus making the battlefield three times as bloody as it was before; but science does not teach brotherly love.[56]

- Bryan joined the American Association for the Advancement of Science in 1924. A well-attended session at their annual meeting that year was entitled "Darwin and Bryan—A Study in Method." The speaker was Edward Loranus Rice, a biologist of Ohio Wesleyan University who later served as a scientific consultant to Clarence Darrow before the Scopes trial.

  Rice's address conclusion was reported as follows: "The dogmatic method of Mr. Bryan is happily not followed by all theologians; nor, unhappily, does Darwin's scientific method characterize all his followers. It is to be hoped that the outcome of the present controversy may be the alliance of a more scientific religion and a more religious science."[57]

5. INFLUENCING THE CLERGY

While many examples could be provided of Bryan's influencing the clergy, here are three of the most significant:

- **Theistic Evolution**. Many clergymen who espoused liberal theology and higher criticism also embraced Darwinism and claimed it did not conflict with Christianity. To Bryan, however, "the real danger was not atheism or agnosticism which were 'open enemies' but the subversive element within the churches which was attempting to reconcile Christianity and evolution."[58] A label by which this reconciliation is known is "theistic evolution."

"The Descent of the Modernists" by E. J. Pace, from inside front cover of WJB's book, *Seven Questions in Dispute*, 1924[59]

Among Bryan's reasons for disagreeing that churches should embrace theistic evolution are these:

> It *permits* one to believe in a God, but puts the creative act so far away that reverence for a Creator—even belief in Him—is likely to be lost.[60]

> Give the modernist three words, 'allegorical,' 'poetical,' and 'symbolical,' and he can suck the meaning out of every vital doctrine of the Christian Church and every passage in the Bible to which he objects.[61]

> Theistic evolution is an anesthetic: it deadens the pain while the Christian religion is being removed.[62]

> Christians do not object to freedom of speech . . . . They concede the right of ministers to pass from belief to agnosticism or atheism, but they contend that they should be honest enough to separate themselves from the ministry and not attempt to debase the religion which they profess.[63]

- **Fundamentalism.** Bryan played no role in the late 19th and early 20th century formation of Fundamentalism; and Bryan differed with Fundamentalist leaders on some theological and other matters. When Bryan became involved with the Fundamentalists in the early 1920s, he brought with him the issue of anti-evolution, which had been only a periphery issue for the Fundamentalists up to that time. After Bryan's entry, however, "the burden of the Fundamentalist message became the passage of anti-evolution laws in every state. Under the umbrella of the constant press coverage which was his wherever he went, Bryan allowed the various factions of Fundamentalism to work together for common goals."[64]

- **The Presbyterian Church.** In 1923 Bryan, who had served for nearly two decades as an elder or ruling elder at First Presbyterian Church in Lincoln, NE, and for several years as a delegate to the General Assembly of the Presbyterian Church in the USA, ran for the post of moderator of the General Assembly.

After losing to Charles F. Wishart, a college president who endorsed the teaching of evolution, Bryan introduced several resolutions from the floor. The delegates accepted his resolution to add to their articles of faith, a statement on the inerrancy of the Bible. Another of his resolutions was accepted as a compromise. Bryan's version—that no denominational funds should be spent to support schools that permitted the teaching of evolution "as a proven fact"—was reduced to a statement that they would warn teachers against allowing materialistic evolution to be taught.[65]

He wrote his daughter Grace on June 3, 1923: "I think my defeat for Moderator was providential. I did far more on the floor than I could have done in the chair. . . . I got through four resolutions besides helping to secure a statement of the Church position on **five important doctrines** [emphasis added]. It was a great victory for orthodox Christianity—other churches will follow. It means a new awakening of the Church. It was much better than being Moderator."[66]

Shortly after Bryan's participation in the Presbyterian General Assembly (PGA) meeting, he published a book entitled *Orthodox Christianity Versus Modernism*, where he

- Presents a defense of the PGA's position taken on the **five important doctrines** to which he referred in his letter to Grace; namely, the inerrant verbal inspiration of the Bible, the virgin birth of Jesus Christ, the substitutionary atonement through His death, His bodily resurrection, and the validity of biblical miracles.[67]

- Begins the second section, entitled "Evolution," as follows:

> But what is it that thus, progressively, whittles away the Word of God and destroys its vitality? I venture to assert that the unproven hypothesis of evolution is the root cause of nearly all the dissension in the church over the five points under discussion. . . . Not all evolutionists are dissenters, but all dissenters are evolutionists,—some theistic evolutionists and some atheistic evolutionists.[68]

- Concludes with an abstract of an address he delivered before the West Virginia State Legislature, April 23, 1923, entitled "Science Versus Evolution."[69]

6. USING THE PRESS

Bryan received much negative press for his creation stand from such newspapers as the *Chicago Post*, which "crucified him"; the *New York Herald*, which said his success would lead to "the Inquisition and heretic-hunting"; and *The New York Times*, which derided "Mr. Bryan's curious array of prejudices."[70] Despite the negativity, he was still able to use the press in positive ways.

For example, Bryan accepted a *New York Times* invitation to participate in a debate series that was widely reprinted by newspapers and the religious press, which fiercely fanned the flames of the creation–evolution controversy. The debate began on Sunday, February 26, 1922, when *The New York Times* published Bryan's article "God and Evolution."[71] On successive Sundays the following rebuttal articles appeared by scientists, a clergyman, and a law professor:

- "Evolution and Religion," Henry Fairfield Osborn, Columbia University and the New York Museum of Natural History[72]
- "Bryan and Evolution," Professor Grant Edwin Conklin, Princeton University[73]
- "Attacks W. J. B.," Harry Emerson Fosdick, a prominent liberal minister of the early 20th century and central figure in the Fundamentalist–Modernist controversy[74]
- "No Non-Man Ancestry," Francis P. LeBuffe, Fordham University School of Law professor[75]

Here are two interesting postscripts to the 1922 debate series:

- About three years later, Bryan had a different view of this strategy. The day Bryan died, he responded to a newspaper editor's question about whether he was going to accept the offer by a New York syndicate to write a series of articles on his position on the evolution controversy in answer to a series Clarence Darrow had written.

  Bryan declared that he had no intention of accepting the offer. "I do not intend to do anything to add to the publicity of the views of such men . . . . My fight is not with the agnostics or the atheists. I am not engaged in a controversy with them. My fight is with the so-called 'modernists' of the Christian Church over a matter of Christian doctrine and belief, and in this battle I am not concerned with the views of agnostics or infidels."[76]

- More than a decade later Rev. Harry Emerson Fosdick had also changed his view when he admitted in 1935 that Modernists had "watered down the thought of the Divine, and, may we be forgiven for this, left souls standing like the ancient Athenians, before an altar to an Unknown God! . . . We have been all things to all men long enough. We have adapted and adjusted and accommodated and conceded long enough. We have at times gotten so low down that we talked as though the highest compliment that could be paid to Almighty God was that a few scientists believed in him."[77]

7. LITIGATING A LAWSUIT

The first six anti-evolution strategies provide context for understanding Bryan's seventh strategy, his involvement in the Scopes trial, the subject of the next chapter.

15 | THE SCOPES TRIAL

> Causes stir the world, and this cause has stirred the world. It is because it goes deep. It is because it extends wide, and because it reaches into the future beyond the power of man to see. . . . There can be no settlement of a great cause without discussion, and people will not discuss a cause until their attention is drawn to it.
>
> —William Jennings Bryan
> Scopes Trial (21 July 1925)

INTRODUCTION [1]

In the era following World War I, known as "The Roaring Twenties," teaching evolution in state-funded public schools triggered a dizzying array of debates. These included such matters as separation of church and state; the social implications of Darwin's concept of survival of the fittest (eugenics and racism); the authority of the Bible vs. the soundness of Darwin's theory; academic freedom vs. popular control over public education; fundamentalism vs. modernism in the church; and traditional vs. modern views and values in society.

This debate over the public schools' teaching of evolution, along with its widespread implications, was central to the *State of Tennessee v. John Thomas Scopes* (1925). The Scopes trial, like other famous courtroom cases fought over controversial causes, such as *Roe v. Wade* (1973) and *Brown v. Board of Education* (1954), is a cultural icon for its cause. While most such cases are remembered primarily for their decisions, the Scopes trial is remembered primarily for its trial—the people, drama, and atmosphere. Commonly referred to as the Scopes Monkey Trial, it has inspired numerous stage and screen adaptations and novels, as well as non-fiction books and scholarly articles.

The "Trial of the Century" was held at the Rhea County Courthouse in Dayton, TN, nestled into the foothills of the Cumberland Mountains. It drew much attention to the small town and was reported on by about "200 American and international reporters, newsreel and still photographers, editorial cartoonists, and 65 telegraph operators in Dayton who dispatched over 2,000,000 words by wire and airplane to 2310 daily newspapers in the U.S. alone."[2] More words were cabled to Europe and Australia than had ever been sent about any other American event.

In addition, the crew of WGN, the radio voice of the *Chicago Tribune*, produced the first national broadcast of an American trial. Defendant John T. Scopes' alleged crime, violating Tennessee's Butler Act by teaching evolution, only counted as a misdemeanor—no more significant than a charge of petty theft or producing illegal liquor. But the trial and cause for which it stood did indeed, as Bryan stated, "stir the world." In announcing the broadcast, the *Tribune* stated, "This is not a criminal trial . . . . It is more like the opening of a summer university. . . . The defendant, Scopes, is already a negligible factor. Nothing serious can happen to him. The contest is entirely over ideas."[3]

Notice the WGN microphone in the foreground and newsreel camera in the background. Standing in the middle (L-R) are prosecuting attorneys Wallace Haggard and Herbert Hicks and defense attorney Dudley Field Malone. (BCA)

The eight-day trial that started with jury selection on Friday, July 10, ended abruptly on Tuesday, July 21, when Clarence Darrow asked the jury to find his client guilty. Darrow's request denied Bryan two opportunities: to cross-examine Darrow and to give his carefully crafted summation speech. The request also ensured the defense could file an appeal with a higher court. The jury deliberated nine minutes and found Scopes guilty; Judge John Raulston fined Scopes $100 (equivalent to nearly $1,440 in 2019). Scopes did not pay the fine. However, several conflicting accounts have left historians uncertain about who ultimately paid the fine: (1) "H. L. Mencken, acting in behalf of the Baltimore *Evening Sun*, either paid or guaranteed the payment of the fine."[4] (2) Bryan offered to pay Scopes' fine.[5] (3) The American Civil Liberties Union (ACLU) paid Scopes' bill for court costs totaling $343.87.[6]

Scopes' lawyers challenged the conviction on appeal before the Tennessee Supreme Court. However, the court ruled on January 15, 1927, that the Butler Act was constitutional but overturned Judge Raulston's decision on a technicality: The jury, not he, should have assessed the fine.[7] Shortly thereafter, the Attorney General announced he would not seek a retrial, denying Darrow and the defense team the opportunity to take the case to the U.S. Supreme Court.

This chapter will look at the trial from four perspectives, each of which will emphasize Bryan's role in the trial: (1) Scopes trial facts, (2) Scopes trial legends, (3) Scopes trial's impact, and (4) Bryan's final days in Dayton.

SCOPES TRIAL FACTS

This section tells the Scopes trial story in four parts: an 18-month chronology of events that led up to the start of the trial, an introduction to the trial's cast of characters, an explanation of the strategies employed by both legal teams, and highlights of the eight-day trial.

CHRONOLOGY: THE ROAD TO THE SCOPES TRIAL

The following timeline begins with Bryan's delivery of a speech that helped set the stage for the Scopes trial, and it ends on the trial's first day.

■ **January 24, 1924:** Bryan delivered his lecture "Is the Bible True?"[8] at Ryman Auditorium, Nashville, TN, after which 500 copies of the lecture were sent to Tennessee legislators; and Representative John Washington Butler, an admirer of Bryan, was one of the recipients.

● **January 21, 1925:** Representative Butler introduced in the House of Representatives TN House Bill 185, known as the Butler Act. Bryan's lecture was once again sent to members of the state legislature.[9]

● **January 28, 1925:** The Butler Act passed the House.

● **March 13, 1925:** The Butler Act passed the Senate.

● **March 21, 1925:** Governor Austin Peay signed the Butler Act into law, making Tennessee the first state to ban the teaching of human evolution, thereby setting the stage for the Scopes trial. The Butler Act, however, fell short on two of Bryan's standards for anti-evolution legislation at the state level:

  - *Legislation should contain no penalties*: Violation of the Butler Act was considered a misdemeanor and subject to a $100–$500 fine for each offense.

  - *Legislation should prohibit only the teaching of evolution as a fact*: The Butler Act stated that "it shall be unlawful for any teacher in any of the . . . public schools . . . to teach any theory that denies the story of the Divine Creation of man as taught in the Bible, and to teach instead that man has descended from a lower order of animals."

● **May 4, 1925:** The *Chattanooga Times* published the following notice from the ACLU: "We are looking for a Tennessee teacher who is willing to accept our services in testing this law in the courts. Our lawyers think a friendly test case can be arranged without costing a teacher his or her job. Distinguished counsel have volunteered their services. All we need now is a willing client."[10]

● **May 5, 1925:** In response to the ACLU offer, New Yorker George W. Rappleyea, who moved to Dayton in 1922 to coordinate the shutdown and sale of the failing Cumberland Coal and Iron Co., hatched a scheme to increase publicity for Dayton. Rappleyea convinced Frank Earle (F. E.) Robinson, drugstore owner and chair of the local school board, that it would be a good idea to bring the test case to Dayton. They summoned John Scopes, the 24-year-old Rhea Central High School coach and general science instructor, to the meeting where he agreed to be indicted even though he had been only a substitute teacher in the science class that used Hunter's *Civic Biology*. The textbook described evolution as "the belief that simple forms of life on the earth slowly and gradually gave rise to those more complex and that thus ultimately the most complex forms came into existence." After the meeting Rappleyea signed the complaint that led to Scopes' "arrest" for violating the Butler Act; Scopes never spent any time in jail.

The Dayton trial leaders reenacted their original meeting at Robinson's drugstore for press photographers. Seated: (L-R) Herbert Hicks (prosecutor), John Scopes (defendant), Walter White (superintendent of Rhea County Schools), Gordon McKenzie (prosecutor). Standing: (L-R) Burt Wilbur (constable), Wallace Haggard (prosecutor), W. E. Morgan (later produced with F. E. Robinson a 28-page booklet "Why Dayton of All Places?"[11]), George Rappleyea (originator of publicity stunt), Sue Hicks (prosecutor), and F. E. Robinson (chairman of local school board and owner of drugstore) (BCA)

May 9, 1925: The first attempt to transfer the case to a different city occurred during the preliminary hearing. John Neal "suggested transferring the case to Knoxville or Chattanooga, which could provide more dignified facilities for the event and adequate accommodations for visitors. *The Chattanooga News* even tried to instigate a new case in its city . . . [if] the transfer fell through. Daytonians responded by threatening to boycott Chattanooga merchants and preparing their town for the trial."[12]

May 13, 1925: William Bell Riley, president of the World Christian Fundamentals Association, telegrammed Bryan asking him to go to Dayton to join the prosecution team on the association's behalf. Bryan volunteered his services and wired his acceptance back from Pittsburgh, where he was on a speaking tour. The next day Clarence Darrow announced his intention to join the defense team.

July 4, 1925: The second attempt to transfer the case occurred when Secretary of State Bainbridge Colby, an early member of the defense team, convinced the ACLU to seek an injunction to move the case to a federal court. A federal judge denied the last-minute petition, and Colby quietly resigned from the case.[13]

July 7, 1925: Bryan and his wife, Mary, arrived in Dayton by train. That evening Bryan delivered a lengthy speech at a banquet given in his honor by Dayton's Progressive Club (DPC) at Hotel Aqua.

July 9, 1925: Darrow, Hays, and Malone arrived by train, and the DPC hosted a similar banquet for Darrow, at which Darrow delivered an address.

July 10, 1925: Before the official opening for the first day of the trial, Bryan was given a standing ovation on what was the 29th anniversary of his famous "Cross of Gold" speech (see page 52).[14]

After Bryan's arrival in Dayton, he and fellow prosecutors went to F. R. Rogers' home on Market Street. During their stay in Dayton, this is the home that Bryan, his wife, and their entourage rented for $25 per week and is where Bryan died five days after the trial ended. (L-R) Wallace Haggard, Gordon McKenzie, F. R. Rogers, Bryan, brothers Sue and Herbert Hicks, and Ben McKenzie. (BCA)

MAJOR PLAYERS

In addition to the defendant, **John Thomas Scopes**, other major players included the circuit court judge for the 18th district, **John T. Raulston**; the *Baltimore Sun's* **H. L. Mencken**, the most well-known reporter who covered the trial and is credited with coining the moniker "Monkey Trial" (see "H. L. Mencken" on page 45); and **William Jennings Bryan** and **Clarence Darrow**, the public figures who embodied the opposing viewpoints, which are succinctly described as follows:

 In the same way that . . . modernism and fundamentalism were incompatible, Bryan and Darrow were irreconcilable. For Bryan, the Darwinian idea that random chance was at the center of an obviously ordered nature was simply a self-evident contradiction. For Darrow, it was equally self-evident that Scriptural validity should be subjected to the same critical scrutiny as any other text or set of facts.[15]

Members of the Scopes trial prosecution team reviewing court documents: (L-R) Tom Stewart; William Jennings Bryan, Jr; and William Jennings Bryan. (BCA)

The prosecution team had eight attorneys of record:

- **Tom Stewart**, current attorney general for the 18th district, led the prosecution.

- **Sue Hicks,** named after his mother who died after giving birth to him, and his brother, **Herbert Hicks**, were both Dayton attorneys.

- **Wallace Haggard**, F. E. Robinson's brother-in-law, was a young Dayton lawyer.

- **Ben McKenzie**, retired attorney general for the 18th district, and his son, **Gordon McKenzie**, formed one of two father-son duos on the team.

- **William Jennings Bryan**, for whom the trial was a natural, if unintended, next step in his anti-evolution campaign (see Figure 14-3 on page 102), recruited his son, **William Jennings Bryan, Jr.**, in a letter dated June 17, 1925: "In the first place, this trial will become one of the greatest trials in history and I want your name associated with it. In the second place, the issue will be raised in every state and I want you to be in a position to take up my work and carry it on in this matter. I can't return to the practice of law but you can take my place in the various states. The fact that you are my son, added to your connection with the case, will give you a standing no one else can have. Every attack from our opponents draws the orthodox Christians more closely to me, and you will share in the benefits. Don't fail to come; it would be a very grave mistake for you to miss this opportunity."[16]

Clarence Darrow (left) and William Jennings Bryan during the Scopes trial (BCA)

The defense team had six attorneys of record:

- **John R. Neal**, a former law professor at the University of Tennessee, led the defense.
- **Arthur Garfield Hays**, a wealthy Park Avenue attorney, regularly defended free-speech cases for the ACLU.
- **Dudley Field Malone**, a wealthy divorce lawyer drawn to the spotlight of the Scopes litigation, acted as the third assistant secretary of state reporting to Secretary of State Bryan for seven months in 1913.[17]
- **Clarence Darrow** was one of the most formidable and controversial attorneys in America in the 1910s and 1920s. He brought with him the public's memories from his recent courtroom appearance as defense counsel for Nathan Leopold and Richard Loeb, wealthy University of Chicago students who had kidnapped and murdered 14-year-old Bobby Franks in Chicago. Darrow's 12-hour summation was credited with saving the two young men from the death penalty. While the Scopes trial was the first and last time Darrow offered free legal aid, he agreed to volunteer his service for the defense only after he heard that Bryan had volunteered. Darrow "saw a chance to grab the limelight and debunk Christianity." He later wrote that his "object was to focus the attention of the country on the programme of Mr. Bryan and the other fundamentalists in America."[18]
- **W. O. Thompson** was Darrow's law partner.
- **F. B. McElwee** was Neal's former student.

STRATEGIES EACH SIDE EMPLOYED

PROSECUTION [19]	DEFENSE [20]
• Stewart tried to keep his team and the trial focused on the narrow legal limits that John Scopes had broken the law. He hoped to keep the proceedings from veering off into debates about biblical authority or the merits of evolution being taught in Tennessee classrooms. He, therefore, objected to the defense including any expert witnesses.	• Darrow's focus was putting Bryan on the defensive by saying such things to the press as "Nero tried to kill Christianity with persecution and law. Bryan would block enlightenment with law." Darrow behaved toward Bryan as though Bryan instead of Scopes were the accused. "It was a simple theme and one Darrow kept reiterating until he hounded his target in the witness chair at Dayton."
• During day seven's famous exchange between Darrow and Bryan, Stewart raised objections more than ten times, reminding the judge that Bryan's testimony as an expert on the Bible had no pertinence to the trial; but Bryan demanded the right to answer Darrow's challenges, and the judge allowed the questioning to continue.	• Neal kept the focus on academic freedom. • Malone focused on the defense's position that the theory of evolution did not conflict with the biblical account of creation. • Hays supported his defense team colleagues in expanding the fight for individual liberty against majority control to include scientific evidence for evolution and religious theories of biblical interpretation.

EACH TRIAL DAY'S HIGHLIGHT [21]

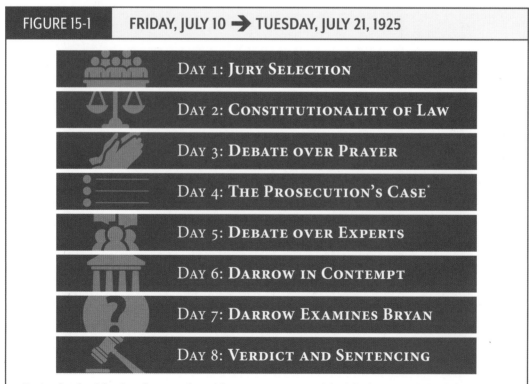

FIGURE 15-1	FRIDAY, JULY 10 ➡ TUESDAY, JULY 21, 1925

Day 1: **Jury Selection**

Day 2: **Constitutionality of Law**

Day 3: **Debate over Prayer**

Day 4: **The Prosecution's Case**[*]

Day 5: **Debate over Experts**

Day 6: **Darrow in Contempt**

Day 7: **Darrow Examines Bryan**

Day 8: **Verdict and Sentencing**

*During their lunch break on day 4, members of the prosecution team and the defendant enjoyed a break from the heat when Scopes, Haggard, and Bryan, Jr., went swimming in nearby Pocket Wilderness's "Blue Hole."[22] See #45 on page 155.

SCOPES TRIAL LEGENDS

Many of the Scopes trial legends and myths originated with the 1955 stage play *Inherit the Wind* that opened at Broadway's National Theatre in April 1955 and ran through June 1957. It was revived on Broadway twice (1999 and 2007). The film version (1960), the made-for-TV movies (1965, 1988, and 1999), and the countless community and school theaters that have produced the play since its release have also contributed to the widespread misinformation about the trial.

Jerome Lawrence and Robert E. Lee's play was based loosely on the historical record of the trial and was meant to be an indictment against McCarthyism. The play's two main characters, Matthew Harrison Brady and Henry Drummond, representing Bryan and Darrow, respectively, bear little resemblance to the real-life participants; and factual errors can be found in almost every scene. Yet academics and others continue to promote *Inherit the Wind* as a "useful tool for 'supporting an understanding of the Scopes trial.'"[23]

Inherit the Wind's courtroom scene in which Darrow questioned Bryan came to represent a triumph for the defense and dramatically took over the original Scopes trial narrative. In fact, the notion that the Scopes trial had "dismantled the Fundamentalist campaign against evolution, or that Bryan was crushed and lost whatever moral authority he had enjoyed, did not begin to take hold until the 1930s and only became the received interpretation of the trial with the success of *Inherit the Wind*—the play and, especially, the movie."[24]

On day seven of the trial, when relief from an overcrowded courtroom and extreme temperatures was needed, Judge Raulston moved court proceedings to the platform outside the courthouse. Darrow (standing) grilled Bryan (seated on left) for 90 minutes before the judge ended the questioning. Bryan had agreed to take the stand on the condition that he would have the same opportunity to question the defense team attorneys. The promised questioning never took place; the following morning the judge expunged Bryan's testimony from the record, and the trial ended later that day.
(Smithsonian Institution Archives. Image # SIA2007-0123)

Biographer Lawrence Levine responded to some commentators' views that the Scopes trial left Bryan an exhausted and broken man by pointing out that Bryan "did a masterly job of concealing it during the five days of life remaining to him."[25] A commentary by a New Orleans *Times-Picayune* reporter provides a response to the claim that the Fundamentalist anti-evolution campaign was dismantled: "Mr. Darrow, with his sneering, 'I object to prayer!' and with his ill-natured and arrogant cross-examination of Bryan on the witness stand, has done more to stimulate 'antievolution' legislation in the United States than Mr. Bryan and his fellow literalists, left alone, could have hoped for."[26]

An examination of what happened after the Scopes trial, the topic in the next section, sheds some light on which side could claim victory and whether the trial was the beginning of the end of the campaign against evolution.

AFTERMATH OF THE SCOPES TRIAL

Immediately after the trial, both sides claimed victory—the prosecution, a legal victory; the defense a moral one. *New York Times* reporter Russell D. Owen concluded, "Each side withdrew at the end of the struggle satisfied that it had unmasked the absurd pretensions of the other."[27]

Victory can be more clearly determined by analyzing outcomes in the following four areas:

TRIAL'S IMPACT ON EVOLUTION CONTENT IN BIOLOGY TEXTBOOKS

An examination of biology textbooks published in the 35 years following the Scopes trial (1925–1960) provides evidence that the trial influenced how the topic of evolution was treated. Two perspectives on the trial's impact are provided in this section. In the first study, author Randy Moore provides evidences that by 1960 evolution had all but disappeared from biology textbooks, and attributes this change to the after-effects of the Scopes trial. A few details are as follows: [28]

- Soon after Scopes was indicted, Tennessee abandoned George Hunter's popular textbook *Civic Biology*. Hunter's publisher gave the next edition a new title, *New Civic Biology*; and Hunter "eliminated charts showing the evolution of species and added vague qualifiers such as 'suggested' and 'believed' when describing evolution." Within a few months of the trial's end, Texas Governor Miriam Ferguson "ordered her state's textbook commission to delete the theory of evolution from its high school biology books." Louisiana took a similar step the following year.

- In the 1930s Baker and Mills' *Dynamic Biology* (1933) was the best-selling biology textbook; it did not include the word evolution, claimed that Darwin's theory was no longer generally accepted, and included a tribute to God.

- "In the late 1940s, many authors reduced their treatments of human evolution."

- "As the 1950s came to a close, there was no evidence in textbooks that evolution was regarded as a major concept in biology. On the contrary, biology textbooks and biology teaching in public schools [according to famed biologist H. J. Muller's 1959 article "One Hundred Years Without Darwinism Are Enough"] were dominated by 'antiquated religious traditions.'"

Ronald P. Ladouceur, the author of the second study, proposes that although "pressure from anti-evolutionists certainly had some influence on how the topic of evolution was treated in textbooks," the trial's "impact has been greatly exaggerated." He provides evidence that the textbooks during this period were not "limited and censored works," but rather were "fair reflections of social attitudes among educators and scientists." Ladouceur also suggests that exaggerating the trial's impact obscures a more important story, a few highlights of which follow:[29]

- Ella Thea Smith's *Exploring Biology*, published by Harcourt, Brace and Company (1938, 1942, and 1949), is evidence of an educator who was able to "simultaneously present the latest science [Smith's 1949 edition was the first American high school biology textbook to present the modern evolutionary synthesis], empower her students, work to counter social injustices, and compete successfully in the commercial textbook market."

- Smith's and similar textbooks do not support the premise Ladouceur calls the "myth of Scopes," which says that biology textbooks prior to the Scopes trial had fairly presented the theory of evolution using concepts similar to how we understand the theory today; however, Christian fundamentalists pressured authors and publishers, resulting in the systematic removal of references to the topic over the next 35 years.

- The myth of Scopes also benefited the Biological Sciences Curriculum Study (BSCS) that was established in 1958 with federal funding from the National Science Foundation. The myth served to "differentiate, defend, and promote" the 1963 publication of three BSCS biology textbooks. The BSCS was "incorrectly credited for 'reintroducing the topic of evolution into the high school curriculum, and exalted for being more 'scientific,' meaning less culturally bound, than their post-Scopes predecessors."

TRIAL'S IMPACT ON ANTI-EVOLUTION LEGISLATION IN TENNESSEE

The Butler Act stayed on Tennessee's books for another 42 years, after which the Tennessee legislature repealed it in 1967 based on a challenge to its constitutionality. However, that decision did not put the matter to rest. In 1974 Tennessee legislators approved a bill requiring equal time for various origins theories, including creationism. In 1996 the world watched as the Tennessee General Assembly debated a bill that would prohibit teaching evolution as a "fact." That bill, however, was defeated in the Senate. In 2012, a new law was passed by the state legislature that protected teachers who allowed students to challenge controversial scientific ideas such as evolution.[30]

TRIAL'S IMPACT ON ANTI-EVOLUTION LEGISLATION IN THE UNITED STATES

The Scopes trial proved that anti-evolution laws could be passed and upheld; and before the decade ended, 23 state legislatures had debated such legislation. Mississippi's anti-evolution law was enacted in 1926. Of the 18 anti-evolution bills presented in 1927, all were defeated, with most dying in committee. Then Arkansas' anti-evolution law passed in 1928. "By 1929, most states of the old Confederacy had imposed restrictions against evolutionary teaching by law, legislative resolution, or administrative ruling." However, efforts in the North met with defeat, and each side occupied its respective territories. For the most part over the next three decades the battle subsided with evolutionists not seeking to overturn existing legislation and creationists not pursuing further state legislative initiatives. Therefore, during this period efforts to restrict evolutionary teaching occurred at the local school district level rather than at the state level.[31]

The debate was relaunched with the 1967 *Epperson v. Arkansas* case that challenged Arkansas' 1928 statute that prohibited the teaching of human evolution in the public schools. The U.S. Supreme Court declared the statute unconstitutional because it violated the Establishment Clause of the First Amendment that prohibits the government from making any law "respecting an establishment of religion."

Anti-evolution bills in the 21st century introduced in the U.S. Congress and State legislatures have centered on academic freedom, seeking protection of teachers, students, and college professors who face intimidation and retaliation when discussing scientific criticisms of evolution. While most of the bills have been unsuccessful, the Louisiana Science Education Act was enacted in 2008. Critics argued against the bill, saying it "would unleash an assault against scientific integrity, leaving students confused about the fundamental nature of science and unprepared to excel in a work force that increasingly requires science-related skills." Critics also argued against the bill's proponents saying, "Their aim is clear: Erode students' understanding and trust of science by sowing confusion and doubt, and count on religious ideas to fill the void."[32]

Evolutionists' current dubbing of creationism as an "assault against scientific integrity" undermining faith in science ironically mirrors Bryan's view of Darwinism as a menace undermining faith in God. In Bryan's eyes the teaching of human evolution left students confused about God's existence.[33] Now, only 100 years later, the situation has entirely reversed, since creationism is the one accused of muddling "the fundamental nature of science."

Bryan's words to reporters at the beginning of the Scopes trial proved prophetic: "It is not the decision but the discussion which will follow that I consider important. It will bring the issue before the attention of the world."[34] The creation–evolution debate continues today across the land and around the world in large part due to Bryan's anti-evolution crusade that culminated with the Scopes trial and brought to the world's attention that

- many church leaders and academicians believed and taught that science, not the Bible, explains man's origins;

- young people being taught that the evolutionary theory of the origin of man was factual and that the first 11 chapters of Genesis are symbolical, allegorical, or poetical caused many to doubt the entire Bible and turn to agnosticism or atheism;

- the survival-of-the-fittest philosophy was influencing the growth of eugenics and racism at home and abroad; see "Social Implications of Darwinism" on page 98.

Since the 1925 Scopes trial, scientists—whether coming from a creation-, evolution-, or theistic evolution-based perspective—have answered many questions that couldn't be answered 100 years ago, have asked and answered new questions, and continue to seek answers to new origins questions.

The Scopes trial was clearly a major catalyst that "stirred the world" to discuss and debate the origin of man. It increased the awareness that all origins belief systems are based upon foundationally different presuppositions, such as scriptural inerrancy or the reliability of science (see "Answering the Human Origins Question" on page 92).

Evolutionists put their faith in science that science will eventually answer all the unanswered questions. Creationists put their faith in God and his supernatural acts that are beyond the scope of the human mind to comprehend. In addition, creationists have developed organizations that promote creation science and provide answers to complex scientific origins questions, like those Darrow grilled Bryan about in 1925.[35] The following are four such organizations:

- Creation Research Society (creationresearch.org) – established 1963
- Institute for Creation Research (icr.org) – established 1970
- Answers in Genesis (answersingenesis.org) – established 1993
- Core Academy of Science (coresci.org) – established 2013

BRYAN'S FINAL DAYS

Following the trial's end on Tuesday, July 21, Bryan and his wife had planned on staying the remainder of the week in Dayton and spending the next week vacationing in the Smoky Mountains. Despite the grueling demands and pressures of the 8-day trial, Bryan was busier than ever from the trial's end until his death five days later.

- He immediately issued a press statement with nine questions to the defense attorneys that he was not permitted to ask at the trial, and Darrow responded shortly afterward with answers that affirmed his agnosticism.[36]

- He polished his 15,000-word anti-evolution speech (originally intended to be delivered during his closing statements at the trial) to prepare it for publication.

- He inspected prospective sites around Dayton for what would become Bryan College.

Bryan was driven to Dayton on Sunday, July 26, after spending the previous night at Chattanooga's newly opened Hotel Ross. He appeared unannounced at Dayton Methodist Episcopal Church (South), known today as First United Methodist Church, where he had preached two weeks prior. He led in prayer but did not preach. This is the last photograph taken of Bryan; he died later that day. (BCA)

- He traveled several hundred miles to deliver speeches to crowds totaling 50,000 people. His last speech was delivered in Winchester, TN,[37] after which he told a reporter, "If I should die tomorrow, I should feel that much has been accomplished in the greatest cause for enlightening humanity ever known. I believe that on the basis of the accomplishments of the past few weeks, I could truthfully say, well done."[38]

- He had a physical examination, reporting to his wife afterward that according to all the test results, "I have several more years to live."[39]

- Newspapers reported that Bryan was a board of regents member for the University of Miami, which had recently begun construction on its initial buildings.[40] (See "University of Miami" on page 159.)

- He reviewed galley proofs with Chattanooga printers for the publication of his intended Scopes trial speech.

- On Sunday, July 26, after leading a prayer at the Methodist church in Dayton, he returned to the private residence where he had been staying and ate lunch. After lunch he told the editor of a Chattanooga newspaper, "My fight is not with the agnostics or atheists. I am not engaged in a controversy with them. My fight is with the so-called 'Modernists' of the Christian Church over the matter of Christian doctrine and beliefs, and in this battle I am not concerned with the views of the agnostics or infidels."[41] After the telephone conversation, he took a nap and died in his sleep.

- Some newspapers reported that he died of "apoplexy," the term used then for a stroke or cerebral hemorrhage. Other accounts cited heart attack or diabetes mellitus.[42]

- On July 28 Bryan's memorial service was held on the lawn of the Rogers' home in Dayton where Bryan and his entourage had stayed for more than two weeks. Early the next morning his flag-draped casket was taken to the train station and was loaded on a special Pullman car for transport to Washington, DC, with stops in Knoxville, Bristol, Roanoke, Lynchburg, and other cities where throngs of people came to pay their respects.[43]

- On July 30 his body lay in repose at the New York Avenue Presbyterian Church, located three blocks from the White House. It is estimated that more than 20,000 mourners visited the church while Bryan lay in state. See photo on next page.

Bryan's funeral was broadcast by radio nationwide on July 31. Joseph R. Sizoo delivered the eulogy; see "Individuals' Expressions" on page 76. President Calvin Coolidge ordered that all American flags be flown at half-staff that day in tribute to Bryan. Bryan was buried during a rainstorm atop a hill in Arlington National Cemetery.[44] (LOC.gov/pictures/item/2016850552)

In what became known after Bryan's death as *The Last Message*, he laid out his five indictments against evolution, all of which have been covered to some degree in Chapter 14. To read Bryan's full remarks about each in *The Last Message*, refer to the eBook accessed via the *Web Companion*.[45]

INDICTMENTS AGAINST EVOLUTION	PAGES
1. "It disputes the truth of the Bible account of man's creation and shakes the faith in the Bible as the Word of God. . . . [I]t disputes the Bible doctrine of reproduction according to kind—the greatest scientific principle known."	31
2. "Evolutionists attack the truth of the Bible, not openly at first, but by using weasel-words like 'poetical,' 'symbolical' and 'allegorical' to suck the meaning out of the inspired record of man's creation. . . . It is belief in evolution that has caused so many scientists and so many Christians to reject the miracles of the Bible, and then give up, one after another, every vital truth of Christianity."	32–51
3. "It diverts attention from pressing problems of great importance to trifling speculation. . . . Evolution is deadening the spiritual life of a multitude of students. Christians do not desire less education, but they desire that religion shall be entwined with learning so that our boys and girls will return from college with their hearts aflame with love of God and love of fellow-men and prepared to lead in the altruistic work that the world so sorely needs. The cry in the business world, in the industrial world, in the professional world, in the political world—even in the religious world—is for consecrated talents—for ability *plus* a passion for service."	51–53
4. "By paralyzing the hope of reform, it discourages those who labor for the improvement of man's condition." Bryan explained the power of the gospel for individual regeneration that can lead to the regeneration of society: "It is this fact that inspires all who labor for man's betterment." He contrasted the evolutionary view that improvement comes "slowly through unfolding ages" with the power of the gospel to change a heart "in the twinkling of an eye" by a merciful God who gives everyone an opportunity to "turn from sin to righteousness."	53–56
5. "If taken seriously and made the basis of a philosophy of life, it would eliminate love and carry man back to a struggle of tooth and claw," threatening "the very existence of the doctrine of brotherhood." He quoted from a popular book within the eugenics movement, Albert Wiggam's *The New Decalogue of Science* (1922), that says, "Evolution is a brutal business, but civilization tries to make it a pink tea. Barbarism is the only process by which man has ever organically progressed, and civilization is the only process by which he has organically declined." Wiggam advised that unless we allow the "beneficent hand of natural selection" to work its will, we will "bungle the whole task."	56–65

After a lifetime of writing and speech making, Bryan's final words in his *Last Message* were these:

Science is a magnificent material force, but it is not a teacher of morals. . . . [N]ow we are told that newly discovered instruments of destruction will make the cruelties of the late war seem trivial in comparison with the cruelties of wars that may come in the future. If civilization is to be saved from the wreckage threatened by intelligence not consecrated by love, it must be saved by the moral code of the meek and lowly Nazarene. His teachings, and His teachings alone, can solve the problems that vex the heart and perplex the world.

The world needs a Saviour more than it ever did before, and there is only one "Name under heaven given among men whereby we must be saved." It is this Name that evolution degrades, for, carried to its logical conclusion, it robs Christ of the glory of a virgin birth, of the majesty of His deity and mission, and of the triumph of His resurrection. It also disputes the doctrine of the atonement. . . .

Again force and love meet face to face, and the question, "What shall I do with Jesus?" must be answered. A bloody, brutal doctrine—evolution—demands, as the rabble did nineteen hundred years ago, that He be crucified. That cannot be the answer of this jury representing a Christian State and sworn to uphold the laws of Tennessee. Your answer will be heard throughout the world; it is eagerly awaited by a praying multitude. If the law is nullified, there will be rejoicing wherever God is repudiated, the Saviour scoffed at and the Bible ridiculed. . . . If, on the other hand, the law is upheld and the religion of the school children protected, millions of Christians will call you blessed and, with hearts full of gratitude to God, will sing again that grand old song of triumph:

> *Faith of our fathers, living still,*
> *In spite of dungeon, fire and sword;*
> *O how our hearts beat high with joy*
> *Whene'er we hear that glorious word—*
> *Faith of our fathers—holy faith;*
> *We will be true to thee till death!* [46]

Governor Woodrow Wilson was a guest (October 5–6) at the Bryans' home during his 1912 presidential campaign and is shown here (left) on the steps of Fairview with Bryan and Bryan's grandson John. The two lions that frame the entrance of their home were gifts the Bryans received from the emperor of Korea on their 1905–1906 world tour. Bryan noted in his book *The Old World and Its Ways* that one lion has his mouth shut and the other has his mouth open, representing the "eternal conflict between the positive and the negative—one says yes, the other no." (BCA, Lawrence Puckett's Wire Photo Collection)

16 | BRYAN'S HOMES

> " Real estate is the best investment for small savings. More money is made from the rise in real estate values than from all other causes combined.
>
> —William Jennings Bryan
> *Munsey's Magazine*, September 1907

INTRODUCTION

The Bryans used their real estate investments to make a difference. They developed, improved, and expanded their properties; their homes were well known places of hospitality; and they donated property to be used for civic and charitable purposes.

- The Bryans' primary residences were in Illinois, Nebraska, and Florida. They owned additional real estate in several other states, including California, Texas, North Carolina, and Idaho.

- They donated Bryan's Salem, IL, birthplace property for a public library and their Lincoln, NE, Fairview property for a park and a hospital.

- They built nine homes in five states.[1]

- The five Bryan homes featured in this chapter have been awarded historical designations. The following table outlines the places Bryan called home when he was not traveling.

PRIMARY RESIDENCE	1860–1887: ILLINOIS	1887–1920: NEBRASKA	1921–1925: FLORIDA
Homes with Historical Designations	**1** **Salem, IL** Birthplace	**2** **Lincoln, NE** Fairview (primary residence)	**5** **Miami, FL** Villa Serena
		3 **Mission, TX** Winter home	
		4 **Asheville, NC** Secondary residence	
		5 **Miami, FL** Villa Serena (winter home)	
Other Residences[2]	• **Jacksonville, IL** Student at Whipple Academy and Illinois College (1875–1881) and first home with Mary (1884–1887) • **Chicago, IL** Student at Union College of Law (1881–1883)	• **Lincoln, NE,** 1625 D Street (1888–1903); ran 1896 and 1900 presidential campaigns from this home • **Washington, DC** Congressman (1891–1895) and Secretary of State (1913–1915)	• **Coconut Grove, FL** Marymont (1924–1925)

1

BIRTHPLACE AND BOYHOOD HOME

408 South Broadway, Salem, Illinois

1852 Built by Bryan's father | **1975** Added to *National Register of Historic Places*

Bryan lived in this home with his family until he was six years old (1866), when the family moved to a larger home nearby. This 1896 photo shows Bryan visiting his birthplace with his three children.

In the early 1900s Bryan purchased his boyhood home and gave it to the City of Salem for a museum to house the artifacts and memorabilia of his life. Philo S. Bennett, a wealthy tea merchant from Connecticut, held Bryan and his politics in high esteem; a friendship developed between the two men. Upon Bennett's passing in 1903, his estate provided $1,500, an amount that Bryan matched, for the building of a library at Bryan's birthplace. The house was moved "a few feet to the west in order to give room for the erection of the Bryan-Bennett Library" next to the house. Construction of the library was completed in 1909, and Bryan contributed $500 toward the purchase of the library's first books.[3]

RECENT TIMES: Since the Bryan-Bennett Library moved to a larger location in 1986, the building has housed a variety of businesses. The City of Salem operates Bryan's birthplace home as a museum where visitors enjoy seeing Bryan memorabilia and learning about Bryan, his politics, and his times.[4]

A small portion of the Bryan-Bennett Library is visible on the left in this 2005 photo of the William Jennings Bryan Boyhood Home. (Stephen P. H. Frakes)

2 FAIRVIEW
4900 Sumner Street, Lincoln, Nebraska

1901–1903 Built | **1903–1921** Primary Residence | **1963** Designated a *U.S. National Historic Landmark*
1966 Added to *National Register of Historic Places*

Friends gather at Fairview, July 14, 1908, following ceremonies held at the Nebraska State Capitol officially notifying Bryan that he was the Democratic Party's presidential nominee for the third time. (NSHS RG3198-45-02)

The Bryans broke ground for Fairview on their wedding anniversary, October 1, 1901, celebrated their 18th anniversary there a year later, and moved into their finished home in 1903. Among the politicians who visited the Bryans at Fairview were Champ Clark, speaker of the House of Representatives; John Kern, Bryan's 1908 running mate; and Woodrow Wilson (see Part 5 photo on page 127).

Overlooking a 160-acre farm, the 11,000-square-foot home had several guest rooms, a dining room that could seat 24, and a full complement of servants. It was the site for political rallies, lawn parties, and the Bryans' 25th wedding anniversary party in 1909 with their 600 guests. The farm produced much of the food for the Bryan table. Although hired hands did the farming, Bryan enjoyed an occasional day in the fields.

In 1906 Bryan donated a tract of land along Antelope Creek to the city for the establishment of Antelope Park.[5] When the Bryans made Miami their primary residence in 1921, they donated Fairview and ten acres to the Nebraska Conference of the United Methodist Church to establish a hospital. The 60-bed Bryan Memorial Hospital (known today as Bryan Medical Center; see page 155) opened on June 6, 1926. The Bryan School of Nursing (known today as Bryan College of Health Sciences) opened the same year with 37 students, and Fairview became the student dormitory.[6]

In this 2013 photo, Fairview is surrounded by several buildings that are part of the Bryan Medical Center's East Campus; see page 154. The Bryan statue, formerly located on the north side of the Nebraska State Capitol, was moved to Fairview in 1967; see page 142. (Bryan Health)

RECENT TIMES: Fairview was restored in 1994 and today houses the Bryan Museum and the William Jennings Bryan Institute. The museum portion features rooms furnished to depict the family's life during the early 1900s, and the institute consists of the Center for Bioethics, the Center for Advancing Nursing Practice, and the Center for Quality.

1909 Built | **1913** Sold | **1936** Awarded a *Texas Historical Marker*

1912

At the urging of Mission founder and developer John J. Conway, the Bryans purchased 240 acres near the Rio Grande where they built a home and planted a fruit orchard. During the two winters they spent in Mission, Bryan enjoyed daily horseback rides and duck hunting.

Bryan used his influence to encourage people to move to the Lower Rio Grande Valley. For example, *The Commoner* ran a full-page advertisement in 1909 promoting the farming opportunities in the area.[8]

FOR SALE
An Improved Texas Farm

I OFFER for Sale 240 acres of land, three miles from Mission, Texas, on the Rio Grande, 200 acres are cleared and under irrigation. The improvements, consisting of a $2500.00 house with barns, fences, etc., have cost over $5,000.00 Easy terms will be given on deferred payments. I would not care to sell to anyone unless purchaser makes a personal examination of the property. Apply to owner for price and terms.

W. J. Bryan, Lincoln, Neb.

Bryan ran this notice on page 14 of *The Commoner* on February 14, 1913.

Following a confluence of circumstances—several cold snaps that killed some of their orange and grapefruit trees, the 1911 Pancho Villa raids that required Texas forces be sent to the town, and Bryan's appointment as secretary of state—the Bryans sold their Texas winter home.[9]

RECENT TIMES: In 2015 The Bryan House opened as a bed and breakfast and social event center.[10]

The Bryan House Bed & Breakfast, 2015[7]

4 WILLIAM JENNINGS BRYAN HOUSE
107 Evelyn Place, Asheville, North Carolina

1917 Built | **1920** Sold | **1983** Added to *National Register of Historic Places*

William Jennings Bryan House, 2014 [11]

Bryan visited Asheville during his 1896 presidential campaign and again in December 1912 and July 1913 to deliver speeches. He and Mrs. Bryan went to Asheville several times for rest and relaxation while he was secretary of state (1913–1915) and then again shortly after his resignation.

Beginning in 1914, the Bryans made several purchases of acreage near Sunset Mountain, in Chunns Cove, and in Grove Park, after which they decided to build a home in Grove Park.

The Bryans lived in Asheville for approximately two years. Bryan taught a Sunday school class at the First Presbyterian Church and wrote for several magazines and newspapers while an Asheville resident. After it became evident that the mountain climate was not beneficial to Mrs. Bryan's health, they decided to move to Florida and make Villa Serena their permanent residence.[12]

RECENT TIMES: Today the home is a private residence and part of the Grove Park Historic District.

During the Bryans' 1913 visit to Asheville for Bryan's keynote speech at the grand opening of Grove Park Inn, Fred Seely, Bryan's friend and head of construction for Grove Park Inn, led the motorcade in the 1913 Packard. Bryan is seated next to Seely; Mrs. Bryan is behind her husband; and Seely's wife, Evelyn Grove Seely, is seated in the middle back. (North Carolina Collection, Pack Memorial Public Library, Asheville, NC)

5 VILLA SERENA

3115 Brickell Avenue, Miami, Florida

1913 Built | **1913–1920** Winter Home | **1921–1924** Permanent Residence
2012 Added to *National Register of Historic Places*

Front elevation—Biscayne Bay side, c. 1920 (State Archives of Florida/Fishbaugh)

The Bryans often opened their waterfront mansion Villa Serena to the public on Friday afternoons, attracting as many as 500 guests to hear Bryan speak. Bryan touted the virtues of south Florida, praising the city's winter climate, promoting tourism and the development of Coral Gables, and advocating for the establishment of a local university (see "Lectures" on page 88 and "University of Miami" on page 159). They entertained many dignitaries at Villa Serena, including Warren G. Harding (see photo on next page), Greece's Premier Eleftherios Venizelos, and Franklin D. Roosevelt.[13]

In 1924 the Bryans moved about three miles south to a home on Main Highway in Coconut Grove. Named for Bryan's wife, Marymont was located near their daughter Ruth's home, Chota Khoti.[14]

Bryan's children, Ruth and William, Jr. (both are in the Harding photo), were executors of Bryan's estate. They sold Villa Serena in 1933 to a grandson of the co-founder of the Maxwell House Coffee Company, William Cheek, who owned it until his death in 1970. Gaspar Nagymihaly, a Miami general contractor and builder, owned Villa Serena from 1971–2007.[15]

RECENT TIMES: Villa Serena is among the last of the remaining Biscayne Bay waterfront mansions in an area known in the early 20th century as "Millionaires' Row." Businesswoman and philanthropist Adrienne Arsht, whose own home is located next door to Villa Serena, purchased Villa Serena in 2007 for $12 million. Ms. Arsht spent several million dollars over the next four years restoring Villa Serena and surrounding property. Today the meticulously and elegantly restored Villa Serena serves as Ms. Arsht's guesthouse and entertaining space.[16]

Rear elevation—street side, 2011

While on a Florida cruise in February 1921, President-elect Warren G. Harding visited Bryan at Villa Serena. Front row (L-R) Dr. Albert H. Ely; Senator Joseph S. Frelinghuysen, Sr., of NJ; William Jennings Bryan, Jr.; Ruth Bryan Owen; Harding; Bryan; and Harding's secretary, George B. Christian, Jr. (BCA, Lawrence Puckett's Wire Photo Collection)

17 | STATUES HONORING BRYAN

> " Bryan was a great crusader, with all the religious fervor of the ancient crusaders directed on behalf of the people. He never separated his moral sense, his private conscience from his public or national acts. . . . [A] man finally is measured for the Immortal Hall of Fame by what he thought and tried to do, and not by the crown he won.
>
> —Gutzon Borglum, Sculptor and Artist
> At the unveiling ceremony of his Bryan statue (1934)

INTRODUCTION

The following chart provides an overview of the four statues commissioned to honor the memory of William Jennings Bryan.

ORIGINAL LOCATION	UNVEILED	CURRENT LOCATION	ARTIST	COMMISSIONED BY
1 Washington, DC	5/3/1934	Salem, IL Bryan Memorial Park	Gutzon Borglum	William Jennings Bryan Memorial Association
2 Washington, DC National Statuary Hall, U.S. Capitol	4/27/1937	Washington, DC	Rudulph Evans	State of Nebraska
3 Lincoln, NE Nebraska State Capitol	9/1/1947	Lincoln, NE Fairview	Rudulph Evans	Bryan Memorial Commission
4 Dayton, TN Rhea County Courthouse	10/1/2005	Dayton, TN	Cessna Decosimo	Bryan College

ABOUT THE ARTIST

Gutzon Borglum was the famed sculptor of Mount Rushmore, Black Hills, SD.

INSCRIPTION

"You shall not press down upon the brow of labor this crown of thorns. You shall not crucify mankind upon a cross of gold."

TRIVIA

- President Franklin Roosevelt delivered the dedicatory address; see excerpts in this section.

- At its original Washington, DC, location, the "statue was the butt of many jokes because this representation of Bryan, a noted advocate of temperance, stood with its hand upraised, pointing toward the nearby Christian Heurich Brewery."[1]

- The statue was removed for construction of Theodore Roosevelt Bridge c. 1958.

Bryan's youngest grandson, David Hargreaves (front center), unveiled his grandfather's statue at the May 3, 1934, ceremony. (LOC.gov/item/2016879971)

- While Bryan's birthplace city, Salem, IL, won its appeal to be the new location for the statue and was moved there in 1961, four others put in bids, including William Jennings Bryan College in Dayton, TN, and Mission, TX, where Bryan once had a home.[2]

William Jennings Bryan Memorial Association commissioned the first Washington, DC, statue of Bryan. Members are pictured here at their September 11, 1925, meeting at Hotel Lafayette, Washington, DC. Josephus Daniels, in front of the door in dark suit with hat in right hand, was president of the association and Bryan's friend. Daniels served with Bryan on Woodrow Wilson's cabinet when Bryan was secretary of state and Daniels was secretary of the navy.[3] (BCA)

DEDICATION SPEECH EXCERPTS

No man of his time was or could have been more constantly in the limelight than he; yet we can look back and scan his record without being able to point to any instance where he took a position that did not accord with his conscience or his belief.

He did not have to dare to do what to him seemed right; he could not do otherwise.

I think that we would choose the word "sincerity" as fitting him most of all. . . . [I]t was that sincerity that served him so well in his life-long fight against sham and privilege and wrong. It was that sincerity which made him a force for good in his own generation and kept alive many of the ancient faiths on which we are building today.

We . . . can well agree that he fought the good fight; that he finished the course; and that he kept the faith.[4]

—Franklin D. Roosevelt
U.S. President (1933–1945)
May 3, 1934

The statue that once stood in Washington, DC, was moved to the city of Bryan's birth and dedicated on Labor Day 1961. It is located across the street from Bryan Memorial Park, Salem, IL. (Photo by Lori D. Smith, 2019)

ABOUT THE ARTIST

Rudulph Evans was the famed sculptor of the Thomas Jefferson statue in the Jefferson Memorial, Washington, DC, and the Robert E. Lee statue, Virginia State Capitol.

INSCRIPTION

William Jennings Bryan
Nebraska

TRIVIA

- Nebraska Governor Roy L. Cochran presented the statue to the federal government during a ceremony held in the U.S. Capitol Rotunda on April 27, 1937.

- The next day it was moved from the Capitol Rotunda to the National Statuary Hall.

- Bryan's statue is one of 35 statues located in National Statuary Hall. The remaining 65 statues in the collection are on display elsewhere throughout the United States Capitol.

Bryan's great-granddaughters, Katherine and Helen, unveiled the statue in the U.S. Capitol Rotunda. (L-R) Senator George W. Norris of Nebraska, Katherine Lehman, Helen Lehman, Governor Roy L. Cochran of Nebraska, and Carl Morton (LOC LC-DIG-hec-29219)

DEDICATION SPEECH EXCERPT

 If Bryan were here today, he would be standing by the side of the great president in the White House, thinking and fighting for the rights of the common man. The old Bryan smile would cheer us on our way—the smile which all America loved. The old Bryan fire would be there—the fire which flamed because of love of country and his fellowmen. He would still be the battle-scarred veteran of the common people, for he never retreated.[5]

—Arthur J. Weaver
Nebraska Governor (1929–1931)
April 27, 1937

The Bryan statue is one of 100 in the U.S. Capitol's National Statuary Hall Collection that honors men and women who are "illustrious for their historic renown."[6]

3   LINCOLN, NE, CAPITOL (1947) ➜ FAIRVIEW (1967)

ABOUT THE ARTIST

The State of Nebraska commissioned Rudulph Evans to create his second statue of Bryan.[7]

INSCRIPTION

"The humblest citizen in all the land, when clad in the armor of a righteous cause, is stronger than all the hosts of error."[8]

TRIVIA

- Dorothy Bryan Harnsberger, Bryan's great-niece, unveiled the statue at the Labor Day 1947 ceremony on the north approach of the Nebraska State Capitol.

- The statue was moved in 1967 to Fairview, Bryan's home in East Lincoln, on the grounds of Bryan Medical Center, formerly known as Bryan Memorial Hospital. See Chapter 19.

- In 1971, four years after the removal of the Bryan statue from its state capitol location, Bryan was elected to the Nebraska Hall of Fame; and a bust of Bryan was placed in the Nebraska State Capitol's Hall of Fame.[9]

The statue for the first 20 years was located on the north side of the Capitol. However, before and after its installation, there were political and esthetic controversies about its placement. For example, some Republicans protested having a Democrat on the steps of the Capitol, and architects claimed it blocked the view of the 19-story Capitol. In 1967 the statue was relocated to nearby Fairview, a U.S. National Historic Landmark; see Chapter 16.[10] (BCA)

DEDICATION SPEECH EXCERPT

> " Ah, what a dreary world this world would be were it without men to dream, speak and pray! What a dreary world this would be without men to infuse its millions to new faith, to restore their strength and to re-awaken them to decent impulses of civilized living. What a dreary world this would be without men stout of heart and courage to brave the ridicule and to face the criticism of those of lesser faith that in the ultimate the decency of mankind will triumph over evil.[11]

—"W. J. Bryan Comes Home"
James E. Lawrence, Editor
The Lincoln Star (1922–1957)
Labor Day, 1947

The statue was relocated in 1967 to the front of Bryan's Fairview home on the east campus of the Bryan Medical Center. (Author's photo)

---

4   DAYTON, TN (2005), SCOPES TRIAL SITE

(Photo by Curtis Jolley)

ABOUT THE ARTIST

Bryan College commissioned Chattanooga-based sculptor Cessna Decosimo to create a Bryan statue at the Rhea County Courthouse (photo on page 144), site of the Scopes trial and designated a National Historic Landmark in 1977.[12]

INSCRIPTIONS

- "The humblest citizen in all the land, when clad in the armor of a righteous cause, is stronger than all the hosts of error." THE CROSS OF GOLD 1896[13]

- "Destiny is not a matter of chance; it is a matter of choice; it is not a thing to be waited for, it is a thing to be achieved." AMERICA'S MISSION 1899[14]

TRIVIA

- The statue was given to Dayton and Rhea County by Bryan College on the college's 75th anniversary.

- The statue was unveiled on October 1, 2005, William and Mary Bryans' 121st wedding anniversary.

- On July 14, 2017, the Freedom from Religion Foundation installed a statue of Clarence Darrow on the Rhea County Courthouse lawn across from Bryan's statue. Bryan and Darrow were the most famous names associated with the Scopes trial (see Chapter 15).

DEDICATION SPEECH EXCERPT

Mr. Bryan was no mere politician; he was truly a Christian statesman. His eloquence and oratory sprang from a heart of conviction that was guided by his courageous advocacy for truth and justice. He was a great leader because his concerns were his Creator's concerns. He lived for principles that ennoble every human being; and he believed that we as individuals, and collectively through the power and persuasion of governments and nations, exist to further the ends for which we were all created.[15]

—Stephen D. Livesay, President
Bryan College (2003–present)
October 1, 2005

The statue depicts Bryan in 1891, the year the Rhea County Courthouse (in background) was built and Bryan's first year serving as a U.S. congressman from Nebraska. (Photo by Curtis Jolley)

18 | BOOKS ABOUT BRYAN

"We should be remembered for the things we do. The things we do are the most important things of all. They are more important than what we say or what we look like. The things we do outlast our mortality. The things we do are like monuments that people build to honour heroes after they've died. . . . Only instead of being made out of stone, they're made out of the memories people have of you. That's why your deeds are like your monuments. Built with memories instead of with stone.

—R. J. Palacio, author of *Wonder*

Bryan during his 1908 presidential campaign (NSHS RG3198-47-16)

Since 1896, authors have been drawn to write about Bryan's life and work. Some have come along to analyze and critique what he did and who he was, others to promote and praise, and still others to mock and belittle. Nevertheless, all of them—whatever their perspective or purpose may have been—thought Bryan worthy enough of their time to add to the story of how he used his influence to make a difference. As a result, each new generation of readers has had the opportunity to learn about Bryan's life of significance.

Three factors provide context for this chapter.

- The only criterion that was used for including a book is whether Bryan's name is in the title.
- The titles cover the entire range on the not-scholarly-to-very-scholarly continuum.
- The *Web Companion* includes the following: citations for every title, eBook links when available, and additional titles that do not have Bryan's name in the title yet include significant information about him.

1890s

1896   *The Boomerang: Or, Bryan's Speech with the Wind Knocked Out*

1896   *Bryan and Sewall, the Great Issue of 1896*

1896   *Bryan the Brave, the Light of Silver Freedom*

1896   *Bryan, Sewall and Honest Money Will Bring Prosperity*

1896   *Civilization: Bryan and the Times*

(L-R) Louisiana Governor Newton Blanchard, Judge T. J. Kernan, Bryan, and Rev. Dr. John H. Fox, Washington, DC, c. 1908 (LOC LC-DIG-ggbain-00417)

1960s

1960   *The Trumpet Soundeth: William Jennings Bryan and His Democracy, 1896–1912*

1961   *William Jennings Bryan: The Great Commoner*

1963   *The Whirligig of Politics: The Democracy of Cleveland and Bryan*

1964   *McKinley, Bryan and the People*

1964   *William Jennings Bryan, Vol. 1: Political Evangelist, 1860–1908*

1965   *Defender of the Faith, William Jennings Bryan: The Last Decade, 1915–1925*

1967   *Bryan and Darrow at Dayton*

1968   *William Jennings Bryan: A Profile*

1969   *Bryan and World Peace*

1969   *William Jennings Bryan, Vol. 2: Progressive Politician and Moral Statesman, 1909–1915*

1969   *William Jennings Bryan, Vol. 3: Political Puritan, 1915–1925*

Bryan and Henry Ford, founder of Ford Motor Company, c. 1915, discussing Ford's Peace Ship expedition[1]

1970s

1980s

1990s

2000s

2010s

2020

Bryan and Detroit Tigers outfielder Ty Cobb pictured at Navin Field, later known as Tiger Stadium, May 1, 1921. In 1936 Cobb received the most votes among the inaugural inductees to the National Baseball Hall of Fame.

19 | NAMESAKES AND HONORS

> **"** The human measure of a human life is its income; the divine measure of a life is its outgo—its overflow—its contribution to the welfare of all.
>
> —William Jennings Bryan
> *The Fruits of the Tree* (1910)

Bryan's namesakes and honors demonstrate the high esteem to which Bryan was held. They also reveal the wide diversity of influence Bryan had on American life and are presented here under seven categories—Education, Literature, Music, People, Healthcare, Community, and Tributes. See more information about each item in the *Web Companion*.

EDUCATION

1. **Bryan College**, Dayton, TN (originally known as William Jennings Bryan University; see Chapter 20); Bryan Opportunity Scholarship Program; The Great Commoner Award (see photo).

2. **Bryan College of Health Sciences**, affiliated with Bryan Medical Center, Lincoln, NE.

3. **Bryan Community Focus Program** at Hawthorne, Lincoln, NE, was formerly known as Bryan Community School.

4. **Bryan Elementary School**, Mission, TX.

5. **Bryan Lounge**, Florida Union, University of Florida, Gainesville. The original student union was dedicated in 1936, and the main lounge was named in recognition of Bryan's fundraising efforts on behalf of the university; see "University of Florida" on page 159.

6. **Bryan Middle School**, Omaha, NE.

7. **Bryan Society** (originally known as William Jennings Bryan Literary Society), Bob Jones University, Greenville, SC. Bob Jones was a member of the National Campaign Committee that raised money for the founding of William Jennings Bryan University (see page 162).

8. **W. J. Bryan Elementary Museums Magnet School**, North Miami, FL.

9. **William Jennings Bryan Award,** Indiana University, Bloomington. Award founded in 1888 by Bryan, to be given annually for the best essay on a subject relating to "The Principal Underlying our Form of Government." Today, the prize is awarded to political science students with outstanding honors theses. See "Essay Prizes" on page 158.

10. **William Jennings Bryan Award,** University of Arkansas, Fayetteville.

11. **William Jennings Bryan Award**, University of Wisconsin, Madison.

12. **William Jennings Bryan Award for Outstanding Honors Thesis**, Indiana University, Bloomington.

Bryan College's 128-acre hilltop campus, located in the foothills of the Cumberland Mountains, includes 19 buildings (academics, sports, administration, library, student activities, dining, residence halls, and auditorium). Bryan offers nearly 35 associate's, bachelor's, and master's degrees in over 50 areas of study and has three nationally ranked athletic teams among its eleven NAIA and three coed sports teams.

13. **William Jennings Bryan Debate and Speech Scholarship**, Creighton University, Omaha, NE.

14. **William Jennings Bryan High School**, Omaha, NE.

15. **William Jennings Bryan Prize**, University of Illinois, Urbana.

16. **William Jennings Bryan Prize,** University of Michigan, Ann Arbor. Given consistently since 1936, this award was funded out of a speaker's fee Bryan gave to the university in 1896.

17. **William Jennings Bryan Prize**, University of Minnesota, Minneapolis.

18. **William Jennings Bryan Prize,** University of Texas at Austin. Established in 1898 with $250 (nearly $7,700 in 2019), the William Jennings Bryan Prize was the university's very first endowment. The Department of Government recognizes the top thesis or theses in each year's honors class.

19. **William Jennings Bryan Prize for Best Paper in American Politics and Political Theory**, The Ohio State University, Columbus.

20. **William Jennings Bryan Scholar,** University of Iowa, Iowa City.

LITERATURE

21. Mary Dillon's 1906 novel, ***The Leader***, was reviewed in *The New York Times* stating as follows: "The story is concerned mainly with the career of a statesman, in whom it is the author's evident intention to picture William J. Bryan, who has made himself the leader and the idol of the masses of his party. A large part of the narrative is taken up with events connected with the last Democratic national convention."[1]

22. Vachel Lindsay's poem, **"Bryan, Bryan, Bryan, Bryan"** (1919), chronicles Bryan's 1896 presidential campaign.

23. Ernest Hemingway's *The Sun Also Rises* (1926) refers to Bryan's death.

24. In Thomas Wolfe's debut 1929 autobiographical novel about his youth in Asheville, NC, *Look Homeward, Angel*, Bryan's prospective move to Asheville is briefly discussed by local townspeople; and Bryan has conversations with the local minister and a newspaper reporter. Bryan also appears as a character in Wolfe's 1932 short story **"The Web of Earth,"** in which Bryan's real estate ventures are at the center of the dialog; see "William Jennings Bryan House" on page 133.

25. In John Dos Passos' *USA Trilogy* (1930), Bryan has a biographical part and appears in all three novels.

26. John Steinbeck's *East of Eden* (1952) mentions Bryan.

27. In Jerome Lawrence and Robert Edwin Lee's 1955 play (and 1960 movie), *Inherit the Wind*, a highly fictionalized account of the Scopes trial, Bryan is cruelly satirized as the oafish Matthew Harrison Brady.

28. In Chapter 16 of Harper Lee's *To Kill a Mockingbird* (1960), Lee includes this Bryan allusion: "On the day of Tom Robinson's public trial, Miss Stephanie Crawford passes a large gathering of people outside the Maycomb courthouse and says, 'Look at all those folks—you'd think William Jennings Bryan was speakin'.'"

29. In 1964, historian Henry Littlefield's "The Wizard of Oz: Parable on Populism" was published in *American Quarterly*. Littlefield and other scholars asserted that L. Frank Baum's popular children's fairy tale, *The Wonderful Wizard of Oz* (1900) was a metaphor for the Populist movement and a critique of the national monetary policy debates. Comparisons include the following:

    - Dorothy, naive, young, and simple: the American people, led astray and seeking the way back home
    - The Wicked Witch of the East: eastern industrialists and bankers
    - The Yellow Brick Road: the gold standard
    - Dorothy's silver shoes (changed to red in the 1939 Technicolor film): Democratic/Populist demand for silver coinage
    - The Scarecrow: western farmers
    - The Tin Woodman: the downtrodden eastern workers
    - The Cowardly Lion: William Jennings Bryan

    Besides the obvious rhyming connection, reasons Bryan is associated with the Cowardly Lion are these: (a) Bryan had an imposing physical presence and powerful oratory; (b) Bryan's anti-imperialist opposition to the Spanish–American War was seen by some as cowardly; and (c) the Cowardly Lion fought bravely to protect his friends just as Bryan courageously stuck to positions he believed were in the best interest of his loyal supporters even though doing so led to his repeated presidential losses.[2]

30. Robert Heinlein's **Job: A Comedy of Justice** (1984) uses Bryan's unsuccessful or successful runs for the presidency as the "splitting off" events of the alternate histories through which the protagonists travel.

Sheet music cover (LOC.gov/item/ihas.200155623)

MUSIC

31. Bryan is a biographical character in Douglas Moore's opera, *The Ballad of Baby Doe* (1956).

32. Presidential campaign music was a popular means of communicating the campaign message and spreading the message across the country.

    - 1896: **"Dad's Old Silver Dollar Is Good Enough for Me"** and **"Upon a Cross of Gold"** (see photo)

    - 1900: **"Gold Bug Politician"** and **"The Jeffersonian Banner"**

    - 1908: **"The People's Choice,"** **"Billie Bryan is the Man for Me,"** and **"Billy Bryan is the Boy"**

33. Bryan's role in the Scopes trial inspired songs such as the following, both of which were recorded by Country Music Hall of Famer Vernon Dalhart: **"William Jennings Bryan's Last Fight"** and **"The John T. Scopes Trial."**

PEOPLE

34. Cataloged among the WJB Papers in the Library of Congress are **over a thousand namesake letters Mr. Bryan received from late 1896 and early 1897.** Some included photographs; for example, a set of triplets was named "William," "Jennings," and "Bryan."

35. **Jennings Randolph** (1902–1998), a political leader, statesman, and humanitarian from West Virginia.

36. **William Jennings Bryan "Billy" Herman** (1909–1992), Baseball Hall of Famer who played second base for the Chicago Cubs, Brooklyn Dodgers, Boston Braves, and Pittsburgh Pirates.

37. **William Jennings Bryan "Ben" Weber** (1916–1979), an American composer.

38. **William Jennings Bryan Dorn** (1916–2005), a South Carolina representative and senator and U.S. congressman (see photo).

Official portrait of William Jennings Bryan Dorn with his namesake's portrait hanging in the background (Oil on canvas, Robert Bruce Williams, 1974, Collection of the U.S. House of Representatives)

Bryan Medical Center East Campus Entrance, 1600 South 48th Street, Lincoln, NE (Bryan Health)

Bryan Medical Center West Campus Entrance, 2300 South 16th Street, Lincoln, NE (Bryan Health)

HEALTHCARE

39. **Bryan Medical Center**, Lincoln, NE. In 1922 the Bryans gave their home, Fairview, and ten acres of land to the Nebraska Conference of the United Methodist Church for establishing a new hospital, originally known as the Lincoln Methodist Hospital. After Bryan's death, the hospital board voted to change the name of the facility to commemorate Bryan and the gift. Bryan Memorial Hospital opened on June 6, 1926. The hospital changed its name to BryanLGH Medical Center after its merger with Lincoln General Hospital in 1997. Today the Bryan Medical Center has two campuses about 3 miles apart; the east campus is on the property Bryan donated, and the west campus is the former Lincoln General Hospital (see photos of both locations).

40. **Bryan College of Health Sciences,** Lincoln, NE. Originally known as the Bryan School of Nursing when it opened in 1926. The first class had 37 students with Fairview operating as the student dormitory and administrative center for the school (read more about Fairview in Chapter 16).

COMMUNITY

41. **Bryan-Bennett Library**, Salem, IL (see photo). Bryan purchased his birthplace and moved the home to allow room for construction of the town's first library in 1908. He funded half of the construction monies, and the other half came from the estate of his friend Philo S. Bennett; see "Birthplace and Boyhood Home" on page 129.

42. **Bryan County**, OK, was named for Bryan, who advised the Oklahoma Constitutional Convention to consult existing state constitutions, the proceedings of the Sequoyah Convention, and the U.S. Constitution as the basis for writing the Oklahoma State Constitution.

43. **Bryan Memorial Methodist Church**, Miami, FL. Just weeks after Bryan's death, the church construction was completed on Main Highway frontage land that was part of the Bryans' Marymont property that they sold to the congregation in 1924. Bryan participated in the church's design, evidenced by the ground level entrances whereby his wife who was confined to a wheelchair could have easy access to worship services. The church represents a rare period example of accessibility for a religious building. Another evidence of Bryan's influence is the outdoor pulpit where he planned to conduct Bible classes. The church was dedicated on Easter Sunday, 1928. It is today the home of the Chabad of Miami.

44. **Bryan Memorial Park** and **Bryan Park Nature Trail**, Salem, IL.

45. **Bryan Overlook**, along the Laurel-Snow section of the Cumberland Trail, known as "Pocket Wilderness," Dayton, TN.

46. **Bryan Point**, north side of Snake River Canyon, Twin Falls, ID (one of Bryan's favorite fishing holes).

47. **Bryan Road**, Mission, TX.

Bryan-Bennett Library, Salem, IL, with a small portion of Bryan's birthplace home shown on the right.

48. Bryan was named **Famous Honorary Rotarian** by the Rotary Global History Fellowship c. 1921.

49. **W. J. Bryan Highway**, Dayton, TN.

TRIBUTES

50. The Denver Zoo was founded in 1896 with a gift to the mayor of Denver—an **American black bear cub** named Billy Bryan.

51. A **World War II Liberty ship**, the SS *William J. Bryan*, was put into service in 1943 (see photo).

52. In Salem, IL, (Bryan's birthplace), there are many tributes, including its newspaper being named the *Times-Commoner* after the city and county newspapers merged in 1955 and its radio station launched in 1956 using Bryan's initials, **WJBD**.

53. Bryan was named to the **Nebraska Hall of Fame** in 1971. A bust of him was dedicated in 1974 and is featured in the Capitol's Hall of Fame collection.

54. The United States Postal Service honored Bryan with a *Great Americans* **series $2 postage stamp** issued May 19, 1986.

55. In 2013 Bryan was inducted into the **Gennett Records Walk of Fame** to commemorate his recording of the "Cross of Gold" speech; see page 52.

The SS *William J. Bryan*, a WW II Liberty ship, was built in Panama City, FL, and delivered May 20, 1943. (State Archives of Florida PR13545)

20 | THE FOUNDING OF BRYAN COLLEGE

> " The purpose of education is not merely to develop the mind; it is to prepare men and women for society's work and for citizenship. . . . The measure of a school cannot be gathered from an inspection of the examination papers; the conception of life which the graduate carries away must be counted in estimating the benefits conferred. . . . The heart plays as large a part as the head in the teacher's work, because the heart is an important factor in every life and in the shaping of the destiny of the race.
>
> —William Jennings Bryan
> *The Price of a Soul* (1914)

This account of the founding of Bryan College (originally known as William Jennings Bryan University) begins with stories from throughout Bryan's career that demonstrate his heart for young people and his support of higher education. The focus then shifts to the people who desired to honor his memory by starting a university. The chapter concludes with an overview of the plans, fund-raising highlights, responses to critics, and significant dates.

A DIFFERENCE MAKER IN HIGHER EDUCATION

The following examples demonstrate how Bryan's lifelong and diverse connections with higher education came together after his death in Dayton, TN, to create a catalyst for what would become the establishment of a college that would "present Christ first."

DEGREES

In addition to Bryan's earned Bachelor of Arts (B.A.) and Bachelor of Laws (LL.B.) degrees, Bryan was awarded a Master of Arts (M.A.) degree and seven honorary Doctor of Laws (LL.D.) degrees from such schools as McKendree College (1897), Illinois College (1905), Nebraska Wesleyan University (1905), University of Arizona (1912), and University of Florida (1923).[1]

SPEECHES ON COLLEGE CAMPUSES

While Chapters 8 and 10 also address the time that Bryan spent on college campuses throughout his career, these two accounts illustrate just how impactful his visits were.

University of North Carolina at Greensboro (known originally as the State Normal and Industrial College). The school's founder and first president, Charles Duncan McIver, was so impressed after meeting Congressman Bryan that he asked him to deliver the commencement address to the class of 1894. Greensboro citizens were thrilled to have the "silver-tongued orator" coming to their town. They covered their streetcars, storefronts, and homes with the school colors of yellow and white. Bryan spoke to an over-capacity crowd for almost two hours on the theme of the reinstatement of silver coinage. McIver's hope that inviting Bryan to speak would increase student interest in his new college was realized the following semester when the school received hundreds more applications than the previous year.[2]

Bryan (standing under umbrella near the right single column) tried to speak, but was heckled, at the Washtenaw County Courthouse, Ann Arbor, Michigan, 1900.

University of Michigan. In 1900 on the courthouse steps in Ann Arbor, students with opposing political beliefs disrupted the occasion to the point that police dragged several of the hecklers off to jail, which resulted in Bryan not delivering his address.

"[W]hen Mr. Bryan was leaving town and learned of the students in jail, big and generous and kindly man that he was, he sent word to the officers to 'release the boys. They meant no harm.'"

The following February Bryan was invited to Ann Arbor on Washington's birthday, and "at University Hall those same hecklers and many other students listened in rapt attention as the 'Boy Orator of the Platte' paid a magnificent tribute to the Father of our Country."[3]

ESSAY PRIZES [4]

In his *Memoirs* Bryan wrote about his youth, "I felt the lure of prizes from the start and took part in every contest for which I was eligible. A prize always stirred me to activity, and a recollection of its influence upon my studies has led me in later days to stimulate students to similar activity by the establishing of prizes in a number of institutions of learning." By 1900 Bryan had established annual prizes in 19 colleges in 19 states to be given for the best essay discussing the principles of free government. More than half of those prizes continue to be given today; see "Education" on page 150.

Using three $10,000 funds left in a trust to Bryan following the 1903 death of his friend Philo S. Bennett, Bryan established the following:

- The Bennett Prize for annual essay winners at 25 colleges in 25 states different from the states where the Bryan Prize colleges were located, including Harvard University, University of Tennessee, University of California Berkeley, Yale University, Brown University, and Princeton University.

- An educational fund for boys at 18 colleges, including Illinois College, College of William and Mary, and University of the South.

- An educational fund for girls at 20 colleges selected by Mrs. Bryan, including Baylor University, Tulane University, University of Arizona, and University of New Mexico.

DESIRE FOR A BIBLE-BASED, CHRIST-CENTERED COLLEGE

In 1933 Evelyn McClusky (1889–1994) founded the Miracle Book Club, a U.S.-based high school para-church ministry with about 2,000 high school chapters around the world. For over 50 years McClusky was publisher of *The Conqueror* monthly that "served as a communication link among Fundamentalist Christians concerned with the youth of the nation and set the stage for the Youth for Christ movement of the 1940s."[5] McClusky recalled Bryan telling her in 1905, "People are not paying attention to the Bible. I wish for a college that would present Christ first."[6]

UNIVERSITY OF FLORIDA (GAINESVILLE)

Bryan lectured frequently at the University of Florida. He delivered his first speech in 1916 entitled "Lessons Gleaned from the European War." His last formal appearance on the campus was in 1924 when he delivered a series of six lectures on money and its place and value in society; government, which he defined as "the people at work"; religion; and public speaking. Bryan and the university's president, Albert A. Murphree, were close friends and both were well known as men of faith.

In 1923 President Murphree asked Bryan to serve as campaign chairman to raise money for a YMCA religious activities center for the university. Bryan agreed and traveled the state, making speeches, appealing to the press, and reaching out to his friends for donations. Bryan raised $40,000 in cash and over $173,000 in pledges and personally contributed $1,000 to the project. The Great Depression, however, derailed fundraising efforts, and most of the pledges were never honored. By the time the building was finished more than a decade later, the concept had changed from a religious building to a student activity building, and the Florida Union opened in 1936.[7] See "Bryan Lounge" on page 150.

UNIVERSITY OF MIAMI (FLORIDA)

During ceremonies to lay the University of Miami's cornerstone on February 4, 1926, Bryan was recognized posthumously by Board of Regents President William E. Walsh as the first person to envision the creation of the school. Bryan's involvement in the founding of the school included the following:

- As early as 1916 Bryan advocated for a "Pan American College of Commerce" in Miami to serve students from North America and Latin America. After World War I he resumed promoting the idea, which gained momentum during the 1920's real estate boom in Miami.

- By June of 1925 the 15-member founding board of regents, which included Bryan and his daughter Ruth Bryan Owen, had a charter, a campus site, and the backing of many significant Miami citizens. For example, real estate developer George Merrick provided a gift of 160 acres in Coral Gables and an additional $5 million if matched by the community. One such community matching gift was for $1 million for a W. J. Bryan School of Diplomacy and Public Affairs. However, a school named after Bryan as well as many of the early plans for the university did not occur because of the 1926 Great Miami Hurricane and Florida's land bust.

- After Bryan's death, Ruth was vice chair of the board of regents and taught public speaking during the university's first three years of operation, using her salary to establish scholarships.[8]

SETTING THE STAGE FOR A UNIVERSITY IN DAYTON, TENNESSEE

The day before he left Miami for the Dayton Scopes trial, July 5, 1925, Bryan wrote and signed his will at his Marymont home. In the eleventh bequest he wrote, "I have saved for the last my bequest for religious education." He designated that $50,000 "will be set aside for Christian education." Bryan explained:

> Next to religion I am most interested in education, because education can and should increase one's capacity for service. But education will not be a benefit to its possessor and a blessing to society unless it is wisely used. I am very anxious that each intellectual ship shall be equipped with a moral rudder sufficient to control its course on life's stormy sea. My chief interest is, therefore, in Christian education—the entwining of the spiritual with the intellectual. . . . I would like special attention given to citizenship and applied Christianity so that the graduates may be prepared for leadership in both state and church. . . . I regard supernatural and revealed religion as given in the Bible as the only religion that exerts a controlling influence on our lives.[9]

On July 8, 1925, thousands arrived in Dayton for the Scopes trial. The jury was selected on July 10. On July 12, the Sunday morning papers carried reports of "a proposal to ban Tennessee public school graduates from attending New York City's Columbia University." Superintendent of Rhea County Schools Walter White responded to the outrageous proposal by suggesting that Dayton found its own university and name it for William Jennings Bryan.

On a walk with friends in the scenic hills two days after the trial concluded and three days before his death, Bryan voiced his wish that a Christian school be established there in Dayton.[10]

FOUR CITIES PROPOSE TO ESTABLISH A UNIVERSITY TO HONOR BRYAN

Following Bryan's death, three groups, in addition to the group in **Dayton, TN**, lobbied for their respective cities to be the site of a fundamentalist university to honor Bryan.

1. The establishment of Christian Fundamentalist University in **Chicago, IL**, was proposed by individuals associated with Wheaton College, Chicago, IL, and by William Bell Riley, a Baptist pastor who founded in 1902 what is today known as University of Northwestern, St. Paul, MN. The proposal included various schools in the Christian Fundamentalist University, such as Bryan Law School; Blanchard Theological School, named in honor of Wheaton's president Charles A. Blanchard; and Wheaton College of Letters and Arts. A map of the proposed university depicts Bryan Memorial Chapel at the center of the campus.

2. Due to Bryan's significant ties to **Miami, FL**, another group proposed that Miami would be the best location.

3. A group of Presbyterian men in **Dallas, TX**, offered seed money of $76,000 (about $1.1 million in 2019) for a Presbyterian university to be established in Bryan's memory in their city.[11]

While each of these had good reasons for their respective locations being chosen, ultimately Mrs. Bryan's support for her husband's expressed desire for a Christian school to be established in Dayton, TN, was the deciding factor. The remainder of the chapter tells the story of how William Jennings Bryan University came to be.

THE PEOPLE AND THE PLANS [12]

Within a couple months of Bryan's death, F. E. Robinson had organized the Bryan Memorial University Association (BMUA), secured its charter, and appointed Malcolm Lockhart of Atlanta as director of BMUA's campaign for funds. Although they had similar names and started about the same time, the BMUA was different from the William Jennings Bryan Memorial Association that was responsible for the first statue that was commissioned to honor Bryan; see "Washington, DC (1934)" on page 138.

An attractive 12-page prospectus was published that outlined the BMUA plan, including the following:

- Included on its cover were these words:

Bryan Memorial University
DAYTON, TENNESSEE

AN INSTITUTION FOUNDED UPON THE CONVICTION THAT THE BIBLE IS THE WORD OF GOD

- Its stated goal: To "launch a national drive for five million dollars to found a great University as a Memorial to William Jennings Bryan and to stand for the faith for which he fought. Half of this amount is to be used for equipment and half for endowment."

- Details about the national campaign to identify "Fifty thousand fundamentalists for the faith of our fathers."

- A rendering of the proposed building program to erect 14 buildings, the first of which was to be the Administration Building.

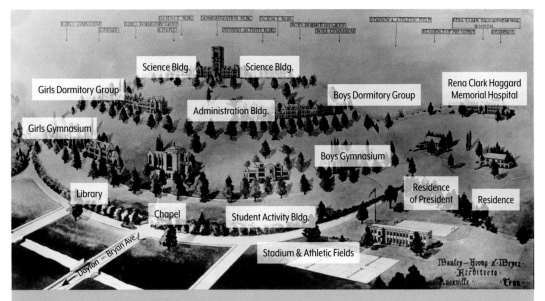

The BMUA commissioned a Knoxville architectural firm to produce an artistic rendering of the hilltop campus to include in the 12-page prospectus. The building labels are across the top; the white labels have been added to improve readability. Of particular note is the inclusion of two science buildings at the top of the hill. (BCA)

The National Campaign Committee initially included 52 members, among whom were the following:

- **Mary Harris Armor**, president of the Woman's Christian Temperance Union

- **Victor Donahey**, governor of Ohio

- **Charles F. Horner**, founder of the Redpath-Horner Chautauqua and Lyceum Bureau in 1906, executive assistant to the administrator of the National Recovery Administration (1933), and president of the National Aeronautics Association

- **T. C. Horton**, co-founder of Biola University in Los Angeles

- **Bob Jones**, founder of Bob Jones University (1927)[13]

- **J. P. McCallie**, co-founder of McCallie School in Chattanooga

- **Austin Peay**, governor of Tennessee

- **John T. Raulston**, judge for the Scopes trial

- **Paul Rader**, pastor of Moody Church, Chicago (1914–1921), president of the Christian & Missionary Alliance

- **C. M. Rosser**, founder of Dallas' first medical school (which became Baylor Medical College) and president of Texas State Medical Society in 1925

- **William D. Upshaw**, congressman (1919–1927; D-GA) and 1932 Prohibition Party candidate for the presidency

While many people sacrificed their time, talent, and treasure to establish William Jennings Bryan University (WJBU),[A] F. E. Robinson, Joe F. Benson (see photo), and Henry Herman Frasa were engaged in a minimum of four of the leadership groups responsible for the founding of William Jennings Bryan University:

BMUA INCORPORATORS (19 MEMBERS)	F. E. Robinson	Joe F. Benson	H. H. Frasa
NATIONAL CAMPAIGN COMMITTEE (52 MEMBERS)	F. E. Robinson	—	H. H. Frasa
WJBU CHARTER INCORPORATORS (7 MEMBERS)	F. E. Robinson	Joe F. Benson	H. H. Frasa
WJBU FOUNDERS [B] (52 MEMBERS)	Mr. & Mrs. F. E. Robinson	Mr. & Mrs. Joe F. Benson	—
WJBU TRUSTEES [C] (16 MEMBERS)	F. E. Robinson, Chairman, 1930–1956	Joe F. Benson, 1930–1942	H. H. Frasa

[A] In 1958 its name was changed to William Jennings Bryan College and in 1993 was shortened to Bryan College.

[B] Part of the reason why the college is not affiliated with a denomination is that its founders represented at least eight denominations, including Presbyterians, Baptists, Episcopalians, Methodists, Lutherans, Brethren, Christian Missionary Alliance, and Methodist Episcopal. Many names in this group included spouses and families. The other four groups included only individuals' names.

[C] Bryan's youngest child, Grace Bryan Hargreaves (also known as Grace Dexter Bryan), was a WJBU trustee from 1930–1942.

(L-R) F. E. Robinson, Ruth Bryan Owen (Bryan's oldest child), and Joe F. Benson survey the future site of WJBU, June 14, 1927. (BCA)

FUNDRAISING HIGHLIGHTS [14]

- While equally large (and larger) pledges had been made by October 5, 1925, the first cash gift of $1,000 was received from C. A. Dagley, a Florida realtor, who was a former Chattanoogan and Rhea County citizen.

- The fundraising campaign began in Rhea County (TN) on October 30, 1925, with a goal of raising $100,000. At the end of the 10-day drive, gifts and pledges totaling $202,000 had been received (nearly $3 million in 2019).

- Donations came from notable individuals such as Mrs. Thomas A. Edison, author Grace Livingston Hill (who was also a WJBU founder), and Franklin D. Roosevelt. FDR gave $50 in 1927 and $50 in 1928 prior to beginning his first term as New York governor in 1929. He indicated that he did not wish for his name to be used because he wanted "to see how the teachers and the teaching work out."

- Donations from cities where Bryan had lived include the following: Asheville, NC, pledged $17,000; Miami, FL, pledged $13,000.

- By June 14, 1926, $450,000 had been pledged.

- By July 5, 1928, $750,000 had been pledged from 29 states even though active campaigns had been conducted in parts of only 5 states.

- By March 22, 1930, $900,000 had been pledged and about $225,000 collected.

- A report dated July 31, 1930, listing the 16 leading states shows a pledged total of $980,681.59 (nearly $15 million in 2019).

- The effects of the Great Depression resulted in many unpaid pledges, thus halting the construction of the Administration Building.

RESPONSES TO CRITICS [15]

Many outspoken critics derided the purpose and establishment of WJBU. Their central argument was that a college dedicated to the truth and infallibility of the Bible, especially with reference to human origins, would be an enemy to true science and scientific research.

F. E. Robinson, trustee chairman, was quoted by the press in March 1930 as follows: "Sure, we are going to teach science—and why not? We are going to teach the theory of evolution, too—but, mind you, I say the theory. We put that question to Mrs. Bryan a short time before she died. She said 'Surely, teach science, but teach fact as fact and theory as theory.' We haven't any quarrel with the evolutionists. If they want to believe they descended from monkeys, we don't care. But we do object to scientists presenting mere theories to our children as cold facts."[16]

The WJBU 1931–1932 *Catalogue*[17] includes this description on the inside cover page: "An Institution Which Recognizes Revelation and Accepts the Supernatural." In it are listed the following 100- and 200-level science courses:

Biology 101 Phanerogamic Botany   **Chemistry 101–103** General Inorganic Chemistry

Biology 102 Crytogamic Botany   **Chemistry 201–202** Qualitative Analysis

Biology 103 Invertebrate Zoology   **Chemistry 203** Quantitative Analysis

Biology 201 Vertebrate Zoology   **Physics 201** Physics

Biology 202 Paleontology   **Physics 202** Heat

Biology 203 Evolution   **Physics 203** Magnetism and Electricity

SIGNIFICANT DATES [18]

June 23, 1926: The debate regarding which of five suggested Dayton sites would serve as the WJBU location was decided by an advisory committee composed of Lewis Paper, commissioner of state institutions, Nashville; John Zeigler, superintendent of Chattanooga city schools; Charles Keffer, University of TN landscape artist and engineer, Knoxville; P. L. Harned, state superintendent of education, Nashville; and Ernest Haston, Tennessee's secretary of state.

The committee inspected the possible sites, considering the university's present needs and future development, and recommended the 81-acre Matthews site. J. T. Matthews offered the property at one-half the appraised value; and after paying Matthews $6,654.33, Dayton citizens presented the deed to the BMUA. (The campus site has since expanded to 128 acres.)

November 5, 1926: Tennessee Governor Austin Peay turned the first shovel of earth on top of Matthews Hill (now Bryan Hill).

Excerpts from his address follow:

- There is no doubt that Bryan University should take its place quickly among the notable institutions of the South and nation.

- It will bear a magic name—a name that for more than a quarter of a century was a household word with the world. It is a name that conjured the admiration and affection of millions in our country from the moment he first appeared in our public life until his lamented death here amid these beautiful hills of East Tennessee.

Governor Peay is in dark coat holding a shovel, on far left is Malcolm Lockhart, and on right is F. E. Robinson. (BCA)

- In many particulars of courage and sincerity, the public and private life of the Great Commoner was a conspicuous example. He came into action at a crucial time in the politics and economics of the nation. Privilege was fast gaining an arrogant control. The government was more and more being seized and used by special interests.

- Fortunate will be your university to bear the name of Bryan. Worthily it must bear it. Nothing is needed except religious and God-fearing teachers. Science in their hands can, and will, be taught hand and hand with the Bible. Whenever there is conflict, that trouble is neither in science nor Holy Writ. In every case the teacher is the trouble. Let the teachers in our schools be Christian men and women and the problem is solved.[19]

By May 1927: The land had been cleared and excavated, and the concrete foundation was laid for the 440-by-54-foot, three-story Administration Building.

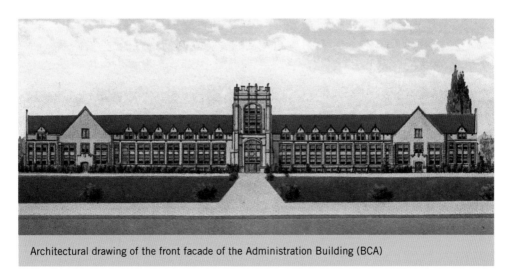

Architectural drawing of the front facade of the Administration Building (BCA)

March 4, 1930: The contract with Knoxville contractor V. L. Nicholson was signed for the construction of the Administration Building that was to cost approximately $350,000.[20] However, due to the challenges of the Great Depression and pledges not being fulfilled, construction began later than scheduled and then proceeded slowly. The first seven classrooms on the first floor were first used in the fall of 1935. The remainder of the three-story building was built in stages until the entire building was enclosed by 1952.[21]

July 9, 1930: F. E. Robinson announced the first president of WJBU, Dr. George E. Guille, a former Presbyterian pastor who had taught at Dallas Theological Seminary and Moody Bible Institute.

July 24, 1930: The Charter of Incorporation, filed with the Tennessee secretary of state, stated that WJBU was founded "for the purpose of establishing, conducting and perpetuating a University for the higher education of men and women under auspices distinctly Christian and spiritual, as a testimony to the supreme glory of the Lord Jesus Christ, and to the Divine inspiration and infallibility of the Bible."[22]

September 18, 1930: WJBU opening exercises were held in the Rhea County court room where the Scopes trial had been held. Administrators, faculty, several campaign committee members, the Dayton mayor, and other prominent men of the town were on the platform when the town turned out to attend the exercises. The program included the following:

- The singing of "Onward Christian Soldiers" and "Faith of Our Fathers"
- An explanation of courses and credits for the coming year
- A violin solo by the wife of one of the instructors
- An inaugural address by President Guille entitled "Wisdom, Human and Divine"

Newspaper reporter Annie Cole stated, "It was a most inspiring address. Let us hope and pray that this institution, so newly organized, may become a storehouse of knowledge and truth to the people now and to future generations of this and many other parts of the world."[23]

September 30, 1930: With first quarter enrollment of 27 students (second quarter was 74),[24] WJBU classes began in the former Rhea Central High School. The building, leased by BMUA, was the same building in which John Scopes was said to have taught evolution.

A 1933 student publication stated as follows:

The William Jennings Bryan University was founded as a memorial to the Great Commoner, but even more it is a memorial to that which made him great—his Christian ideals and his faith in the Bible as God's Word. He trusted in God and in His Son, Jesus Christ. That was his righteousness. In the future, as the memory of Mr. Bryan is dimmed with time, we can still find in God's Word the spiritual food that built Mr. Bryan.[25]

SPEECH CONCLUDING DEBATE ON THE CHICAGO PLATFORM*

DELIVERED BEFORE THE NATIONAL DEMOCRATIC CONVENTION IN CHICAGO, ILLINOIS

JULY 9, 1896

Mr. Chairman and Gentlemen of the Convention—I would be presumptuous indeed to present myself against the distinguished gentleman to whom you have listened if this were a mere measuring of abilities; but this is not a contest between persons. The humblest citizen in all the land, when clad in the armor of a righteous cause, is stronger than all the hosts of error. I come to speak to you in defense of a cause as holy as the cause of liberty—the cause of humanity.

When this debate is concluded a motion will be made to lay upon the table the resolution offered in commendation of the Administration, and also the resolution offered in condemnation of the Administration. We object to bringing this question down to the level of persons. The individual is but an atom; he is born, he acts, he dies; but principles are eternal, and this has been a contest over a principle.

Never before in the history of this country has there been witnessed such a contest as that through which we have just passed. Never before in the history of American politics has a great issue been fought out as this issue has been by the voters of a great party. On the 4th of March, 1895, a few Democrats, most of them members of Congress, issued an address to the Democrats of the nation, asserting that the money question was the paramount issue of the hour; declaring that a majority of the Democratic party had the right to control the action of the party on this paramount issue, and concluding with the request that the believers in the free coinage of silver in the Democratic party should organize, take charge of and control the policy of the Democratic party. Three months later, at Memphis, an organization was perfected, and the silver Democrats went forth openly and courageously proclaiming their belief, and declaring that, if successful, they would crystallize into a platform the declaration which they had made. Then began the conflict. With a zeal approaching the zeal which inspired the crusaders who followed Peter the Hermit, our silver Democrats went forth from victory unto victory, until they are now assembled, not to discuss, not to debate, but to enter up the judgment already rendered by the plain people of this country. In this contest brother has been arrayed against brother, father against son. The warmest ties of love, acquaintance and association have been disregarded; old leaders have been cast aside when they have refused to give expression to the sentiments of those whom they would lead, and new leaders have sprung up to give direction to this cause of truth. Thus has the contest been waged, and we have assembled here under as binding and solemn instructions as were ever imposed upon representatives of the people.

We do not come as individuals. As individuals we might have been glad to compliment the gentleman from New York [Senator Hill], but we know that the people for whom we speak would never be willing to put

---

*In 1896, the first time in the history of American politics, a candidate was nominated for President who was not seriously discussed for the position before the convention met, but who won his nomination by a single oratorical effort, who enthused the convention and swept it from its original moorings. Mr. Bryan was not even a delegate to the convention when it met. He was in the position of a contestant, but on the second day he and his friends were admitted, and in an address of surpassing eloquence, which we give herewith, he won the nomination, even against the most earnest opposition, and stood to its guns until the last shot was fired. A single speech thus made Mr. Bryan a candidate for President, who in the campaign electrified the country by his eloquent and tireless speeches.—Publishers.

him in a position where he could thwart the will of the Democratic party. I say it was not a question of persons; it was a question of principle, and it is not with gladness, my friends, that we find ourselves brought into conflict with those who are now arrayed on the other side.

The gentleman who preceded me [ex-Governor Russell] spoke of the State of Massachusetts; let me assure him that not one present in all this convention entertains the least hostility to the people of the State of Massachusetts, but we stand here representing people who are the equals, before the law, of the greatest citizens in the State of Massachusetts. When you (turning to the gold delegates) come before us and tell us that we are about to disturb your business interests, we reply that you have disturbed our business interests by your course.

We say to you that you have made the definition of a business man too limited in its application. The man who is employed for wages is as much a business man as his employer; the attorney in a country town is as much a business man as the corporation counsel in a great metropolis; the merchant at the crossroads store is as much a business man as the merchant of New York; the farmer who goes forth in the morning and toils all day—who begins in the spring and toils all summer—and who by the application of brain and muscle to the natural resources of the country creates wealth, is as much a business man as the man who goes upon the Board of Trade and bets upon the price of grain; the miners who go down a thousand feet into the earth, or climb two thousand feet upon the cliffs, and bring forth from their hiding places the precious metals to be poured into the channels of trade are as much business men as the few financial magnates who, in a back room, corner the money of the world. We come to speak for this broader class of business men.

Ah, my friends, we say not one word against those who live upon the Atlantic coast, but the hardy pioneers who have braved all the dangers of the wilderness, who have made the desert to blossom as the rose—the pioneers away out there (pointing to the West), who rear their children near to Nature's heart, where they can mingle their voices with the voices of the birds—out there, where they have erected schoolhouses for the education of their young, churches where they praise their Creator, and cemeteries where rest the ashes of their dead—these people, we say, are as deserving of the consideration of our party as any people in this country. It is for these that we speak. We do not come as aggressors. Our war is not a war of conquest; we are fighting in the defense of our homes, our families and posterity. We have petitioned, and our petitions have been scorned; we have entreated, and our entreaties have been disregarded; we have begged, and they have mocked when our calamity came. We beg no longer, we entreat no more, we petition no more. We defy them.

The gentleman from Wisconsin has said that he fears a Robespierre. My friends, in this land of the free you need not fear that a tyrant will spring up from among the people. What we need is an Andrew Jackson to stand, as Jackson stood, against the encroachments of organized wealth.

They tell us that this platform was made to catch votes. We reply to them that changing conditions make new issues; that the principles upon which Democracy rests are as everlasting as the hills, but that they must be applied to new conditions as they arise. Conditions have arisen, and we are here to meet those conditions. They tell us that the income tax ought not to be brought in here; that it is a new idea. They criticise us for our criticism of the Supreme Court of the United States. My friends, we have not criticised;

 Scan QR code to hear a recording of Mr. Bryan giving an abbreviated version of "Cross of Gold" in observance of the speech's 25th anniversary in 1921 (see #55 on page 156). *The italicized text indicates content omitted for the recording .*

we have simply called attention to what you already know. If you want criticisms read the dissenting opinions of the court. There you will find criticisms. They say that we passed an unconstitutional law; we deny it. The income tax law was not unconstitutional when it was passed; it was not unconstitutional when it went before the Supreme Court for the first time; it did not become unconstitutional until one of the judges changed his mind, and we cannot be expected to know when a judge will change his mind. The income tax is just. It simply intends to put the burdens of government justly upon the backs of the people. I am in favor of an income tax. When I find a man who is not willing to bear his share of the burdens of the government which protects him, I find a man who is unworthy to enjoy the blessings of a government like ours.

They say that we are opposing national-bank currency. It is true. If you will read what Thomas Benton said you will find he said that, in searching history, he could not find but one parallel to Andrew Jackson; that was Cicero, who destroyed the conspiracy of Cataline and saved Rome. Benton said that Cicero only did for Rome what Jackson did for us when be destroyed the bank conspiracy and saved America. We say in our platform that we believe that the right to coin and issue money is a function of government. We believe it. We believe that it is a part of sovereignty, and can no more with safety be delegated to private individuals than we could afford to delegate to private individuals the power to make penal statutes or levy taxes. Mr. Jefferson, who was once regarded as good Democratic authority, seems to have differed in opinion from the gentleman who has addressed us on the part of the minority. Those who are opposed to this proposition tell us that the issue of paper money is a function of the bank, and that the Government ought to go out of the banking business. I stand with Jefferson rather than with them, and tell them, as he did, that the issue of money is a function of government, and that the banks ought to go out of the governing business.

They complain about the plank which declares against life tenure in office. They have tried to strain it to mean that which it does not mean. What we oppose by that plank is the life tenure which is being built up in Washington, and which excludes from participation in official benefits the humbler members of society.

Let me call your attention to two or three important things. The gentleman from New York says that he will propose an amendment to the platform providing that the proposed change in our monetary system shall not affect contracts already made. Let me remind you that there is no intention of affecting those contracts which, according to present laws, are made payable in gold; but if he means to say that we cannot change our monetary system without protecting those who have loaned money before the change was made, I desire to ask him where, in law or in morals, he can find justification for not protecting the debtors when the act of 1873 was passed, if he now insists that we must protect the creditors.

He says he will also propose an amendment which will provide for the suspension of free coinage if we fail to maintain the parity within a year. We reply that when we advocate a policy which we believe will be successful we are not compelled to raise a doubt as to our own sincerity by suggesting what we shall do if we fail. I ask him, if he would apply his logic to us, why he does not apply it to himself. He says he wants this country to try to secure an international agreement. Why does he not tell us what he is going to do if he fails to secure an international agreement? There is more reason for him to do that than there is for us to provide against the failure to maintain the parity. Our opponents have tried for twenty years to secure an international agreement, and those are waiting for it most patiently who do not want it at all.

And now, my friends, let me come to the paramount issue. If they ask us why it is that we say more on the money question than we say upon the tariff question. I reply that if protection has slain its thousands, the gold standard has slain its tens of thousands. If they ask us why we do not embody in our platform all the things that we believe in, we reply that when we have restored the money of the Constitution all other necessary reforms will be possible, but that until this is done there is no other reform that can be accomplished.

Why is it that within three months such a change has come over the country? Three months ago, when it was confidently asserted that those who believe in the gold standard would frame our platform and nominate our candidates, even the advocates of the gold standard did not think that we could elect a President. And they had good reason for their doubt, because there is scarcely a State here today asking for the gold standard which is not in the absolute control of the Republican party. But note the change. Mr. McKinley was nominated at St. Louis upon a platform which declared for the maintenance of the gold standard until it can be changed into bimetallism by international agreement. Mr. McKinley was the most popular man among the Republicans, and three months ago everybody in the Republican party prophesied his election. How is it today? Why, the man who was once pleased to think that he looked like Napoleon—that man shudders today when he remembers that he was nominated on the anniversary of the battle of Waterloo. Not only that, but as he listens he can hear with ever-increasing distinctness the sound of the waves as they beat upon the lonely shores of St. Helena.

Why this change? Ah, my friends, is not the reason for the change evident to anyone who will look at the matter? No private character, however pure, no personal popularity, however great, can protect from the avenging wrath of an indignant people a man who will declare that he is in favor of fastening the gold standard upon this country, or who is willing to surrender the right of self-government and place the legislative control of our affairs in the hands of foreign potentates and powers.

We go forth confident that we shall win. Why? Because upon the paramount issue of this campaign there is not a spot of ground upon which the enemy will dare to challenge battle. If they tell us that the gold standard is a good thing we shall point to their platform and tell them that their platform pledges the party to get rid of the gold standard and substitute bimetallism. *If the gold standard is a good thing, why try to get rid of it?* I call your attention to the fact that some of the very people who are in this convention today, and who tell us that we ought to declare in favor of international bimetallism— thereby declaring that the gold standard is wrong and that the principle of bimetallism is better—these very people four months ago were open and avowed advocates of the gold standard, and were then telling us that we could not legislate two metals together, even with the aid of all the world. If the gold standard is a good thing we ought to declare in favor of its retention, and not in favor of abandoning it, and if the gold standard is a bad thing, why should we wait until other nations are willing to help us to let go? *Here is the line of battle, and we care not upon which issue they force the fight; we are prepared to meet them on either issue or on both.* If they tell us that the gold standard is the standard of civilization, we reply to them that this, the most enlightened of all the nations of the earth, has never declared for a gold standard, and that both the great parties this year are declaring against it. *If the gold standard is the standard of civilization, why, my friends, should we not have it? If they come to meet us on that issue we can present the history of our nation.* More than that—we can tell them that they will search the pages of history in vain to find a single instance where the common people of any land have ever declared themselves in favor of the gold standard. They can find where the holders of fixed investments have declared for a gold standard, but not where the masses have.

Mr. Carlisle said in 1878 that this was a struggle between "the idle holders of idle capital" and "the struggling masses, who produce the wealth and pay the taxes of the country," *and, my friends, the question we are to decide is, upon which side will the Democratic party fight—upon the side of "the idle holders of idle capital," or upon the side of "the struggling masses?" That is the question which the party must answer first, and then it must be answered by each individual hereafter. The sympathies of the Democratic party, as shown by the platform, are on the side of the struggling masses who have ever been the foundation of the Democratic party. There are two ideas of government. There are those who believe that if you will only legislate to make the well-to-do prosperous their prosperity will leak through on those below. The Democratic idea, however, has been that if you legislate to make the masses prosperous their prosperity will find its way up through every class which rests upon them.*

You come to us and tell us that the great cities are in favor of the gold standard; we reply that the great cities rest upon our broad and fertile prairies. Burn down your cities and leave our farms, and your cities will spring up again as if by magic; but destroy our farms, and the grass will grow in the streets of every city in the country.

My friends, we declare that this nation is able to legislate for its own people on every question without waiting for the aid or consent of any other nation on earth, and upon that issue we expect to carry every State in the Union. I shall not slander the inhabitants of the fair State of Massachusetts nor the inhabitants of the State of New York by saying that, when they are confronted with the proposition, they will declare that this nation is not able to attend to its own business. It is the issue of 1776 over again. Our ancestors, when but 3,000,000 in number, had the courage to declare their political independence of every other nation; shall we, their descendants, when we have grown to 70,000,000, declare that we are less independent than our forefathers? No, my friends, that will never be the verdict of our people. Therefore, we care not upon what lines the battle is fought. If they say bimetallism is good, but that we cannot have it until other nations help us, we reply that, instead of having a gold standard because England has, we will restore bimetallism, and then let England have bimetallism because the United States has it. If they dare to come out in the open field and defend the gold standard as a good thing we will fight them to the uttermost. Having behind us the producing masses of this nation and the world, supported by the commercial interests, the laboring interests and the toilers everywhere, we will answer their demand for a gold standard by saying to them: You shall not press down upon the brow of labor this crown of thorns; you shall not crucify mankind upon a cross of gold.

SOURCE: William Jennings Bryan and Mary Baird Bryan, *Life and Speeches of Hon. Wm. Jennings Bryan* (Baltimore, MD: R. H. Woodward Company, 1900), 247–252.

Richard Cornelius's critique* of Bryan's most popular speech begins with a statement made by Bryan: "My greatest speech, and the one I wish to be remembered by longest is the 'Prince of Peace.'" Cornelius continued:

- A chief explanation for this popularity undoubtedly was the attractiveness of the focal Person and the typical Bryanesque positive and exuberant outlook on Him, as seen in this quotation: "Christ came not to narrow life, but to enlarge it—not to rob it of its joy, but to fill it to overflowing with purpose, earnestness and happiness."

- This oration—along with "The Value of an Ideal"—is a seminal one. Subsequent speeches and essays reflect the style which marks "The Prince of Peace": extensive parallelism and balance; numerous figures of speech and rhetorical devices; Biblical, historical, and literary allusions; good organization, smooth transitions, and clear reasoning; a blend of seriousness and humor and of both emotional and rational appeals.

- [Although] Bryan worked hard to prepare his orations, he was enough of a realist to admit that "A sermon may be answered; the arguments presented in a speech may be disputed, but no one can answer a Christian life."

- In subject matter this oration is also seminal. It contains both personal testimony and general principles. For the rest of his life, Bryan wrote and spoke in greater detail about topics introduced in "The Prince of Peace": the person of Christ, personal and governmental peace, Darwinism, politics, the role of religion, morality, the trials of life, miracles, the virgin birth, faith, God as Creator, materialism, salvation through the sacrifice of Christ, immortality, the resurrection of Christ, love, the abundant Christian life, and forgiveness ("the most difficult of all the virtues to cultivate is the forgiving spirit.").

I offer no apology for speaking upon a religious theme, for it is the most universal of all themes. The science of government is interesting, but I am more interested in religion than in government. Making a political speech is enjoyable—I have made a good many and shall make more— but I would rather speak on religion than on politics. I commenced speaking on the stump when only twenty, but commenced speaking in the church six weeks earlier—and shall be in the church even after I am out of politics. I feel sure of my ground when making a political speech, but am more certain of my ground when making a religious speech. If this address were upon the subject of law, the lawyers might be interested; if upon the science of medicine, it might interest the physicians; in like manner merchants might be interested in comments on commerce, and farmers in matters pertaining to agriculture; but no one of these subjects appeals to all. Even the science of government, tho broader than any profession or occupation, does not embrace the whole sum of life, and those who think upon it differ so among themselves that one could not speak upon the subject so as to please a part of the audience without displeasing others. While to me the science of government is intensely absorbing, I recognize that the most important things in life lie outside of the realm of government and that more depends upon what the individual does for himself than upon what the government does or can do for him. Men can be miserable under the best government and they can be happy under the worst government.

---

* Richard M. Cornelius, ed., *Selected Orations of William Jennings Bryan* (Dayton, TN: Bryan College, 2000), 37.

Government affects but a part of the life which we live here and does not deal at all with the life beyond, while religion touches the infinite circle of existence as well as the small arc of that circle which we spend on earth. No greater theme, therefore, can engage our attention. When discussing questions of government I must secure the cooperation of a majority before my ideas can be put into practise, but if, in speaking on religion, I can touch one human heart for good, I have not spoken in vain no matter how large the majority may be against me.

Man is a religious being; the heart instinctively seeks for a God. Whether he worships on the banks of the Ganges, prays with his face upturned to the sun, kneels toward Mecca or, regarding all space as a temple, communes with the Heavenly Father according to the Christian creed, man is essentially devout.

There are honest doubters whose sincerity we recognize and respect, but occasionally I find young men who think it smart to be skeptical; they talk as if it were an evidence of larger intelligence to scoff at creeds and to refuse to connect themselves with churches. They call themselves "liberal," as if a Christian were narrow minded. Some go so far as to assert that the "advanced thought of the world" has discarded the idea that there is a God. To these young men I desire to address myself.

Even some older people profess to regard religion as a superstition, pardonable in the ignorant but unworthy of the educated. Those who hold this view look down with mild contempt upon such as give to religion a definite place in their thoughts and lives. They assume an intellectual superiority and often take little pains to conceal the assumption. Tolstoy administers to the "cultured crowd" (the words quoted are his) a severe rebuke when he declares that the religious sentiment rests not upon a superstitious fear of the invisible forces of nature, but upon man's consciousness of his finiteness amid an infinite universe and of his sinfulness; and this consciousness, the great philosopher adds, man can never outgrow. Tolstoy is right; man recognizes how limited are his own powers and how vast is the universe, and he leans upon the Arm that is stronger than his. Man feels the weight of his sins and looks for One who is sinless.

Religion has been defined by Tolstoy as the relation which man fixes between himself and his God, and morality as the outward manifestation of this inward relation. Every one, by the time he reaches maturity, has fixt some relation between himself and God and no material change in this relation can take place without a revolution in the man, for this relation is the most potent influence that acts upon a human life.

Religion is the foundation of morality in the individual and in the group of individuals. Materialists have attempted to build up a system of morality upon the basis of enlightened self-interest. They would have man figure out by mathematics that it pays him to abstain from wrongdoing; they would even inject an element of selfishness into altruism, but the moral system elaborated by the materialists has several defects. First, its virtues are borrowed from moral systems based upon religion. All those who are intelligent enough to discuss a system of morality are so saturated with the morals derived from systems resting upon religion that they can not frame a system resting upon reason alone. Second, as it rests upon argument rather than upon authority, the young are not in a position to accept or reject. Our laws do not permit a young man to dispose of real estate until he is twenty-one. Why this restraint? Because his reason is not mature; and yet a man's life is largely molded by the environment of his youth. Third, one never knows just how much of his decision is due to reason and how much is due to passion or to selfish interest. Passion can dethrone the reason—we recognize this in our criminal laws. We also recognize the bias of self-interest when we exclude from the jury every man, no matter how reasonable or upright he may be, who has a pecuniary interest in the result of the trial. And, fourth, one whose morality rests upon a nice calculation of benefits to be secured spends time in figuring that he should spend in action. Those who keep a book account of their good deeds seldom do enough good to justify keeping books. A noble life can not be built upon an arithmetic; it must be rather like the spring that pours forth constantly that which refreshes and invigorates.

Morality is the power of endurance in man; and a religion which teaches personal responsibility to God gives strength to morality. There is a powerful restraining influence in the belief that an all-seeing eye scrutinizes every thought and word and act of the individual.

There is wide difference between the man who is trying to conform his life to a standard of morality about him and the man who seeks to make his life approximate to a divine standard. The former attempts to live up to the standard, if it is above him, and down to it, if it is below him—and if he is doing right only when others are looking he is sure to find a time when he thinks he is unobserved, and then he takes a vacation and falls. One needs the inner strength which comes with the conscious presence of a personal God. If those who are thus fortified sometimes yield to temptation, how helpless and hopeless must those be who rely upon their own strength alone!

There are difficulties to be encountered in religion, but there are difficulties to be encountered everywhere. If Christians sometimes have doubts and fears, unbelievers have more doubts and greater fears. I passed through a period of skepticism when I was in college and I have been glad ever since that I became a member of the church before I left home for college, for it helped me during those trying days. And the college days cover the dangerous period in the young man's life; he is just coming into possession of his powers, and feels stronger than he ever feels afterward—and he thinks he knows more than he ever does know.

It was at this period that I became confused by the different theories of creation. But I examined these theories and found that they all assumed something to begin with. You can test this for yourselves. The nebular hypothesis, for instance, assumes that matter and force existed—matter in particles infinitely fine and each particle separated from every other particle by space infinitely great. Beginning with this assumption, force working on matter—according to this hypothesis—created a universe. I have as much right to assume as they do, and I prefer to assume, a Designer back of the design—a Creator back of the creation; and no matter how long you draw out the process of creation, so long as God stands back of it you can not shake my faith in Jehovah. In Genesis it is written that, in the beginning, God created the heavens and the earth, and I can stand on that proposition until I find some theory of creation that goes farther back than "the beginning." We must begin with something—we must start somewhere—and the Christian begins with God.

I do not carry the doctrine of evolution as far as some do; I am not yet convinced that man is a lineal descendant of the lower animals. I do not mean to find fault with you if you want to accept the theory; all I mean to say is that while you may trace your ancestry back to the monkey if you find pleasure or pride in doing so, you shall not connect me with your family tree without more evidence than has yet been produced. I object to the theory for several reasons. First, it is a dangerous theory. If a man links himself in generations with the monkey, it then becomes an important question whether he is going toward him or coming from him—and I have seen them going in both directions. I do not know of any argument that can be used to prove that man is an improved monkey that may not be used just as well to prove that the monkey is a degenerate man, and the latter theory is more plausible than the former.

It is true that man, in some physical characteristics resembles the beast, but man has a mind as well as a body, and a soul as well as a mind. The mind is greater than the body and the soul is greater than the mind, and I object to having man's pedigree traced on one-third of him only—and that the lowest third. Fairbairn, in his "Philosophy of Christianity," lays down a sound proposition when he says that it is not sufficient to explain man as an animal; that it is necessary to explain man in history—and the Darwinian theory does not do this. The ape, according to this theory, is older than man and yet the ape is still an ape while man is the author of the marvelous civilization which we see about us.

One does not escape from mystery, however, by accepting this theory, for it does not explain the origin of life. When the follower of Darwin has traced the germ of life back to the lowest form in which it appears—and to follow him one must exercise more faith than religion calls for—he finds that scientists differ. Those who reject the idea of creation are divided into two schools, some believing that the first germ of life came from another planet and others holding that it was the result of spontaneous generation. Each school answers the arguments advanced by the other, and as they can not agree with each other, I am not compelled to agree with either.

If I were compelled to accept one of these theories I would prefer the first, for if we can chase the germ of life off this planet and get it out into space we can guess the rest of the way and no one can contradict us, but if we accept the doctrine of spontaneous generation we can not explain why spontaneous generation ceased to act after the first germ was created.

Go back as far as we may, we can not escape from the creative act, and it is just as easy for me to believe that God created man *as he is* as to believe that, millions of years ago, He created a germ of life and endowed it with power to develop into all that we see to-day. I object to the Darwinian theory, until more conclusive proof is produced, because I fear we shall lose the consciousness of God's presence in our daily life, if we must accept the theory that through all the ages no spiritual force has touched the life of man or shaped the destiny of nations.

But there is another objection. The Darwinian theory represents man as reaching his present perfection by the operation of the law of hate—the merciless law by which the strong crowd out and kill off the weak. If this is the law of our development then, if there is any logic that can bind the human mind, we shall turn backward toward the beast in proportion as we substitute the law of love. I prefer to believe that love rather than hatred is the law of development. How can hatred be the law of development when nations have advanced in proportion as they have departed from that law and adopted the law of love?

But, I repeat, while I do not accept the Darwinian theory I shall not quarrel with you about it; I only refer to it to remind you that it does not solve the mystery of life or explain human progress. I fear that some have accepted it in the hope of escaping from the miracle, but why should the miracle frighten us? And yet I am inclined to think that it is one of the test questions with the Christian.

Christ can not be separated from the miraculous; His birth, His ministrations, and His resurrection, all involve the miraculous, and the change which His religion works in the human heart is a continuing miracle. Eliminate the miracles and Christ becomes merely a human being and His gospel is stript of divine authority.

The miracle raises two questions: "Can God perform a miracle?" and, "Would He want to?" The first is easy to answer. A God who can make a world can do anything He wants to do with it. The power to perform miracles is necessarily implied in the power to create. But would God *want* to perform a miracle?—this is the question which has given most of the trouble. The more I have considered it the less inclined I am to answer in the negative. To say that God *would not* perform a miracle is to assume a more intimate knowledge of God's plans and purposes than I can claim to have. I will not deny that God does perform a miracle or may perform one merely because I do not know how or why He does it. I find it so difficult to decide each day what God wants done now that I am not presumptuous enough to attempt to declare what God might have wanted to do thousands of years ago. The fact that we are constantly learning of the existence of new forces suggests the possibility that God may operate through forces yet unknown to us, and the mysteries with which we deal every-day warn me that faith is as necessary as sight. Who would have credited a century ago the stories that are now told of the wonder-working electricity? For ages man had known the lightning, but only to fear it; now, this invisible current is generated by a man-made machine, imprisoned in a man-made wire and made to do the bidding of man. We are even able to dispense with the wire and hurl words through space, and the X-ray has enabled us to look through substances which were supposed, until recently, to exclude all light. The miracle is not more mysterious than many of the things with which man now deals—it is simply different. The miraculous birth of Christ is not more mysterious than any other conception—it is simply unlike it; nor is the resurrection of Christ more mysterious than the myriad resurrections which mark each annual seed-time.

It is sometimes said that God could not suspend one of His laws without stopping the universe, but do we not suspend or overcome the law of gravitation every-day? Every time we move a foot or lift a weight we temporarily overcome one of the most universal of natural laws and yet the world is not disturbed.

Science has taught us so many things that we are tempted to conclude that we know everything, but there is really a great unknown which is still unexplored and that which we have learned ought to increase our reverence rather than our egotism. Science has disclosed some of the machinery of the universe, but science has not yet revealed to us the great secret—the secret of life. It is to be found in every blade of grass, in every insect, in every bird and in every animal, as well as in man. Six thousand years of recorded history and yet we know no more about the secret of life than they knew in the beginning. We live, we plan; we have our hopes, our fears; and yet in a moment a change may come over anyone of us and this body will become a mass of lifeless clay. What is it that, having, we live, and having not, we are as the clod? The progress of the race and the civilization which we now behold are the work of men and women who have not yet solved the mystery of their own lives.

And our food, must we understand it before we eat it? If we refused to eat anything until we could understand the mystery of its growth, we would die of starvation. But mystery does not bother us in the dining-room; it is only in the church that it is a stumbling block.

I was eating a piece of watermelon some months ago and was struck with its beauty. I took some of the seeds and dried them and weighed them, and found that it would require some five thousand seeds to weigh a pound; and then I applied mathematics to that forty-pound melon. One of these seeds, put into the ground, when warmed by the sun and moistened by the rain, takes off its coat and goes to work; it gathers from somewhere two hundred thousand times its own weight, and forcing this raw material through a tiny stem, constructs a watermelon. It ornaments the outside with a covering of green; inside the green it puts a layer of white, and within the white a core of red, and all through the red it scatters seeds, each one capable of continuing the work of reproduction. Who drew the plan by which that little seed works? Where does it get its tremendous strength? Where does it find its coloring matter? How does it collect its flavoring extract? How does it develop a watermelon? Until you can explain a watermelon, do not be too sure that you can set limits to the power of the Almighty and say just what He would do or how He would do it.

The egg is the most universal of foods and its use dates from the beginning, but what is more mysterious than an egg? When an egg is fresh it is an important article of merchandise; a hen can destroy its market value in a week's time, but in two weeks more she can bring forth from it what a man could not find in it. We eat eggs, but we can not explain an egg.

Water has been used from the birth of man; we learned after it had been used for ages that it is merely a mixture of gases, but it is far more important that we have water to drink than that we know that it is not water.

Everything that grows tells a like story of infinite power. Why should I deny that a divine hand fed a multitude with a few loaves and fishes when I see hundreds of millions fed every year by a hand which converts the seeds scattered over the field into an abundant harvest? We know that food can be multiplied in a few months' time; shall we deny the power of the Creator to eliminate the element of time, when we have gone so far in eliminating the element of space? Who am I that I should attempt to measure the arm of the Almighty with my puny arm, or to measure the brain of the Infinite with my finite mind? Who am I that I should attempt to put metes and bounds to the power of the Creator?

But there is something even more wonderful still—the mysterious change that takes place in the human heart when the man begins to hate the things he loved and to love the things he hated—the marvelous transformation that takes place in the man who, before the change, would have sacrificed a world for his own advancement but who, after the change, would give his life for a principle and esteem it a privilege to make sacrifice for his convictions! What greater miracle than this, that converts a selfish, self-centered, human being into a center from which good influences flow out in every direction! And yet this miracle has been wrought in the heart of each one of us—or may be wrought—and we have seen it wrought in the hearts and lives of those about us. No, living a life that is a mystery, and living in the midst of mystery and miracles, I shall not allow either to deprive me of the benefits of the Christian religion. If you ask me if I understand everything in the Bible, I answer, no, but if we will try to live up to what we do understand, we will be kept so busy doing good that we will not have time to worry about the passages which we do not understand.

Some of those who question the miracle also question the theory of atonement; they assert that it does not accord with their idea of justice for one to die for all. Let each one bear his own sins and the punishments due for them, they say. The doctrine of vicarious suffering is not a new one; it is as old as the race. That one should suffer for others is one of the most familiar of principles and we see the principle illustrated every-day of our lives. Take the family, for instance; from the day the mother's first child is born, for twenty or thirty years her children are scarcely out of her waking thoughts. Her life trembles in the balance at each child's birth; she sacrifices for them, she surrenders herself to them. Is it because she expects them to pay her back? Fortunate for the parent and fortunate for the child if the latter has an opportunity to repay in part the debt it owes. But no child can compensate a parent for a parent's care. In the course of nature the debt is paid, not to the parent, but to the next generation, and the next— each generation suffering, sacrificing for and surrendering itself to the generation that follows. This is the law of our lives.

Nor is this confined to the family. Every step in civilization has been made possible by those who have been willing to sacrifice for posterity. Freedom of speech, freedom of the press, freedom of conscience and free government have all been won for the world by those who were willing to labor unselfishly for their fellows. So well established is this doctrine that we do not regard anyone as great unless he recognizes how unimportant his life is in comparison with the problems with which he deals.

I find proof that man was made in the image of his Creator in the fact that, throughout the centuries, man has been willing to die, if necessary, that blessings denied to him might be enjoyed by his children, his children's children and the world.

The seeming paradox: "He that saveth his life shall lose it and he that loseth his life for my sake shall find it," has an application wider than that usually given to it; it is an epitome of history. Those who live only for themselves live little lives, but those who stand ready to give themselves for the advancement of things greater than themselves find a larger life than the one they would have surrendered. Wendell Phillips gave expression to the same idea when he said, "What imprudent men the benefactors of the race have been. How prudently most men sink into nameless graves, while now and then a few *forget* themselves into immortality." We win immortality, not by remembering ourselves, but by forgetting ourselves in devotion to things larger than ourselves.

Instead of being an unnatural plan, the plan of salvation is in perfect harmony with human nature as we understand it. Sacrifice is the language of love, and Christ, in suffering for the world, adopted the only means of reaching the heart. This can be demonstrated not only by theory but by experience, for the story of His life, His teachings, His sufferings and His death has been translated into every language and everywhere it has touched the heart.

But if I were going to present an argument in favor of the divinity of Christ, I would not begin with miracles or mystery or with the theory of atonement. I would begin as Carnegie Simpson does in his book entitled, "The Fact of Christ." Commencing with the undisputed fact that Christ lived, he points out that one can not contemplate this fact without feeling that in some way it is related to those now living. He says that one can read of Alexander, of Caesar or of Napoleon, and not feel that it is a matter of personal concern; but that when one reads that Christ lived, and how He lived and how He died, he feels that somehow there is a cord that stretches from that life to his. As he studies the character of Christ he becomes conscious of certain virtues which stand out in bold relief—His purity, His forgiving spirit, and His unfathomable love. The author is correct. Christ presents an example of purity in thought and life, and man, conscious of his own imperfections and grieved over his shortcomings, finds inspiration in the fact that He was tempted in all points like as we are, and yet without sin. I am not sure but that each can find just here a way of determining for himself whether he possesses the true spirit of a Christian. If the sinlessness of Christ inspires within him an earnest desire to conform his life more nearly to the perfect example, he is indeed a follower; if, on the other hand, he resents the reproof which the purity of Christ offers, and refuses to mend his ways, he has yet to be born again.

The most difficult of all the virtues to cultivate is the forgiving spirit. Revenge seems to be natural with man; it is human to want to get even with an enemy. It has even been popular to boast of vindictiveness; it was once inscribed on a man's monument that he had repaid both friends and enemies more than he had received. This was not the spirit of Christ. He taught forgiveness and in that incomparable prayer which He left as a model for our petitions, He made our willingness to forgive the measure by which we may claim forgiveness. He not only taught forgiveness but He exemplified His teachings in His life. When those who persecuted Him brought Him to the most disgraceful of all deaths, His spirit of forgiveness rose above His sufferings and He prayed, "Father, forgive them, for they know not what they do!"

But love is the foundation of Christ's creed. The world had known love before; parents had loved their children, and children their parents; husbands had loved their wives, and wives their husbands; and friend had loved friend; but Jesus gave a new definition of love. His love was as wide as the sea; its limits were so far-flung that even an enemy could not travel beyond its bounds. Other teachers sought to regulate the lives of their followers by rule and formula, but Christ's plan was to purify the heart and then to leave love to direct the footsteps.

What conclusion is to be drawn from the life, the teachings and the death of this historic figure? Reared in a carpenter shop; with no knowledge of literature, save Bible literature; with no acquaintance with philosophers living or with the writings of sages dead, when only about thirty years old He gathered disciples about Him, promulgated a higher code of morals than the world had ever known before, and proclaimed Himself the Messiah. He taught and performed miracles for a few brief months and then was crucified; His disciples were scattered and many of them put to death; His claims were disputed, His resurrection denied and His followers persecuted; and yet from this beginning His religion spread until hundreds of millions have taken His name with reverence upon their lips and millions have been willing to die rather than surrender the faith which He put into their hearts. How shall we account for Him? Here is the greatest fact of history; here is One who has with increasing power, for nineteen hundred years, molded the hearts, the thoughts and the lives of men, and He exerts more influence to-day than ever before. "What think ye of Christ?" It is easier to believe Him divine than to explain in any other way what he said and did and was. And I have greater faith, even than before, since I have visited the Orient and witnessed the successful contest which Christianity is waging against the religions and philosophies of the East.

I was thinking a few years ago of the Christmas which was then approaching and of Him in whose honor the day is celebrated. I recalled the message, "Peace on earth, good will to men," and then my thoughts ran back to the prophecy uttered centuries before His birth, in which He was described as the Prince of Peace. To reinforce my memory I re-read the prophecy and I found immediately following a verse which I had forgotten—a verse which declares that of the increase of His peace and government there shall be no end. And, Isaiah adds, that He shall judge His people with justice and with judgment. I had been reading of the rise and fall of nations, and occasionally I had met a gloomy philosopher who preached the doctrine that nations, like individuals, must of necessity have their birth, their infancy, their maturity and finally their decay and death. But here I read of a government that is to be perpetual—a government of increasing peace and blessedness—the government of the Prince of Peace— and it is to rest on justice. I have thought of this prophecy many times during the last few years, and I have selected this theme that I might present some of the reasons which lead me to believe that Christ has fully earned the right to be called the Prince of Peace—a title that will in the years to come be more and more applied to Him. If he can bring peace to each individual heart, and if His creed when applied will bring peace throughout the earth, who will deny His right to be called the Prince of Peace?

All the world is in search of peace; every heart that ever beat has sought for peace, and many have been the methods employed to secure it. Some have thought to purchase it with riches and have labored to secure wealth, hoping to find peace when they were able to go where they pleased and buy what they liked. Of those who have endeavored to purchase peace with money, the large majority have failed to secure the money. But what has been the experience of those who have been eminently successful in finance? They all tell the same story, viz., that they spent the first half of their lives trying to get money from others and the last half trying to keep others from getting their money, and that they found peace in neither half. Some have even reached the point where they find difficulty in getting people to accept their money; and I know of no better indication of the ethical awakening in this country than the increasing tendency to scrutinize the methods of money-making. I am sanguine enough to believe that the time will yet come when respectability will no longer be sold to great criminals by helping them to spend their ill-gotten gains. A long step in advance will have been taken when religious, educational and charitable institutions refuse to condone conscienceless methods in business and leave the possessor of illegitimate accumulations to learn how lonely life is when one prefers money to morals.

Some have sought peace in social distinction, but whether they have been within the charmed circle and fearful lest they might fall out, or outside, and hopeful that they might get in, they have not found peace. Some have thought, vain thought, to find peace in political prominence; but whether office comes by birth, as in monarchies, or by election, as in republics, it does not bring peace. An office is not considered a high one if all can occupy it. Only when few in a generation can hope to enjoy an honor do we call it a great honor. I am glad that our Heavenly Father did not make the peace of the human heart to depend upon our ability to buy it with money, secure it in society, or win it at the polls, for in either case but few could have obtained it, but when He made peace the reward of a conscience void of offense toward God and man, He put it within the reach of all. The poor can secure it as easily as the rich, the social outcasts as freely as the leader of society, and the humblest citizen equally with those who wield political power.

To those who have grown gray in the church, I need not speak of the peace to be found in faith in God and trust in an overruling Providence. Christ taught that our lives are precious in the sight of God, and poets have taken up the thought and woven it into immortal verse. No uninspired writer has exprest it more beautifully than William Cullen Bryant in his Ode to a Waterfowl. After following the wanderings of the bird of passage as it seeks first its southern and then its northern home, he concludes:

> Thou art gone; the abyss of heaven
> Hath swallowed up thy form, but on my heart
> Deeply hath sunk the lesson thou hast given,
> And shall not soon depart.
>
> He who, from zone to zone,
> Guides through the boundless sky thy certain flight,
> In the long way that I must tread alone,
> Will lead my steps aright.

Christ promoted peace by giving us assurance that a line of communication can be established between the Father above and the child below. And who will measure the consolations of the hour of prayer?

And immortality! Who will estimate the peace which a belief in a future life has brought to the sorrowing hearts of the sons of men? You may talk to the young about death ending all, for life is full and hope is strong, but preach not this doctrine to the mother who stands by the death-bed of her babe or to one who is within the shadow of a great affliction. When I was a young man I wrote to Colonel Ingersoll and asked him for his views on God and immortality. His secretary answered that the great infidel was not at home, but enclosed a copy of a speech of Colonel Ingersoll's which covered my question. I scanned it with eagerness and found that he had exprest himself about as follows: "I do not say that there is no God, I simply say I do not know. I do not say that there is no life beyond the grave, I simply say I do not know." And from that day to this I have asked myself the question and have been unable to answer it to my satisfaction, how could anyone find pleasure in taking from a human heart a living faith and substituting therefor the cold and cheerless doctrine, "I do not know."

Christ gave us proof of immortality and it was a welcome assurance, altho it would hardly seem necessary that one should rise from the dead to convince us that the grave is not the end. To every created thing God has given a tongue that proclaims a future life.

If the Father deigns to touch with divine power the cold and pulseless heart of the buried acorn and to make it burst forth from its prison walls, will he leave neglected in the earth the soul of man, made in the image of his Creator? If he stoops to give to the rose bush, whose withered blossoms float upon the autumn breeze, the sweet assurance of another springtime, will He refuse the words of hope to the sons of men when the frosts of winter come? If matter, mute and inanimate, tho changed by the forces of nature into a multitude of forms, can never die, will the imperial spirit of man suffer annihilation when it has paid a brief visit like a royal guest to this tenement of clay? No, I am sure that He who, notwithstanding his apparent prodigality, created nothing without a purpose, and wasted not a single atom in all his creation, has made provision for a future life in which man's universal longing for immortality will find its realization.

In Cairo I secured a few grains of wheat that had slumbered for more than thirty centuries in an Egyptian tomb. As I looked at them this thought came into my mind: If one of those grains had been planted on the banks of the Nile the year after it grew, and all its lineal descendants had been planted and replanted from that time until now, its progeny would to-day be sufficiently numerous to feed the teeming millions of the world. An unbroken chain of life connects the earliest grains of wheat with the grains that we sow and reap. There is in the grain of wheat an invisible something which has power to discard the body that we see, and from earth and air fashion a new body so much like the old one that we can not tell the one from the other. If this invisible germ of life in the grain of wheat can thus pass unimpaired through three thousand resurrections, I shall not doubt that my soul has power to clothe itself with a body suited to its new existence when this earthly frame has crumbled into dust. I am as sure that we live again as I am sure that we live to-day.

A belief in immortality not only consoles the individual, but it exerts a powerful influence in bringing peace between individuals. If one actually thinks that man dies as the brute dies, he will yield more easily to the temptation to do injustice to his neighbor when the circumstances are such as to promise security from detection. But if one really expects to meet again, and live eternally with, those whom he knows to-day, he is restrained from evil deeds by the fear of endless remorse. We do not know what rewards are in store for us or what punishments may be reserved, but if there were no other it would be some punishment for one who deliberately and consciously wrongs another to have to live forever in the company of the person wronged and to have his littleness and selfishness laid bare. I repeat, a belief in immortality must exert a powerful influence in establishing justice between men and thus laying the foundation for peace.

Again, Christ deserves to be called the Prince of Peace because He has given us a measure of greatness which promotes peace. When His disciples quarreled among themselves as to which should be greatest in the Kingdom of Heaven, He rebuked them and said: "Let him who would be chiefest among you be the servant of all." Service is the measure of greatness; it always has been true; it is true to-day, and it always will be true, that he is greatest who does the most of good. And how this old world will be transformed when this standard of greatness becomes the standard of every life! Nearly all of our controversies and combats grow out of the fact that we are trying to get something from each other—there will be peace when our aim is to do something for each other. Our enmities and animosities arise largely from our efforts to get as much as possible out of the world—there will be peace when our endeavor is to put as much as possible into the world. The human measure of a human life is its income; the divine measure of a life is its outgo, its overflow—its contribution to the welfare of all.

Christ also led the way to peace by giving us a formula for the propagation of truth. Not all of those who have really desired to do good have employed the Christian method—not all Christians even. In the history of the human race but two methods have been used. The first is the forcible method, and it has been employed most frequently. A man has an idea which he thinks is good; he tells his neighbors about it and they do not like it. This makes him angry; he thinks it would be so much better for them if they would like it, and, seizing a club, he attempts to make them like it. But one trouble about this rule is that it works both ways; when a man starts out to compel his neighbors to think as he does, he generally finds them willing to accept the challenge and they spend so much time in trying to coerce each other that they have no time left to do each other good.

The other is the Bible plan—"Be not overcome of evil but overcome evil with good." And there is no other way of overcoming evil. I am not much of a farmer—I get more credit for my farming than I should, and my little farm receives more advertising than it deserves. But I am farmer enough to know that if I cut down weeds they will spring up again; and farmer enough to know that if I plant something there which has more vitality than the weeds I shall not only get rid of the constant cutting, but have the benefit of the crop besides.

In order that there might be no mistake in His plan of propagating the truth, Christ went into detail and laid emphasis upon the value of example—"So live that others seeing your good works may be constrained to glorify your Father which is in Heaven." There is no human influence so potent for good as that which goes out from an upright life. A sermon may be answered; the arguments presented in a speech may be disputed, but no one can answer a Christian life—it is the unanswerable argument in favor of our religion.

It may be a slow process—this conversion of the world by the silent influence of a noble example but it is the only sure one, and the doctrine applies to nations as well as to individuals. The Gospel of the Prince of Peace gives us the only hope that the world has—and it is an increasing hope—of the substitution of reason for the arbitrament of force in the settlement of international disputes. And our nation ought not to wait for other nations—it ought to take the lead and prove its faith in the omnipotence of truth.

But Christ has given us a platform so fundamental that it can be applied successfully to all controversies. We are interested in platforms; we attend conventions, sometimes traveling long distances; we have wordy wars over the phraseology of various planks, and then we wage earnest campaigns to secure the endorsement of these platforms at the polls. The platform given to the world by the Prince of Peace is more far-reaching and more comprehensive than any platform ever written by the convention of any party in any country. When He condensed into one commandment those of the ten which relate to man's duty toward his fellows and enjoined upon us the rule, "Thou shalt love thy neighbor as thyself," He presented a plan for the solution of all the problems that now vex society or may hereafter arise. Other remedies may palliate or postpone the day of settlement, but this is all-sufficient and the reconciliation which it effects is a permanent one.

My faith in the future—and I have faith—and my optimism—for I am an optimist—my faith and my optimism rest upon the belief that Christ's teachings are being more studied to-day than ever before, and that with this larger study will come a larger application of those teachings to the every-day life of the world, and to the questions with which we deal. In former times when men read that Christ came "to bring life and immortality to light," they placed the emphasis upon immortality; now they are studying Christ's relation to human life. People used to read the Bible to find out what it said of Heaven; now they read it more to find what light it throws upon the pathway of to-day. In former years many thought to prepare themselves for future bliss by a life of seclusion here; we are learning that to follow in the footsteps of the Master we must go about doing good. Christ declared that He came that we might have life and have it more abundantly. The world is learning that Christ came not to narrow life, but to enlarge it—not to rob it of its joy, but to fill it to overflowing with purpose, earnestness and happiness.

But this Prince of Peace promises not only peace but strength. Some have thought His teachings fit only for the weak and the timid and unsuited to men of vigor, energy and ambition. Nothing could be farther from the truth. Only the man of faith can be courageous. Confident that he fights on the side of Jehovah, he doubts not the success of his cause. What matters it whether he shares in the shouts of triumph? If every word spoken in behalf of truth has its influence and every deed done for the right weighs in the final account, it is immaterial to the Christian whether his eyes behold victory or whether he dies in the midst of the conflict.

> "Yea, tho thou lie upon the dust,
> When they who helped thee flee in fear,
> Die full of hope and manly trust,
> Like those who fell in battle here.

Another hand thy sword shall wield,
Another hand the standard wave,
Till from the trumpet's mouth is pealed,
The blast of triumph o'er thy grave."

Only those who *believe* attempt the seemingly impossible, and, by attempting, prove that one, with God, can chase a thousand and that two can put ten thousand to flight. I can imagine that the early Christians who were carried into the coliseum to make a spectacle for those more savage than the beasts, were entreated by their doubting companions not to endanger their lives. But, kneeling in the center of the arena, they prayed and sang until they were devoured. How helpless they seemed, and, measured by every human rule, how hopeless was their cause! And yet within a few decades the power which they invoked proved mightier than the legions of the emperor and the faith in which they died was triumphant o'er all the land. It is said that those who went to mock at their sufferings returned asking themselves, "What is it that can enter into the heart of man and make him die as these die?" They were greater conquerors in their death than they could have been had they purchased life by a surrender of their faith.

What would have been the fate of the church if the early Christians had had as little faith as many of our Christians have to-day? And if the Christians of to-day had the faith of the martyrs, how long would it be before the fulfilment of the prophecy that "every knee shall bow and every tongue confess"?

I am glad that He, who is called the Prince of Peace—who can bring peace to every troubled heart and whose teachings, exemplified in life, will bring peace between man and man, between community and community, between State and State, between nation and nation throughout the world—I am glad that He brings courage as well as peace so that those who follow Him may take up and each day bravely do the duties that to that day fall.

As the Christian grows older he appreciates more and more the completeness with which Christ satisfies the longings of the heart, and, grateful for the peace which he enjoys and for the strength which he has received, he repeats the words of the great scholar, Sir William Jones:

"Before thy mystic altar, heavenly truth,
I kneel in manhood, as I knelt in youth,
Thus let me kneel, till this dull form decay,
And life's last shade be brightened by thy ray."

SOURCE: William Jennings Bryan, *The Prince of Peace* (New York: Funk & Wagnalls Company, 1914).

NOTES

ABBREVIATIONS FOR NOTES, PHOTO CAPTIONS, AND BIBLE REFERENCES

BCA	Bryan College Archives, Dayton, TN
Coletta	Paola E. Coletta, *William Jennings Bryan* <ul><li>*Vol. 1: Political Evangelist, 1860–1908* (Lincoln: University of Nebraska Press, 1964)</li><li>*Vol. 3: Political Puritan, 1915–1925* (Lincoln: University of Nebraska Press, 1969)</li></ul>
ESV	English Standard Version
Kazin	Michael Kazin, *A Godly Hero: The Life of William Jennings Bryan* (New York, NY: Random House, 2006)
KJV	King James Version
Levine	Lawrence W. Levine, *Defender of the Faith: William Jennings Bryan: The Last Decade, 1915–1925* (New York, NY: Oxford University Press, 1965)
LOC	Library of Congress Prints and Photographs Division, Washington, DC
Memoirs	William J. and Mary B. Bryan, *The Memoirs of William Jennings Bryan* (Chicago, IL: John C. Winston, 1925)
NIV	New International Version
NLT	New Living Translation
NSHS	Nebraska State Historical Society, Lincoln, NE
WC	*Web Companion* (bryan.edu/wjb) or scan QR code
WJB	William Jennings Bryan

CHAPTER 1 – TIMELINE: QUICK FACTS

See **WC** for a variety of resources related to Bryan's life.

CHAPTER 2 – BRYAN'S FAMILY

1. *Memoirs*, 31. Bryan tells the story of his mother's last Christmas as follows: "In the fall of 1895, she was stricken down with an illness that resulted fatally the following June. I shall never forget her last Christmas with us. We took the children (Ruth was about ten, William six, and Grace four) with us to spend the holidays at Salem. Four of her five children were there and five grandchildren also. Mother sat up in bed and distributed the presents. I never saw her happier; her cheerfulness enlivened our Christmas reunion and is a cherished recollection."

2. See **WC** for more about Bryan's parents and siblings.

3. See **WC** for stories of the Bryans' devotion to one another throughout their marriage.

4. *Memoirs*, 282. "The Wedding at Fairview," *The Nebraska State Journal* (Lincoln, NE), 8 June 1911: 2.

5. See **WC** for more information about Ruth's colorful life.

6. "Financial Coup in Art World," *The Times* (San Mateo, CA), 18 January 1975: 41. "Quick Takes: Mel Gibson sells Maxfield Parrish's 'Daybreak' at a Loss," *Los Angeles Times*, 21 May 2010: articles.latimes.com/2010/may/21/entertainment/la-et-quick-20100521. See **WC** for more about Kitty's work with Parrish.

7. John Baird was John Baird Bryan's great grandfather, Mary Bryan's father, who died on May 3, 1905. His namesake was born later that same year on November 16, 1905. John's stage work (1930–1932) included Lorenzo in *The Merchant of Venice* in Chicago and Hemings in *The Passionate Pilgrim* in New York City. The

1935–1936 Hollywood films in which John played minor roles are *A Tale of Two Cities, Camille, The Garden of Allah*, and *Romeo and Juliet*. See **WC** for more information.

8. Rudd Brown, *Ruth Bryan Owen: An Intimate Portrait* (Kindle Edition Paul A. Myers Books, 2014), 196.

9. "Ike Off for 'Real' Vacation," *The Ogden (UT) Standard-Examiner*, 15 September 1954: 1.

10. See **WC** for more information about Rudd Brown.

11. See **WC** for more about William, Jr., and his children.

12. See **WC** for more about Grace and her family.

13. "Little Bryan Leavitt Hides; Gives Grandpa Bryan a Scare," *Montgomery Advertiser*, 22 April 1908: 5.

14. "Bryan Asks for Roosevelt Votes," *The Lincoln (NE) Daily Star*, 27 August 1908: 3.

15. "Latest News," *The Times (Munster, IN)*, 6 October 1913: 1.

16. "Bryan Catches Eleven Fish and Explains What He Means by Words 'Unnecessary Risk,'" *The Billings (MT) Gazette*, 13 July 1915: 1. See **WC** for Bryan's sporting photos.

17. "Bryan and Grandson Hunt," *The New York Times* (23 November 1913): 1.

18. "Bryan Made Pop Call," *Fort Scott Daily Tribune and Fort Scott (KS) Daily Monitor*, 17 August 1920: 1.

19. "Mr. and Mrs. Bryan Keep Wedding Date," *Lincoln (NE) Journal Star*, 6 October 1923: 6. See **WC** for poem.

CHAPTER 3 – PREPARATION

1. WJB, *The First Battle: A Story of the Campaign of 1896* (Chicago, IL: W. B. Conkey, 1896), 45.

2. George R. Poage, "College Career of William Jennings Bryan," *The Mississippi Valley Historical Review*, 15:2 (September 1928): 171, 175. jstor.org/stable/1895643. See **WC** for more on Bryan's education.

3. Lynn McKeown, "Galesburg's Oratory Contest of 1880: When the Great Addams and Bryan Lost to Jimmie Who?" *The Zephyr*, 19 September 2001: thezephyr.com/addamsbryan.htm.

4. Sally Vickers, "Ruth Bryan Owen: Florida's First Congresswoman and Lifetime Activist," *The Florida Historical Quarterly*, 77:4 (Spring 1999): 449–450. jstor.org/stable/30150828.

5. *Memoirs*, 44.

6. Ibid., 27–28, 33.

7. See **WC** for more on Mary Baird Bryan.

8. Kazin, 14.

9. "Ruth Bryan Owen," History, Art & Archives, United States House of Representatives: history.house.gov/People/Detail/19256.

10. Vickers, 446.

CHAPTER 4 – CHRISTIAN STATESMAN

1. These words (or some variation thereof) represent Bryan's common response to those who expressed their sorrow that he had not been rewarded with the presidency after all he had done. For more on Bryan's "unshakable faith that although Wall Street might keep him out of the White House it could not keep him out of history," see Levine, 220–222.

2. William Jennings Bryan, letter to Mr. I. J. Dunn, Chairman of Banquet Committee, Jackson Club, Omaha, Nebraska, 4 January 1895, 2. See **WC** for PDF of original letter.

3. "Bryan, Radical in Politics, Standpat in Religion, Tells Why," *Chicago Daily Tribune*, 28 May 1925: 5.

4. The four constitutional amendments:

   - 16th Amendment: See **WC** for more about how Bryan's support began in Congress in 1894; continued with his influence to include an income tax plank in the 1896, 1900, and 1908 Democratic Party platforms; and culminated in his presence at the White House on October 3, 1913, when President Wilson signed the law that imposed the federal income tax.

   - 17th Amendment: See accompanying photo in Chapter 4 of Bryan signing the proclamation with Mrs. Bryan at his side.

   - 18th and 19th Amendments: See "Political Crusades" on page 82.

5. See **WC** for more on public policy.

6. See **WC** for more on 1902 coal strike.

7. Robert W. Cherny, "William Jennings Bryan and the Historians," *Nebraska History*, 77 (Fall/Winter 1996): 184. See **WC** for link to article.

8. "William Jennings Bryan," Nebraska Studies, nebraskastudies.org/1875-1899/roots-of-progressivism/william-jennings-bryan.

9. Robert W. Cherny, *A Righteous Cause: The Life of William Jennings Bryan* (University of Oklahoma Press, 1985), 201.

10. Laura A. Ackley, *San Francisco's Jewel City: The Panama-Pacific International Exposition of 1915* (Berkeley, CA: Heyday, 2015), 199. Photo credit: 13833-NEG, Edward A. Rogers collection of Cardinell-Vincent Company and Panama-Pacific International Exposition photographs, BANC PIC 2015.013, The Bancroft Library, University of California, Berkeley. See **WC** for uncropped version of photo that shows Bryan's massive audience.

11. The two epigrams on the plowshare photo are from *A Message from Bethlehem* (1914). See **WC** for more about Bryan's leadership on the world stage.

CHAPTER 5 – PRESIDENTIAL CAMPAIGNS

1. Merle Miller, *Plain Speaking: An Oral Biography of Harry S. Truman* (New York, NY: Berkley Publishing Corp., 1974), 80–81.

2. See **WC** for more about the 1896 campaign.

3. Coletta, Vol. 1: 152.

4. *The First Battle*, 529.

5. Jeff Menne, Christian B. Long, eds., *Film and the American Presidency* (New York, NY: Routledge, 2015), 29.

6. Kazin, 82.

7. Glen McGregor, "Putting Your Data on the Map: There's a Way to Use Geographic Information Systems to Find and See Stories Lost in Data," *Media* (Spring 2011): 21.

8. Richard M. Cornelius, *Selected Orations of William Jennings Bryan* (Dayton, TN: Bryan College, 2000), 11.

9. See **WC** for more about the 1900 campaign.

10. See **WC** for more about the 1908 campaign.

11. Michael Kazin, "Past and Present: William Jennings Obama? Once Again, Democrats Meet in Denver to Nominate a Skilled Orator," *U.S. News & World Report*, 28 August 2008: usnews.com/opinion/articles/2008/08/28/past-and-present-william-jennings-obama-once-again-democrats-meet-in-denver-to-nominate-a-skilled-orator.

12. See **WC** for more on Bryan's recordings.

13. Election results retrieved from the following:

    - 1896: en.wikipedia.org/wiki/1896_United_States_presidential_election
    - 1900: en.wikipedia.org/wiki/1900_United_States_presidential_election
    - 1908: en.wikipedia.org/wiki/1908_United_States_presidential_election

14. The turnout—nearly four out of five eligible voters—was not the highest in U.S. history (81.8 percent in 1876 was); however, turnout has not been surpassed since. The significance of the issues in the 1896 election is further evidenced by voter turnout exceeding 95 percent in Iowa, Illinois, Indiana, Ohio, and Michigan.

15. Jeff Taylor, "Of Money and Mouths," *Front Porch Republic*, 10 May 2010: frontporchrepublic.com/2010/05/of-money-and-mouths. See also Coletta, Vol. 1: 197–207, for similar estimates of both candidates' 1896 war chests and also for support of the premise that Bryan was defeated by Republican campaign manager Mark Hanna rather than by McKinley. Because of his centralized organization of resources and fundraising success, Hanna is often credited with creating the modern presidential campaign.

16. McKinley won California and Kentucky; however, one elector from each state cast a vote for Bryan.

17. Bryan won Maryland; however, two electors cast votes for Taft.

CHAPTER 6 – BETWEEN PRESIDENTIAL CAMPAIGNS

1. See **WC** for more 1896–1900 information, including explanation of some of the major themes of his political speeches: bimetallism, the encroachment of the trusts and money power on the rights of the people, and the evils of protective tariffs.

2. Edward H. Worthen, "The Mexican Journeys of William Jennings Bryan, A Good Neighbor," *Nebraska History,* 59 (1978): 486. See **WC** for more on Bryan and Mexico and about the three visits he and Mrs. Bryan made to Mexico in 1897, 1904, and 1922.

3. Outcome: The Supreme Court voided a Nebraska railroad tariff law, declaring that it violated the Fourteenth Amendment to the United States Constitution in that it takes property without the due process of law.

4. See **WC** for video, photos, and more information about the Expo.

5. See **WC** for more 1900–1908 information.

6. RMS *Majestic* was the largest ship in the world until the completion of the SS *Normandie* in 1935.

7. See **WC** for text of two speeches Bryan delivered in London in July 1906—at the Conference of the Interparliamentary Union and at the American Society.

8. "The Home-coming of Mr. Bryan," *The Commoner,* 7 September 1906: 4, 7. Article based on extracts from Associated Press reports. See **WC** for speech text.

CHAPTER 7 – CRITICS AND DETRACTORS

1. See **WC** for more examples of WJB editorial cartoons.

2. "Sidelights on Bryan's Career," *Chicago Daily Tribune,* 27 July 1925: 3.

3. Kazin, 71.

4. Walter Lippmann, *Drift and Mastery: An Attempt to Diagnose the Current Unrest* (New York, NY: Mitchell Kennerley, 1914), 130.

5. Walter Lippmann, *A Preface to Politics* (New York, NY: Macmillan, 1933), 100–101.

6. See **WC** for more on Mencken.

7. H. L. Mencken, *My Life as Author and Editor,* ed. Jonathan Yardley (New York, NY: Alfred A. Knopf, 1993), 34.

8. Terry Teachout, *Skeptic: A Life of H. L. Mencken* (New York, NY: HarperCollins Publishers, Inc., 2002), 217.

9. H. L. Mencken, "The Monkey Trial: A Reporter's Account," *Famous Trials:* famous-trials.com/scopesmonkey/2132-menckenaccount. "Bryan," *The Baltimore Evening Sun,* 27 July 1925: faculty.etsu.edu/history/documents/menckenbryan.htm.

10. Marion Elizabeth Rodgers, *Mencken: The American Iconoclast* (Oxford University Press, 2005), 292.

11. Cherny, "WJB and the Historians," 184–193.

12. James S. Barcus, *The Boomerang or Bryan's Speech with the Wind Knocked Out* (New York, NY: J. S. Barcus & Co., 1896). See **WC** for link to title.

13. H. E. Bartholomew, *Bryan (The Boy Orator of the Platte) Unveiled* (Chicago, IL: The Bartholomew Publishing Co., 1908), 70. See **WC** for link to title.

14. Richard Hofstadter, *The American Political Tradition and the Men Who Made It* (New York, NY: Alfred Knopf, 1948), 370.

15. Richard Challener, "William Jennings Bryan," in *An Uncertain Tradition: American Secretaries of State in the Twentieth Century,* ed. Norman A. Braebner (New York, NY: McGraw-Hill, 1961), 80, 99.

16. Kazin, xiv.

17. More on Bryan's response to his critics: "While the discussion of religious themes has brought down upon me the criticism of some agnostics and infidels, it has brought me into closer contact with the churchgoing element." (*Memoirs,* 452)

18. Kazin, 71.

19. Ibid.

20. Lincoln Steffens, "Why the Newspapers Misrepresent Bryan," *The Lyceum Magazine* (December 1913), 22. (See **WC** for link to article.)

21. *Memoirs,* 289.

CHAPTER 8 – ORATOR

1. See **WC** for more on chapter's opening quotation.

2. *Memoirs,* 248–249.

3. See **WC** for more on the "Cross of Gold" speech.

4. Scott Farris, *Almost President: The Men Who Lost the Race but Changed the Nation* (Lanham, MD: Lyons Press, 2011), 82.

5. Coletta, Vol. 1: 147. One only has to Google "Cross of Gold" to see it continues to be remembered in a similar way as described by Coletta in 1964. For example, Robert Bradley, "2016: Populism revisited and the Cross of Gold Speech," *NewBostonPost,* 7 September 2016: newbostonpost.com/2016/09/07/2016-populism-revisited-and-the-cross-of-gold-speech.

6. See **WC** for more on Milton's "The Story of the Last Message."

7. Bryan's home was located near the Platte River in Nebraska. See **WC** for more nicknames.

8. Kazin, 24–25. See **WC** for more on Bryan's power as a speaker.

9. "William Jennings Bryan," *Washington Post*, 27 July 1925: 4.

10. See **WC** for recordings of Bryan speeches and a video about his oratorical style.

11. Kazin, 71.

12. Brian K. Johnson & Marsha Hunter, *The Articulate Attorney: Public Speaking for Lawyers* (Phoenix, AZ: Crown King Books, 2010), 103.

13. Kazin, 48.

14. Victoria Case and Robert Ormond Case, *We Called It Culture: The Story of Chautauqua* (New York, NY: Doubleday and Company, 1948), 88–89.

15. Donald K. Springen, *William Jennings Bryan: Orator of Small-Town America* (New York, NY: Greenwood Press, 1991), 13–14. Also see *Memoirs*, 301, 455.

16. Kazin, xiv.

17. Ibid., 49.

18. Coletta, Vol. 1: 83.

19. *The First Battle,* 458.

20. *Memoirs*, 281.

21. WJB, "Bryan's Most Famous Lecture, 'The Prince of Peace,'" *The New York Times*, Magazine Section, 7 September 1913: 10. See **WC** for more on Bryan's heart. The wording in the *Times* is a variation of that in the 1914 book (see Appendix B).

22. *Memoirs*, 9.

23. Ibid., 451.

24. Ibid., 287–288.

25. See **WC** for videos, photos, and more on Chautauqua.

26. Jeff DeGraff, "Before There Were TED Talks, There Were Chautauquas," *Inc.,* 20 July 2015: inc.com/jeff-degraff/start-an-innovation-chautauqua.html.

27. Charlotte Canning, "What Was Chautauqua?" *Traveling Culture: Circuit Chautauqua in the Twentieth Century*, The University of Iowa Libraries, December 2000: lib.uiowa.edu/sc/tc.

28. See **WC** for photos and information about Bryan's four visits to the Bay View Association, Petoskey, MI, a Chautauqua that continues to this day.

29. Case & Case, 78.

30. Ibid., 84–85.

31. Charles F. Horner, *Strike the Tents: The Story of the Chautauqua* (Philadelphia, PA: Dorrance & Company, 1954), 127: archive.org/details/strikethetentsth008243mbp.

32. Phyllis H. Winkelman, "Fairview: Home of William Jennings Bryan," *Nebraska History,* 55 (1974): 151–152.

33. C. Allyn Russell, "William Jennings Bryan: Statesman—Fundamentalist," *Journal of Presbyterian History,* 53:2 (1975): 106–107. jstor.org/stable/23327570.

34. "Famous as Lecturer and Leader in Lines of Religious Work," *Chicago Tribune*, 27 July 1925: 4.

35. Levine, 272.

36. *Memoirs,* 452–453.

37. Kazin, 272.

38. See **WC** for more on Bryan and radio.

39. See **WC** for photo.

40. See **WC** for more on Lincoln statue dedication.

41. See **WC** for more on Grove Park Inn.

42. *Memoirs*, 474. See **WC** for more on college addresses.

43. See **WC** for more on mock convention.

44. See **WC** for link to speech text and to learn more about Bryan's impact on Japanese rhetorical theory and practice.

CHAPTER 9 – THE COMMONER

1. WJB, *In His Image* (New York, NY: Fleming H. Revell, 1922), 259–265.

2. Coletta, Vol. 1: 292.

3. See **WC** for more about Orlando Jay Smith's role in the paper's founding.

4. WJB, "A Visit to the East," *The Commoner*, 31 January 1902: 3.

5. *The Commoner* is available online as follows:

    - chroniclingamerica.loc.gov/lccn/46032385/issues
    - nebnewspapers.unl.edu/lccn/46032385

6. WJB, "The Commoner," *The Commoner*, 23 January 1901: 1.

7. Circulation reported by *Rowell's American Newspaper Directory*, as cited in Edward Caudill, *Intelligently Designed: How Creationists Built the Campaign against Evolution* (Chicago: University of Illinois Press, 2013), 21.

8. Coletta, Vol. 3: 158–159.

CHAPTER 10 – BOOKS AND SPEECHES BY BRYAN

1. Richard Hall Williams, *Realigning America: McKinley, Bryan, and the Remarkable Election of 1896* (Lawrence, KS: University Press of Kansas, 2010), 161.

2. *Memoirs,* 451.

3. Ibid., 474.

4. *In His Image,* 8.

5. Ibid., 136.

CHAPTER 11 – MEMORABLE QUOTATIONS

See **WC** for eBook links to the speeches and books from which the quotations are taken.

1. WJB, "Character" (1881), in *The Life and Speeches of Hon. Wm. Jennings Bryan* (Baltimore, MD: R. H. Woodward Company, 1900), 28–29. Graduation speech given June 1881 at Illinois College.

2. Ibid., 30.

3. *In His Image*, 186.

4. WJB, *Man* (New York, NY: Funk & Wagnalls Company, 1914), 22.

5. *In His Image*, 86.

6. Ibid., 26.

7. Ibid., 25.

8. Ibid., 59.

9. Ibid., 47, 53.

10. WJB, "Cross of Gold" (1896) in *Life and Speeches,* 252. Speech given at the Democratic National Convention in Chicago on July 9, 1896.

11. *The First Battle*, 344.

12. *In His Image,* 203.

13. WJB, *The Price of a Soul* (New York, NY: Funk & Wagnalls Company, 1914), 38.

14. WJB, "Oratory" (1877). This essay, written by a teenage Bryan, was found in his mother's papers (Kazin, 3, 309).

15. Albert Liscomb Gale and George Washington Kline, *Bryan the Man: The Great Commoner at Close Range* (St. Louis, MO: The Thompson Publishing Co., 1908), 136.

16. *In His Image*, 250.

17. WJB and Francis W. Halsey, eds., *The World's Famous Orations, Vol. 1* (New York, NY: Funk and Wagnalls Company, 1906), x.

18. WJB, *Orthodox Christianity versus Modernism* (New York, NY: Fleming H. Revell Company, 1923), 31–32.

19. *The World's Most Famous Court Trial: Tennessee Evolution Case, 3rd ed.* (Cincinnati, OH: National Book Company, 175).

20. *In His Image*, 127.

21. Levine, 339. From a speech to the Progressive Club of Dayton, TN, 1925.

22. WJB, "Memorial Day Address (1894), in *Life and Speeches*, 53.

23. WJB, *The Prince of Peace* (New York, NY: Funk and Wagnalls, 1913), 52.

24. WJB, "At the Peace Congress" (1906), in *Speeches of William Jennings Bryan, Vol. 1* (New York, NY: Funk & Wagnalls Company, 1909), 228. Speech given in London on July 26, 1906.

25. *The Price of a Soul*, 64.

26. *In His Image*, 205.

27. Ibid., 139.

28. WJB, "Graduating Oration—Subject: Character" (1881), in *Life and Speeches*, 30. Graduation speech given June 1881 at Illinois College.

29. *In His Image*, 235.

30. *The Menace of Darwinism,* 15.

CHAPTER 12 – INFLUENCER

1. The **WC** provides additional examples of Bryan's influence.

2. Agnes Hooper Gottlieb, Henry Gottlieb, Barbara Bowers & Brent Bowers, *1,000 Years, 1,000 People: Ranking the Men and Women Who Shaped the Millennium* (New York, NY: Kodansha International, 1998), ix, 274.

3. Ross Douthat, "They Made America," *The Atlantic* (December 2006), 60, 64.

4. Scott Farris, *Almost President: The Men Who Lost the Race but Changed the Nation* (Guilford, CT: Lyons Press, 2011), 85.

5. *Memoirs, 297–298.*

6. Farris, 86.

7. Kazin, 245.

8. See **WC** for letter from Neff to Bryan, related correspondence, and seven duck hunting photos.

9. *Memoirs, 453, 456.*

10. Ibid., 491. See **WC** for text of Dr. Joseph Sizoo's address.

11. "Warm Praise of Bryan," *Nebraska State Journal*, 5 December 1925: 1.

12. "Sorrow in the American Home," *The Chicago Daily Tribune*, 27 July 1925: 5. From Chicago Tribune, © 1925. All rights reserved. Used by permission and protected by the Copyright Laws of the United States. The printing, copying redistribution, or retransmission of this Content without express written permission is prohibited.

CHAPTER 13 – CALLINGS AND CRUSADES (1915–1925)

1. "Mr. Bryan on Leaving Washington," *The Commoner*, November 1915: 7. See **WC**.

2. Coletta, Vol. 3: 2.

3. "Applied Christianity," *The Commoner*, May 1919: 11–12. See **WC**.

4. WJB, *The Bible and Its Enemies: An Address Delivered at the Moody Bible Institute of Chicago* (Chicago, IL: The Bible Institute Colportage Association, 1921), 6. See **WC**.

5. "Three Coming Issues," *The Commoner*, December 1915: 5. See **WC**.

6. "Bryan's Speech, Madison Square Garden, NYC, June 24 1915," in *New American Government and Politics: A History, Vol. III,* ed. Arthur Raymond McCook (New History Publisher, 1916), 181.

7. "Bryan's Speech, Madison Square Garden, February 2, 1917," in *Not in Our Name: American Antiwar Speeches, 1846 to the Present,* ed. Jesse Stellato (University Park, PA: Penn State Press, 2012), 84.

8. WJB, "Mr. Bryan's Tender to President Wilson" and "At War," *The Commoner,* April 1917: 3.

9. WJB, "Constitutional Rights," *The Commoner,* October 1917: 1. See **WC**.

10. Kazin, 260.

11. Russell, "WJB: Statesman-Fundamentalist," 97. See **WC** for links to sources that outline Bryan's point-counterpoint approach to presenting his case for prohibition.

12. He wrote in April 1922 that Prohibition Commissioner Haynes reported that since the 18th amendment went into effect, 12 million people had stopped drinking, that $2 billion formerly spent for intoxicants was now available for better uses, and arrests for drunkenness had decreased by 66% ("WJB to Earl Reeves, April 5, 1922, Bryan Papers," in Levine, 208). WJB, "Enforcement of Prohibition," *The Commoner,* April 1922: 1. Charles W. Eliot, "Dr. Eliot for Prohibition," *The Commoner,* February 1922: 12. See **WC** for more examples.

13. Samuel Proctor, "William Jennings Bryan and the University of Florida," *The Florida Historical Quarterly,* Vol. 39., Issue 1 (July 1960): 8–9.

14. "Bryan Extols President," *The New York Times,* 16 June 1916: 1. The following headers were in the *NYT* article: "Draws Volleys of Cheers from Throng by Praise of Wilson; Buries All Differences; Credits Administration with More Popular Laws than Any in Nation's History [tariff revision, the Federal Reserve law, and the strengthening of the anti-trust laws]; Makes Appeal for Peace; Wants the President to Have the Honor of Bringing End to the Conflict."

15. Kazin, 251. See **WC** for speech text.

16. Coletta, Vol. 3: 191–192.

17. Levine, 79–81.

18. Ibid., 81.

19. Levine, 241–242, 307, 323.

20. Ibid., 237.

21. Ibid., 272. See **WC** for more about Miami Sunday school class.

22. Kazin, 265–266.

23. Photo source: floridamemory.com/items/show/28552. See **WC** for more photos.

24. Arva Moore Parks, *George Merrick, Son of the South Wind: Visionary Creator of Coral Gables* (Gainesville, FL: University Press of Florida, 2015), 203, 210, 212, 223. See **WC**.

25. See **WC** for information about Coral Gables' 11 historic landmarks.

26. Levine, 238.

27. Sources vary as to when Bryan joined the law firm. For example, Coletta, 3:147–148 indicates 1919. Others say 1921, such as *Law Notes* (Long Island, NY: Edward Thompson Company), April 1921: 76, as well as "Bryan to Join Law Firm in Washington; Expected to Prosecute Claims in Mexico," *The New York Times,* 26 May 1921: 1.

28. Leslie Rivera, "Cornerstones of Faith: First Presbyterian Church of Miami . . . Before There was a City": brickellhomeowners.com/cornerstones-faith-presbyterian-church-miami-before-city.

29. W. W. Rodgers, "Broadcasting Church Services," *Radio Broadcast* (May 1922), 1:325. Photo from historicpittsburgh.org/islandora/object/pitt:20170320-hpichswp-0048.

30. Edith Waldvogel Blumhofer, *Aimee Semple McPherson: Everybody's Sister* (Grand Rapids, MI: Wm. B. Eerdmans, 1993), 223–224, 263.

31. Michael Pasquier, *Religion in America: The Basics* (New York, NY: Routledge, 2017), 127.

32. WJB, *The Value of an Ideal* (New York, NY: Funk and Wagnalls, 1914), 23, 30–31.

33. Levine, 272, 276. In a speech before the Presbyterian General Assembly, Bryan suggested that the churches ought to take the lead "in arousing public sentiment against the crime of the profiteer," declaring that "we should drive all the profiteers out of the Presbyterian Church so that when they go to the penitentiary, they will not go as Presbyterians." *The Commoner,* September 1920: 8.

34. WJB, *Orthodox Christianity,* 26.

CHAPTER 14 – ON THE ORIGIN OF MAN

1. Levine, 274. Further, it can be argued that "Bryan joined the anti-evolutionists not in order to retreat from politics but in order to combat a force which he held responsible for sapping American politics of its idealism and progressive spirit" (Levine, 270). See **WC** for more on cartoons and evolution.

2. Ibid., 287–288.

3. Allison Flood, "On the Origin of Species Voted Most Influential Academic Book in History," *The Guardian,* 10 November 2015: theguardian.com/books/2015/nov/10/on-the-origin-of-species-voted-most-influ-ential-academic-book-charles-darwin. The survey was conducted by a group of academic booksellers, publishers, and librarians as part of Academic Book Week in the United Kingdom. Tia Ghose, "Darwin's 'Origin of Species' Voted Most Influential Academic Book," *Live Science,* 11 November 2015: livescience.com/52756-darwins-book-most-influential.html.

4. See **WC** for more information about Darwin's books.

5. WJB, "Efforts to Discredit Bible Story of Origin of Species Have Failed, William Jennings Bryan Declares," *The Brooklyn (NY) Daily Eagle,* 17 June 1922: 9. newspapers.com/image/60022514.

6. WJB, *Orthodox Christianity,* 24–25.

7. V. B. Smocovitis, "Unifying Biology: The Evolutionary Synthesis and Evolutionary Biology," *Journal of the History of Biology,* 25:1 (Spring 1992): 1–65. jstor.org/stable/4331201.

8. Book: icr.org/genesis-flood-50th. CRS: creationresearch.org/history-and-aims. The creationist movement of the 1960s drew many ideas from one of Bryan's contemporaries: prolific Seventh-day Adventist author George McCready Price. See Kurt P. Wise, "Contributions to Creationism by George McCready Price" in J. H. Whitmore, ed., *Proceedings of the Eighth International Conference on Creationism* (Pittsburgh, PA: Creation Science Fellowship, 2018), 683–694.

9. The terms were first used in the English-speaking world with the publication of Theodosius Dobzhansky, *Genetics and the Origin of Species* (New York, NY: Columbia University Press, 1937).

10. David Menton, "Is Evolution a Theory, a Fact, or a Law?—or None of the Above?" (8 July 2017): answersin-genesis.org/theory-of-evolution/evolution-theory-fact-or-law. Steven M. Stanley, *Macroevolution: Pattern and Process* (Baltimore, MD: The Johns Hopkins University Press, 1998). See also Todd Charles Wood and Paul A. Garner, eds., *Center for Origins Research Issues in Creation: Genesis Kinds: Creationism and the Origin of Species* (Eugene, OR: Wipf and Stock Publishers, 2009). Todd Charles Wood, *Center for Origins Research Issues in Creation: Animal and Plant Baramins* (Eugene, OR: Wipf and Stock Publishers, 2008).

11. See Chapter 10, "The Social Implications of Darwinism" in Peter J. Bowler, *Evolution: The History of an Idea* (Los Angeles, CA: University of California Press, 1984), 266ff. *Social Darwinism* is a "theory arising in the late nineteenth century that the laws of evolution, which Charles Darwin had observed in nature, also apply to society. Social Darwinists argued that social progress resulted from conflicts in which the fittest or best adapted individuals, or entire societies, would prevail" (Dictionary.com).

12. Stephen Lloyd, "Christian Theology and Neo-Darwinism Are Incompatible: An Argument from the Resurrection" in Graeme Finlay, et al., *Debating Darwin: Two Debates: Is Darwinism True and Does It Matter?* (Colorado Springs, CO: Paternoster, 2009), 15–25. Stephen J. Gould, "Darwin and Paley Meet the Invisible Hand," *Natural History* (November 1990), 8–16. See **WC** for more information on theistic evolution.

13. WJB, "Evolution as Applied to Man," *The Commoner,* March 1922: 2. This piece originally appeared in a letter to the editor of *The New York Times* and was reprinted in *The Commoner.*

14. Ronald L. Numbers, *The Creationists: From Scientific Creationism to Intelligent Design* (Cambridge, MA: Harvard University Press, 2006), 116. See **WC** for more about George McCready Price.

15. GeoChristian, "William Jennings Bryan and the Age of the Earth," 21 September 2009: geochristian.com/2009/09/21/william-jennings-bryan-and-the-age-of-the-earth.

16. WJB, "Mr. Bryan's Rejoinder," *The Forum* (August 1923), 1852. play.google.com/books/reader?id=Lx-4PAAAAMAAJ&hl=en&pg=GBS.PA1852.

17. *Prince of Peace,* 14–20.

18. Levine, 233.

19. *Memoirs,* 457–460.

20. *Memoirs,* 457. Mary also quoted from Bryan's Preface to Volume VIII of *The Writings of Thomas Jefferson*: "He rather lacks reverence who believes that religion is unable to defend herself in contest with error. He places a low estimate upon the strength of religion, who thinks that the wisdom of God must be supplement-ed by the force of man's puny arm." See **WC** for Bryan's full preface.

21. WJB, "The Menace of Darwinism," *The Commoner,* April 1921: 5–6.

22. WJB, *Seven Questions in Dispute* (New York, NY: Fleming H. Revell Company, 1924), 119–121.

23. *Menace of Darwinism,* 56.

24. *Memoirs,* 458–460.

25. Kazin, 264–265.

26. *Memoirs,* 459, 479.

27. Levine, 267–268, as quoted from various newspapers, books, and Bryan papers. See **WC** for more examples.

28. James H. Leuba, *The Belief in God and Immortality, a Psychological, Anthropological and Statistical Study* (Boston, MA: Sherman, French & Company, 1916), 280: moses.law.umn.edu/darrow/documents/Leuba_Belief_in_God_Complete.pdf

29. Ferenc M. Szasz, "William Jennings Bryan, Evolution, and the Fundamentalist–Modernist Controversy," *Nebraska History,* 56 (1975): 261. history.nebraska.gov/sites/history.nebraska.gov/files/doc/publications/NH1975WJBModernist.pdf. See Canon Dyson Hague, "The History of the Higher Criticism" (1910), in *The Fundamentals,* ed. R. A. Torrey: blueletterbible.org/Comm/torrey_ra/fundamentals/01.cfm. See **WC** for another resource on higher criticism.

30. Edward John Larson, *Trial and Error: The American Controversy over Creation and Evolution* (New York, NY: Oxford University Press, Inc., 1989), 41.

31. Ibid., 44–45.

32. *The Bible and Its Enemies,* 15–16. See **WC** for link to eBook.

33. *Eugenics* is "the study of or belief in the possibility of improving the qualities of the human species or a human population, especially by such means as discouraging reproduction by persons having genetic defects or presumed to have inheritable undesirable traits (negative eugenics) or encouraging reproduction by persons presumed to have inheritable desirable traits (positive eugenics)" (Dictionary.com).

34. LeRoy Ashby, *William Jennings Bryan: Champion of Democracy* (Boston, MA: Twayne Publishers, 1987), 183.

35. See **WC** for link to Kidd's book.

36. Stephen Jay Gould, "William Jennings Bryan's Last Campaign," *Nebraska History* 77 (1996), 180. history.nebraska.gov/sites/history.nebraska.gov/files/doc/publications/NH1996Bryan_Last_Campn.pdf.

37. WJB, *The Last Message of William Jennings Bryan* (New York, NY: Fleming H. Revell, 1925), 63.

38. Gould, 181. See **WC** for more about Kellogg's book.

39. Danae M. McGregor, "German and American Eugenics in the pre-World War I Era," *Answers Research Journal,* 6 (2013): 72–73. assets.answersingenesis.org/doc/articles/pdf-versions/arj/v6/german-american-eugenics.pdf

40. Ibid., 73–74.

41. Charles Darwin, *The Descent of Man, and Selection in Relation to Sex* (London: John Murray, Albemarle Street, 1874): 133–134.

42. WJB, *Last Message,* 57–59.

43. *Memoirs,* 479–480.

44. James Gilbert, *Redeeming Culture: American Religion in an Age of Science* (Chicago, IL: University of Chicago Press, 1997), 23. See "H. L. Mencken" on page 45.

45. Louis William Koenig, *Bryan: A Political Biography of William Jennings Bryan* (New York, NY: Putnam, 1971), 613–614.

46. WJB, "Brother or Brute?" *The Commoner,* November 1920: 11. See **WC** for text of speech.

47. The article appears on pp. 5–8: nebnewspapers.unl.edu/lccn/46032385/1921-04-01/ed-1/seq-5.

48. *The Menace of Darwinism,* 15. See **WC** for link to eBook.

49. Larson, *Trial and Error,* 45.

50. Coletta, Vol. 3: 228.

51. Ferenc Morton Szasz, *The Divided Mind of Protestant America, 1880–1930* (Tuscaloosa, AL: University of Alabama Press, 1982), 110–111.

52. See **WC** for April 7, 1925, article about Bryan's visit in *The Harvard Crimson* (college newspaper).

53. Levine, 285–286.

54. "Quotations: William Jennings Bryan on Evolution," *Science*, New Series, 55:1418 (3 March 1922), 242–243. jstor.org/stable/1644502. Published by American Association for the Advancement of Science, a general scientific society founded in 1848.

55. T. V. Smith, "Bases of Bryanism" (13 May 1923), 505. jstor.org/stable/6874. *The Scientific Monthly* merged with *Science* in 1958.

56. WJB, *Last Message*, 20, 66–67.

57. "Report by Herbert W. Rand," *Science* (6 February 1925), 149. jstor.org/stable/1649778.

58. Levine, 281.

59. Unlike the other cartoons in *Seven Questions*, this one had not previously been published. It was based on a letter, archived by the Library of Congress, that Bryan wrote to the editor of the *Sunday School Times* magazine in January 1924. See Edward B. Davis, "Fundamentalist Cartoons, Modernist Pamphlets, and the Religious Image of Science in the Scopes Era," in *Religion and the Culture of Print in Modern America,* ed.s Charles L. Cohen and Paul S. Boyer (Madison, WI: University of Wisconsin Press, 2008), 179–180.

60. *In His Image*, 90.

61. *Seven Questions in Dispute,* 106.

62. WJB, "The Fundamentals," *The Forum* (July 1923), 1678.

63. *Science*, New Series, 242.

64. Szasz, "WJB, Evolution, and the Fundamentalist–Modernist Controversy," 259–260.

65. Coletta, Vol. 3: 222–224. Bryan's main competition for the post was Charles F. Wishart, president of College of Wooster in Ohio, who had endorsed the teaching of evolution at Wooster. Bryan won on the first three ballots; however, on the fourth ballot after the other contenders withdrew and their votes went to Wishart, Bryan lost. L. Gordon Tait, "Evolution: Wishart, Wooster, and William Jennings Bryan," *Journal of Presbyterian History,* 62:4 (Winter 1984), 306–321.

66. Levine, 285.

67. *Orthodox Christianity*, 7–20.

68. Ibid., 21.

69. Ibid., 5.

70. Coletta, Vol. 3: 228.

71. WJB, "God and Evolution," *The New York Times*, 26 February 1922, 7:1. See **WC** for copy of article.

72. *The New York Times*, 5 March 1922, 7:2.

73. Ibid., 7:14.

74. Ibid., 12 March 1922, 7:2.

75. Ibid., 19 March 1922, 8:2.

76. WJB, *Last Message*, 9–10.

77. Herbert Wallace Schneider, *Religion in 20th Century America* (Cambridge, MA: Harvard University Press, 1967), 107–108.

CHAPTER 15 – THE SCOPES TRIAL

1. See **WC** for supplemental resources referred to in the introduction.

2. Cornelius, *Selected Orations*, 87.

3. Edward J. Larson, *Summer for the Gods: The Scopes Trial and America's Continuing Debate Over Science and Religion* (New York, NY: Basic Books, 1997), 142.

4. John Scopes, "Reflections—Forty Years After" (1965). Famous Trials. famous-trials.com/scopesmonkey/2139-reflections.

5. Larson, *Summer for the Gods*, 244

6. Randy Moore, *Evolution in the Courtroom: A Reference Guide* (Santa Barbara, CA: ABC-CLIO, Inc., 2002), 38.

7. "Decision on Scopes' Appeal to the Supreme Court of Tennessee." Famous Trials. famous-trials.com/scopesmonkey/2087-appealdecision.

8. See **WC** for copy of "Is the Bible True?"

9. Russell, "William Jennings Bryan: Statesman-Fundamentalist," 110.

10. Larson, *Summer for the Gods,* 83.

11. See **WC** for "Why Dayton of All Places?"

12. Ibid., 95–96.

13. Ibid., 139.

14. Coletta, Vol. 3: 284.

15. Edward Caudill, *Intelligently Designed: How Creationists Built the Campaign Against Evolution* (Chicago, IL: University of Illinois Press, 2013), 50.

16. WJB, "Letter to William Jennings Bryan, Jr.," from Occidental College Bryan Manuscripts, as quoted in Szasz, *The Divided Mind of Protestant America,* 124.

17. "Dudley Field Malone (1882–1950)." United States Department of State, Office of the Historian. history.state. gov/departmenthistory/people/malone-dudley-field

18. Edward J. Larson, "The Scopes Trial in History and Legend," in *When Science and Christianity Meet,* ed. David C. Lindberg and Ronald L. Numbers (Chicago, IL: The University of Chicago Press, 2003), 254. See **WC** for more about Darrow.

19. Anne Janette Johnson, *Defining Moments: The Scopes "Monkey Trial"* (Detroit, MI: Omnigraphics, 2007), 147. See **WC** for information about Bryan's efforts to secure creation experts to testify at the trial.

20. Larson, *Summer for the Gods,* 103, 106, 133, 138.

21. "State v. Scopes: Trial Excerpts." Famous Trials. famous-trials.com/scopesmonkey/2130-excerpts.

22. Randy Moore, *A Field Guide to the Scopes Trial* (Dayton, TN: Rhea County Historical Society and Genealogical Society, 2016), 51. John T. Scopes, *Center of the Storm: Memoirs of John T. Scopes* (New York, NY: Holt, 1967), 138–139. See #45 in Chapter 19.

23. Andrew Bradbury. "The Scopes Monkey Trial: Inherit the Wind—It Wasn't." The Scopes "Monkey" Trial. Bradburyac.mistral.co.uk/tenness2.html. See **WC** for detailed comparisons of the play and the 1960 film with the real life trial.

24. Javier Lezaun, "Eloquence and Incommensurability: An Investigation into the Grammar of Irreconcilable Differences," *Social Studies of Science,* 40:3 (June 2010), 358. jstor.org/stable/25677412.

25. Levine, 355.

26. Larson, *Summer for the Gods,* 207.

27. Ibid., 201.

28. Randy Moore, "The Lingering Impact of the Scopes Trial on High School Biology Textbooks," *BioScience,* 51:9 (September 2001), 793–794: academic.oup.com/bioscience/article/51/9/790/288261

29. Ronald P. Ladouceur, "Ella Thea Smith and the Lost History of American High School Biology Textbooks," *Journal of the History of Biology,* 41:3 (Fall 2008), 435–438, 442, 466. See **WC** and Joseph W. Francis, "The Effects of the Scopes Trial on Secondary Biology Education," in *Deconstructing Scopes: Unraveling the Mythology of the World's Most Famous Trial* (Dayton, TN: Bryan College, 2006), 26–35. For more about the BSCS textbooks published in 1963, see *The BSCS Story: A History of the Biological Sciences Curriculum Study,* Laura Engleman, ed. (Colorado Springs, CO: BSCS, 2001). The three BSCS titles were released in 1963, with each being referred to by a color:

    - Blue Version: *Biological Science: Molecules to Man* (Boston, MA: Houghton Mifflin Company)
    - Green Version: *High School Biology* (Chicago, IL: Rand McNally & Company)
    - Yellow Version: *Biological Sciences: An Inquiry into Life* (New York, NY: Harcourt, Brace & World)

30. Caudill, *Intelligently Designed,* 43.

31. Larson, *Trial and Error,* 76–84.

32. Alan I. Leshner, "'Academic Freedom' Poses a Threat to State Economy," *The Times (Shreveport, LA),* 25 May 2008, B1. At the time his article was published, Leshner was executive publisher of the journal *Science* and CEO of the American Association for the Advancement of Science.

33. *The World's Most Famous Court Trial: Tennessee Evolution Case,* 3rd ed. (Cincinnati, OH: National Book Company, 1925), 175.

34. Moore, *Evolution in the Courtroom,* 34.

35. See **WC** for more about creation science organizations.

36. "Lawyer Quizzed on His Beliefs: Bryan Propounds Questions to Darrow as Result of Court Ban," *Nevada State Journal,* 22 July 1925, 1. See nine questions/answers in **WC**.

37. Frank A. Pattie "The Last Speech of William Jennings Bryan," *Tennessee Historical Quarterly,* 6:3 (September 1947), 265–283. jstor.org/stable/42620953.

38. "Bryan Called the Work at Dayton 'Well Done,'" *The Des Moines (IA) Register,* 28 July 1925, 3.

39. *Memoirs,* 487.

40. "$15,000,000 University Is Planned for Miami, Florida," *The San Bernardino County (CA) Sun,* 25 July 1925, 12.

41. WJB, *Last Message* (New York, NY: Fleming H. Revell Company, 1925), 10. The speech was published in *The New York Times,* 29 July 1925, under the title "The Last Message," with a foreword by Mrs. Bryan.

42. See **WC** for copy of Bryan's death certificate.

43. Read Mary's heartwarming account of the journey to the nation's capital in *Memoirs,* 488–490.

44. Walter Roderick, "Skies Weep as Bryan Is Laid Beside Heroes," *Chicago Daily Tribune,* 1 August 1925, 1. Randy Moore and William F. McComas, *Images of America: The Scopes Monkey Trial* (Charleston, SC: Arcadia Publishing, 2016), 99–102.

45. Read Bryan's full remarks in the text of *The Last Message:* archive.org/details/TheLastMessage_201903.

46. WJB, *Last Message,* 66–69.

CHAPTER 16 – BRYAN'S HOMES

1. Coletta, Vol. 3: 194. While Coletta did not list all nine homes, the five beyond the four he built that are featured in this chapter (Bryan's father built the birthplace home) are most likely the Bryans' first home in Jacksonville, IL; their first home in Lincoln, NE; Frances (Bryan's sister) and James Baird's home in Lincoln; and homes built for other family members.

2. See **WC** for more on Bryan residences not featured in this chapter.

3. *Memoirs,* 15, 135–136, 442.

4. The museum displays many of Bryan's awards; a chair from Bryan's office in Washington, DC; Bryan's military uniform from the Spanish–American War; several items made of silver; and the Bryans' "life masks" that were made a decade before Bryan's death by sculptor Gutzon Borglum, the sculptor of Mt. Rushmore. See **WC** for more about the Salem house and museum.

5. Phyllis H. Winkelman, "Fairview: Home of William Jennings Bryan," *Nebraska History,* 55 (1974): 149. history.nebraska.gov/sites/history.nebraska.gov/files/doc/publications/NH1974Fairview.pdf

6. See **WC** for Fairview videos, photos, and more.

7. Ariel P. King, "The Bryan House Bed & Breakfast," 2015, photograph.

8. *The Commoner,* 26 February 1909: 14.

9. Kazin, 170, 342. Mason Hart, *Revolutionary Mexico: The Coming and Process of the Mexican Revolution* (Berkeley: University of California Press, 1987), 137. Myron J. Quimby, *Scratch Ankle, U.S.A.: American Place Names and Their Derivation* (New York: A. S. Barnes and Company, 1969), 217.

10. See **WC** for more on Mission, TX, and the Bryans' home.

11. "William Jennings Bryan House" by Karen D. Hoffman is licensed under CC BY SA 3.0 (creativecommons. org/licenses/by-sa/3.0)]: commons.wikimedia.org/wiki/File:William_Jennings_Bryan_House_02.JPG#file.

12. See **WC** for more about the Bryans' Asheville home.

13. Levine, 303. Other noteworthy guests the Bryans entertained were renowned jeweler and designer Louis Comfort Tiffany and multi-millionaire neighbor James Deering, who owned the farm machinery company International Harvester. Kathleen S. Kauffman, *The William Jennings Bryan Residence: 3115 Brickell Avenue: Designation Report* (Miami, FL, Planning Department, 2008), 7: archive.org/details/VillaSerenaFINAL.

14. See **WC** for more about Marymont and Chota Khoti.

15. *National Register of Historic Places Registration Form,* 8:14–15: nps.gov/nr/feature/weekly_features/2012/williamjenningsbryan.pdf. See **WC** for Villa Serena video, photos, and more.

16. Candace Jackson, "A Historic, Period-Perfect, Miami House," *The Wall Street Journal,* 30 January 2014: wsj.com/articles/a-historic-periodperfect-miami-house-1391029455.

CHAPTER 17 – STATUES HONORING BRYAN

1. James M. Goode, *The Outdoor Sculpture of Washington, D.C.* (Washington, DC: Smithsonian Institution Press, 1974), 540.

2. Ibid. See **WC** for more information about statue's relocation to Salem, IL.

3. This association is sometimes confused with the Bryan Memorial University Association responsible for the founding of William Jennings Bryan University in 1930 (see Chapter 20). Josephus Daniels' 1913–1921 tenure as secretary of the navy overlapped with Bryan's 1913–1915 tenure as secretary of state. See more information in **WC**.

4. FDR borrowed from Bryan's speech delivered at the 1904 Democratic National Convention in St. Louis, commonly called the "I Have Kept the Faith" speech: "You may dispute whether I have fought a good fight, you may dispute whether I have finished my course, but you cannot deny that I have kept the faith." See **WC** for PDF of the dedication ceremony program that includes the full text of FDR's speech, as well as other speeches delivered at the ceremony.

5. "Dedicate Statues of W. J. Bryan and Sterling Morton in Capital," *The Lincoln (NE) Star,* 27 April 1937: 1, 12.

6. See **WC** for information about the National Statuary Hall Collection.

7. Tescia Ann Yonkers, "Sculptor Rudulph Evans: His Works on William Jennings Bryan and J. Sterling Morton," *Nebraska History,* 65 (1984): 407. See **WC** for more about sculptor.

8. From Bryan's "Cross of Gold" speech (see Appendix A).

9. See **WC** for more about the Bryan bust in the Nebraska Hall of Fame.

10. See **WC** for more about the statue being moved to Fairview.

11. "Bryan Honored at Unveiling of Statue," *The Lincoln (NE) Star,* 1 September 1947: 1.

12. See **WC** for video of sculptor Cessna Decosimo talking about how he chose to portray Bryan.

13. See Appendix A for text of "Cross of Gold" speech.

14. See **WC** for text of "America's Mission" speech.

15. See **WC** for PDF of Livesay's speech and PDF of the dedication program.

CHAPTER 18 – BOOKS ABOUT BRYAN

See **WC** for complete citations and links to some of the titles.

1. Ford financed a peace mission to Europe to put pressure on the warring nations to convene a peace conference that would end World War I. He chartered the ocean liner Oscar II and invited prominent peace activists to join him. Among the invited guests who were not on board when the Peace Ship left New York on December 4, 1915, were Bryan, Jane Addams, and Thomas Edison. See **WC** for more Peace Ship information.

CHAPTER 19 – NAMESAKES AND HONORS

See **WC** for details on the 55 namesakes and honors presented in this chapter.

1. "John Dalton: The Hero of 'The Leader,' Who Has Been Identified with William Jennings Bryan," *The New York Times*, 22 September 1906, 19.

2. John G. Geer and Thomas R. Rochon, "William Jennings Bryan on the Yellow Brick Road," *The Journal of American Culture,* 16:4 (June 2004), 59–63.

CHAPTER 20 – THE FOUNDING OF BRYAN COLLEGE

1. Levine, 290. WJB, *Last Message,* 276.

2. Kathelene McCarty Smith, "William Jennings Bryan and His Unlikely Connection to UNCG," 7 November 2016: uncghistory.blogspot.com/2016/11/william-jennings-bryan-and-his-unlikely.html

3. *The Michigan Alumnus, 60:* 225. See **WC** for information about other encounters Bryan had with university student hecklers. Additional information is provided about a University of Michigan textbook published in 1921 that includes Bryan as a model of a great orator.

4. *Memoirs,* 85, 141–142. Here's an example of a Bennett Prize still being given: financialaid.berkeley.edu/prizes-and-honors-philo-sherman-bennett-prize-political-science.

5. Mark H. Senter, III, "Christian Educators of the 20th Century: Evelyn MacFarlane McClusky": biola.edu/talbot/ce20/database/evelyn-macfarlane-mcclusky.

6. LaDonna Robinson Olson, *Legacy of Faith: The Story of Bryan College* (Dayton, TN: Bryan College, 1995), 3.

7. The Florida Union moved to a larger location in 1967, after which it was renamed the J. Wayne Reitz Union. The original Florida Union building was repurposed for classrooms and faculty office space and was first renamed the Arts and Science Building and then Dauer Hall. "The History of Unions at the University of Florida" (union.ufl.edu/AboutUs/UnionHistory). Samuel Proctor, "William Jennings Bryan and the University of Florida," *The Florida Historical Quarterly*, 39: 1 (July 1960), 1–15. jstor.org/stable/30139067.

8. Arva Moore Parks, *George Merrick, Son of the South Wind: Visionary Creator of Coral Gables* (Gainesville: University Press of Florida, 2015), 216. "$15,000,000 University Is Planned for Miami, Florida," *The San Bernardino County Sun (CA)*, 25 July 1925: 12. "Ruth Bryan Owen Facts," *Encyclopedia of World Biography* (The Gale Group, 2010): biography.yourdictionary.com/ruth-bryan-owen.

9. Genevieve Forbes Herrick & John Origen Herrick, *The Life of William Jennings Bryan* (Chicago, IL: Buxton Publishing House, 1925), 21–26. In Bryan's lengthy description of how he envisioned the money from this bequest being used, he stated, "I would like to have it used to establish an academy for boys, which shall be under the control of some unit of government, of some Evangelical church, Presbyterian preferred but not absolutely necessary, so that it can be controlled by a recognized religious organization." Based on the terms of the will and the decline in value of Bryan's estate during the Great Depression, the $50,000 bequest was never realized. See **WC** for link to complete text of will and to an image of handwritten first page.

10. Stephen D. Giddens, Ed., *Lions' Pride* (Nashville, TN: The Booksmith Group, 2007), 12, 34–35. Olson, *Legacy of Faith*, 3.

11. Darien Austin Straw, "A Christian University," and William Bell Riley, "A Fundamentalist University in Chicago," *Christian Fundamentals in School and Church*, 8: 1 (January–March 1926), 17–21.

12. *Beginning Bryan College (1925–1930)*, a notebook of newspaper clippings located in BCA. *Legacy of Faith*, 147–153. See **WC** for PDF of 12-page prospectus that includes the architectural rendering of the campus featured in the chapter section titled "The People and the Plans."

13. Bryan College presidents with Bob Jones University degrees: George Guille—honorary (1ˢᵗ president, 1930–1931), Theodore Mercer (4ᵗʰ president, 1956–1986), and Stephen Livesay (7ᵗʰ president, 2003–present).

    • Bryan and Bob Jones, Sr., were friends: "During the Fundamentalist-Modernist controversy of the 1920s, Jones grew increasingly concerned with the secularization of higher education. Children of church members were attending college, only to reject the faith of their parents. Jones later recalled that in 1924, his friend William Jennings Bryan had leaned over to him at a Bible conference service in Winona Lake, IN, and said, 'If schools and colleges do not quit teaching evolution as a fact, we are going to become a nation of atheists.'" Daniel L. Turner, Standing Without Apology: The History of Bob Jones University (Greenville, SC: Bob Jones University Press, 1997), 19.

    • The William Jennings Bryan Society (known as Bryan Society) was one of the four original societies when Bob Jones College was founded in 1927. Today students choose from among 34 societies. "The goal of the camaraderie, activities and prayer meetings is to channel the Gospel and love for each other into a focus on service to the campus, local churches and surrounding communities." (bju.edu/life-faith/get-involved/societies.php). This book's author, Corinne Livesay, is a graduate of Bob Jones University and was a member of the Chi Kappa Delta, whose brother society is Bryan.

14. *Beginning Bryan College (1925–1930)* and *Bryan College Collection, Fundraising, Box 1, BC-FR* located in the Bryan College Archives. See **WC** for related documents.

15. *Beginning Bryan College (1925–1930)*.

16. Robert Talley, "New College to be Opened: Institution Is Outgrowth of Scopes Trial," *Muncie (IN) Evening Press*, 22 March 1930, 6.

17. William Jennings Bryan University, *Annual Catalogue 1931–1932*, 28–31.

18. *Beginning Bryan College (1925–1930)*.

19. "Ground Is Broken for Bryan Memorial University at Dayton," *Tampa (FL) Morning Tribune*, 6 November 1926, 2.

20. "Contract Let for Bryan University," *The Tennessean (Nashville)*, 5 March 1930, 2.

21. Read the Administration Building construction story in Olson, *Legacy of Faith*, 32–35.

22. See **WC** for copy of Charter of Incorporation.

23. Annie M. Cole, "William Jennings Bryan University and Its Beginnings," *Express (Sanford, NC)*, 25 September 1930. Newspaper article located in *Beginning Bryan College 1925–1930*.

24. Olson, *Legacy of Faith*, 6. See **WC** for subsequent years' enrollment numbers.

25. *The Bryan Echo* (student publication), 8 April 1933, 4.

INDEX

About Bryan College

OUR MISSION

Educating students to become servants of Christ to make a difference in today's world

EDUCATING STUDENTS | Located in Dayton, Tennessee, Bryan College is a nationally ranked Christian liberal arts school where earning your education goes deeper than gathering information or passing an exam. At Bryan, we strive to offer our students the best academic professors who encourage students to think critically and creatively about the world around them. Our courses are taught by faculty who foster a love of learning and encourage students in faith through prayer and wisdom. With an average class size of 14, you will never feel like just a number.

SERVING CHRIST | Our goal is to provide students with a campus environment that encourages Christian service, fellowship, and a deeper understanding of who God is and what He is doing in our lives. Through local and international service opportunities, student organizations, and weekly chapel services, students are given the opportunity to live out their faith to make a difference on campus, in the local community, and beyond. We value putting faith into action and truly becoming the hands and feet of Jesus.

FIND YOUR CALLING | With a caring support system from our faculty and staff, we are dedicated to helping you discover and use your gifts to find your calling in life. No matter your talents, you will have the opportunity to use them to glorify God and connect with a vibrant campus community.

CHRIST ABOVE ALL
BRYAN COLLEGE

Want to learn more about Bryan College?
Schedule a campus visit today at **bryan.edu/visit**.

About the Bryan Opportunity Scholarship Program

Proceeds from the sale of this book support the **Bryan Opportunity Scholarship Program** that was instituted in 2007. This program makes Bryan College accessible to all academically qualified Tennessee students who demonstrate significant financial need. Eligible students are guaranteed scholarship and/or grant funds from federal, state, and/or institutional sources that will cover 100 percent of Bryan College's tuition (and room and board if applicable). Several statistics illustrate the impact of this needs-based scholarship program:

- Generous donors have given over $2.5 million.
- The average gross annual family income among recipients is typically less than $20,000.
- 41% of recipients are first-generation college students.
- 288 students have received this scholarship.

About the Author

Corinne Livesay has taught at five colleges and universities during her 30-plus-year teaching career. She has written dozens of business-related books and textbook materials for five college textbook publishers and has created numerous learning resources and curricula for college, continuing education, and corporate training courses. Her passion for Bryan College, breadth of experience, and interest in historical research have uniquely prepared her to write this book. She and Bryan College President Stephen Livesay have been married for 40 years and have three grown children. She enjoys biking and traveling and loves being Grammy to her favorite little "difference makers," Lucas and David.